WHEN A BOUGH BREAKS

MENDING THE FAMILY TREE

WHEN A BOUGH BREAKS

MENDING THE FAMILY TREE

Mary Y. Nilsen

First published October, 1985.

Copyright © 1985, Hazelden Foundation.
All rights reserved. No portion of this publication
may be reproduced in any manner without the written
permission of the publisher.

ISBN: 0-89486-338-X

Printed in the United States of America.

Editor's Note:
Hazelden Educational Materials offers a variety of information on chemical dependency and related areas. Our publications do not necessarily represent Hazelden or its programs, nor do they officially speak for any Twelve Step organization.

To Per

ACKNOWLEDGMENTS

In addition to our son, Per, whose journey through addiction and into sobriety forced us into a painful but fascinating world we would not otherwise have experienced, I am deeply grateful to the other members of my family who have allowed, indeed encouraged, me to take pieces of their lives and give them to the fictitious characters in this book.

I would also like to thank Twin Town and Hazelden, both Minnesota-based treatment centers, for allowing me to experience their family treatment programs. These programs became the framework around which this book was written.

EPIGRAPH

Stop your crying and wipe away your tears
all you have done for your children
will not go unrewarded;
they will return from that enemy's land
there is hope for your future;
your children will come back home.
Jeremiah 31: 16-17

DAY ONE

Dr. Paul Inghram sat stiffly in the taxi staring out the front window as he, his wife, and two of their three children careened through early Monday morning traffic on the freeway linking Minneapolis to St. Paul. He shifted his attention to the meter, watching as the numbers flipped faster than he could read. Then he checked his fingernails, cleaning a black speck from his left thumb, trying to forget why they were there and where they were going. Their destination was a treatment center for chemical dependency where their oldest son, Tom, had been admitted several weeks earlier.

The term *chemical dependency* irritated Paul. He added it to his growing list of irritations. Everyone was chemically dependent. The human body couldn't exist without chemicals. The term was a euphemism, a way of accepting people who are unacceptable: alcoholics, addicts, junkies, winos, pot heads, or, as in the case of their son, kids who got into trouble with the law and that trouble was somehow related to drugs. *But, as irritations go,* Paul thought, *this one was a good one, one with a handle.* He could use it when they got there. Point out to someone the inadequacy of the term. Do it in his most professional voice. Let them know they weren't dealing with some uneducated, skid row family.

The other irritations since arriving in Minneapolis late the evening before had had no such use. They were pure, raw irritants, the kind designed by some perverse god to rub away at a person's good nature. First, there had been confusion over their reservations, and then, he realized how outrageously overpriced the hotel rooms were. This was the Midwest, damn it, not New York. Added to that was a bed too hard for comfortable sleep, and his wife, Beth, who went to sleep, or pretended she was asleep, without so much as saying good night. And his children, Kris and Erik, were sullen and snippy, angry about having to miss a week of school, somehow blaming him.

Then there was the weather — 30 degrees below zero with a windchill factor of minus 70 the weatherman had said. And finally, there was the taxi driver, a friendly but uncouth chap who had nodded knowingly when Paul had given him the address. "Know the place," he had said, and Paul felt exposed.

They had made three left turns since leaving the freeway and Paul, convinced they were going in circles to add more mileage to the meter, was about to ask the driver if he knew what he was doing when the taxi skidded to a stop in front of a pair of small two-story buildings.

"Here you are folks. You go in through that door," he said, pointing to a set of glass doors on the second building. "Know this place well," he added with a grin. "Spent seven weeks here a couple of years ago. Great place."

Paul grimaced as he stared at the cabbie. "What do we owe you?"

"Right there on the meter, sir, six-sixty." Paul reached into his pocket as the cabbie continued talking. "Yup, seven weeks it took, but they were the best weeks of my life. Can't tell you what a mess I was before."

Paul glanced into the back seat as he handed the man eight dollars and smiled at his wife and children. None of them noticed or chose to respond.

Except for the strained, perturbed look on each face, the Inghram family was hardly distinguishable from thousands of upper-middle income families living from coast to coast — parents in their mid-forties, dressed in conservative but expensive clothing, with teenage children in equally expensive designer jeans, jackets, shirts, and shoes.

At fifteen, Erik looked like his father must have 30 years earlier — small-boned, round-faced, with a shock of straw-colored hair. As a small boy he had been labeled *cute* or *darling,* and he was. Twinkly-eyed. Funny. Good-natured. But now, trapped somewhere in the middle of puberty — it had seemed for years — with a crackly voice, bony rib cage, and armpit fuzz, he had begun to take on the cocky defensiveness of a "tough guy."

Kris, unlike her brother, had matured early, both emotionally and physically, and now, at sixteen, appeared almost adult. She was nearly as tall as her father, and attractive in a thin, tight, meticulous way. She had her mother's oval face, slightly turned-up nose, and thick, wavy auburn hair, but she had always reminded people more of her father. Perhaps it was her lack of humor, or maybe it was the way she lived her life — as an orderly progression from one goal to the next, never swerving, never failing.

The taxi driver opened his door, jumped out, and scurried around to open the doors for his passengers. "You folks here for the family program? Didn't have any family when I was here. Nope. Not a soul. Do now though." He grinned. Paul wished the man would keep quiet. But he kept talking as he helped Beth and Kris out the back seat.

"Yup, met my wife at one of the alumni parties. She was just out of treatment at the time . . . needed someone to talk to . . . so we talked and what do you know, we ended up getting married." He didn't seem to notice no one was interested. "You all have a good time," he called after them.

Paul helped his wife over a bank of snow cleared from the street and then followed his family up the short sidewalk and into the reception area. Kris and Erik stood awkwardly to the side, whispering to each other. "God, did you hear that guy? An alumni party? Can you believe it? He makes it sound like getting through this place is some big honor."

"Maybe they have a graduation on the last day," Kris responded. "Can't you see a bunch of drunks in caps and gowns parading up for their diplomas?"

As Paul walked over to the receptionist, he grinned to himself. They were good kids, those two. Too bad they had to be dragged through all this because of Tom. "I'm Dr. Inghram. We're here because our son is in treatment."

"Yes, of course, Dr. Inghram. You're here for the family program. We've been expecting you. Please come back to the lounge."

As she rose to show them the way, he felt dwarfed. He had always envied tall men, not an angry, jealous envy, but a rational, wouldn't-it-be-nice-if admiration. But tall women made him feel inadequate, conscious of the thinning hair on top of his head and the thickness of his rimless glasses. His clothing, which under ordinary circumstances made him feel immaculate and professional, in the presence of tall women turned him into a wooden mannequin. As a protective device, he had established a routine in his office. He would stand only when the woman was sitting or lying on the table. Otherwise he remained seated at his desk, maintaining his authority and image.

As the receptionist smiled down on him, Paul stood a little taller, straightened his tie, and then turned, signaling his family. He followed them through the door separating the lobby from a long hallway. As they walked, Paul pounded the floor with each step, still resentful they had had to travel all the way from New York in order to meet the court's requirement that they join their son in his treatment for chemical dependency.

Three people were already in the lounge as the Inghrams entered. A woman and a young man sat together on the couch looking through folders filled with pamphlets and sheets of paper. Another woman sat by herself in a straight-backed chair in the corner. But it was the woman on the couch who dominated the room. Her short, dark-skinned, energetic body, covered snugly by blue jeans and a low-necked sweater, was the body of a 25-year-old. In fact, the only physical indicators of her true age — somewhere between 35 and 40 — were covered by heavy makeup.

The young man next to her bore no signs of blood relationship. He was tall, brown haired, had the build of an athlete, and was very handsome in a subtle sort of way, his appearance marred only by facial scars, pitted reminders of teenage acne. Heavy brows kept his deep set eyes shadowed, hidden.

The woman in the corner was probably in her early 40s. She wore brown twill pants and a plaid shirt. Her bleached-blonde hair was back-combed and sprayed stiff.

"Good morning, I'm Dr. Inghram and this is my wife, Beth, and my children, Kris and Erik."

"Rick," Erik corrected him.

The three seemed unsure as to how to respond, but finally the woman with the heavy makeup asked, "Do you work here? Are you going to lead our group?"

"No, no. We're here because of our son. Got into a little trouble with the law and they told him he had to go through treatment."

"Well, then, Doc," the woman continued with a twinkle in her eye, "you must have a first name."

Behind Paul his wife and daughter exchanged nervous glances. But Rick, standing to the side, hands stuffed into his pockets, grinned at the woman and said to his father, "Yea, Dad, cut the doctor crap. You're one of the patients here." Paul felt his neck redden but he chose to ignore the comment.

"I'm Paul. And you?" He extended his hand.

"I'm Bonita and this is my stepson Eddie. Eddie's father, my husband, though Lord only knows why I married him, is an alcoholic." Paul shook both hands, amazed at the matter-of-fact attitude she seemed to have toward the problem. As Bonita and Eddie greeted the rest of the Inghrams, Paul turned to the other woman sitting off to the side and extended his hand. "And what's your name?" he asked.

"Connie." Her abrupt response was neither friendly nor unfriendly. She remained seated, legs crossed, her left hand clutching a cloth cigarette case. Then, sensing that some sort of explanation was expected, she went on, "My daughter was picked up by the police, too. Dumb kid . . . should have known better, but you know what teenagers are like these days." She extended her hand.

"Yes, indeed we do," Paul responded, noting how cold her hand was and how weak her grip. As everyone shook hands, the receptionist caught Paul's eye and told him he would have to go to the business office to complete some registration forms.

Beth, Kris, and Rick were given their folders and told they could start reading some of the information.

Paul followed her down the hall to an office which doubled as a library. A friendly young woman asked him to sit down and then began asking all of the usual questions. Finally she said, "You've been informed of the costs of the program. Do you have insurance coverage?" Mention of money renewed the anger Paul had felt when he first realized what all this nonsense was going to cost. It was bad enough that their son had to go through the expensive treatment process, but the additional cost of the family program plus plane fare and hotel expense was absurd.

"I think my policy will cover the treatment costs," he said. "But, do you have any idea what this week is going to cost us?" His anger was apparent, but the woman ignored it.

"You'll just have to think of it as a family vacation," she said as she put the registration form into a folder.

"If we were going to take a vacation in the middle of winter, it would not be to Minnesota, I can tell you that."

Paul regretted saying it as soon as it was out. He didn't usually lash out at people that way. There was just something unsettling about the whole experience. He didn't like it. He felt as if he were losing control.

But the woman, who had heard the comment at least 100 times before, simply laughed and said, "I hope you can find some time to explore the cities in the evenings. There are a lot of interesting things in town, even in the winter."

Paul walked back to the lounge where everyone was sitting in silence reading pamphlets from their folders. He sat down and took one out, but hadn't even opened it when a woman came in and said, "I'm Pat, your counselor for the week. Let's see if everyone is here."

As she read the list of names, Paul noted his first impressions. It was a game he played with himself, and he was getting rather good at it. When a woman would come into his office he would make a mental list of assumptions based on her appearance and her eyes and then, as he got to know her, he would compare the reality against the original impression.

Pat, he guessed, was about 35, had probably graduated from some university with a major in social work, and had belonged to a sorority where she learned how to dress. She was likely married. No, she was probably divorced — that was why her appearance was so important to her. And she was likely the kind of woman who made regular visits to her doctor and tried to turn him into a friend. Paul knew after one glance it would be impossible to think of her as his counselor, but it didn't matter much one way or the other. He followed the group back down the hallway, up a flight of stairs, and into a large meeting room.

Pat sat on a table at the end of the room and asked the group to take seats near the front. She seemed to be watching where people sat, and Paul suddenly felt very self-conscious, wondering where he should sit so she wouldn't make some negative assumption about him. He sat down next to his wife in the front row. Bonita sat in the same row but down a few seats. Kris, Rick, and Eddie spaced themselves across the second row and Connie sat by herself behind them.

Paul watched Pat as she began her introductory talk and wondered why she seemed so nervous. Surely she had done this many times before. His mind wandered in and out catching a little of what she said.

"The people here who are in treatment are called *residents*. We use that term because it implies a certain adult responsibility for the place and for each other and especially for themselves, unlike the word patient, which implies a person is helpless and is here to have something done to him or her.

"But, even though we avoid the word *patient,* that does not mean we do not think of alcoholism as a disease. We are firmly convinced it is a disease, and we operate from that belief. No one chooses to become addicted. It happens randomly, like cancer happens to some people for no apparent reason. It cuts across all religious, socioeconomic, and racial lines, and neither sex is immune.

"We also believe it is a family disease . . . not that families cause it, or can cure it, but that if one person in a family is chemically dependent, any or all of the people in the family can be made emotionally, spiritually, and often physically ill because of their reactions to the behavior of that person. That is why we have this family program and why we encourage the families of all our residents to come here for a week."

Paul glanced at Beth wondering what she was thinking, how she was feeling. He had known for some time she was under great emotional stress, and he had suggested repeatedly that she get out of the house — get involved in bridge or tennis again. But she sat home all day dreaming up things to worry about. *There were advantages in being gone most of the time,* he thought, even though the thought made him feel a little guilty. He had been able to remain unaffected by the home problems — the only reasonable voice around sometimes — because he had another life to concentrate on.

"When we talk about chemical dependency as a family disease, we mean by *family* anyone who is significantly involved with the addict. It might be a boss or a good friend. Certainly it is the people who live with the addict or alcoholic.

"We talk a lot about dysfunction when referring to families of alcoholics. We don't mean the family is not functioning. What we mean is, it's not functioning as well as it could be or needs to be. There's a piece missing. Something is incomplete in the relationships. This is, of course, all very relative. Some families seem, on the surface, to be functioning rather well, while others are reduced to simple survival. But we know because we've seen it one hundred percent of the time, you cannot live with an alcoholic without being affected."

Paul cleared his throat, and Pat glanced at him and then asked if he had a question. Using his most professional tone, he spoke. "You've been busy defining terms, but it seems to me you're very fuzzy in your use of some basic terms. You talk about alcoholism sometimes, chemical dependency other times, and you even used the word *addiction* once, which to me implies heroin addiction. Would you please tell us what you mean by those terms? My son, I know, didn't drink much. All he did was smoke a little pot. If it weren't illegal, we wouldn't be here." Rick snorted from behind, and Pat gave Paul a sympathetic look.

"Thanks for mentioning that. We get so used to those terms we forget that our use of them might be confusing to people new to the program. The term we usually use is *chemical dependency*. That means a person has reached a point in his or her life where certain mood-altering chemicals are seen as necessary for existence." She paused, allowing time for the group to absorb that definition. "That chemical could be alcohol, marijuana, cocaine, Valium, heroin, or any one of dozens of pain-killing or mood-altering drugs. It doesn't really matter. The problems are the same, the disease is the same, and the recovery process is the same."

Paul was about to mention his objections to the term *chemical dependency*, but he couldn't catch her attention. She went on. "We talk about addiction in relation to any of the chemicals, though, I know, especially in New York, the term usually refers to heroin. We have found there is no advantage in differentiating between drugs, as if there's some kind of hierarchy of addiction. Addiction to beer is as big a problem as addiction to heroin." Paul disagreed with her but saw no point in arguing.

"Any other questions about terms?" Pat asked. She looked from person to person receiving either a blank stare or a shake of the head. "About lunch," Pat went on, "you're all welcome to eat here, and we encourage you to do so. You can get tickets at the front desk, but we will need to know each day how many to expect. If you'd rather go out, there are a couple of restaurants in the area. How many of you plan to eat here? Or, let me put it this way, does anyone plan not to?" Pat scanned the group. "Connie?" Connie nodded. "And the rest of you will be here?"

"Trish isn't here so there's no reason for me to eat with the residents. Besides, I dislike institutional food." Paul glanced back at Connie, wondering why she thought it necessary to explain herself.

Pat smiled at her. "It does get a little tiresome. But, any time you change your mind, just let me know."

After reviewing the rules and referring the group to the printed sheet titled "Resident's Rights and Responsibilities and Program Rules and Regulations," Pat told them to find a partner they did not know and to take about a half hour to find out as much as they could about the other person. At 11:00 they would meet in her office and introduce each other.

Paul stood up as she left and glanced at the others. There were seven people: two pairs and one group of three. "Why don't you three kids work together. Beth, maybe you could pair up with Connie . . . ."

"Hey, Doc, relax. You don't need to organize everyone's lives. Come on and sit down. Tell me about your life." Rick laughed as Bonita pulled out a chair for Paul to sit on. It exasperated Paul that his son seemed to find everything she said so amusing.

"Sit down." She patted the seat next to her. "Tell this old Italian mama all about yourself. Wait a minute. Let me guess. You went through college with a three-point-nine GPA, went on to medical school, married a sweet young nursing student who worked to put you through school, and then, at nicely planned intervals, had three children. Am I right?" Her eyes twinkled in a flirtatious way. Paul couldn't help but like her, even though he usually disliked pushy women.

"You're almost right. The GPA wasn't quite that high and the intervals weren't quite that well planned. So, what about you?"

"Well, I'm here because I fell in love with and married an alcoholic . . . a sure sign I need my head straightened out. Why anyone would give up a perfectly good business and, with eyes wide open, marry such a jerk, I don't know. I must be crazy. Maybe it was Eddie I was really concerned about. I hired him when he was just fourteen. He worked for me . . . cleaning up, carrying out, stuff like that. I could see how much the boy needed a mother. I don't know, I must be nuts." She laughed a loud, deep laugh. "But you know, that son of a gun, when he's sober, is the most loving, sensitive human being that ever walked the face of the earth. I guess I thought if I married him I could keep him sober. It lasted about a week. I knew better. I mean, I've been around long enough to know better, but I really thought I could change him. God, what a fool I was. I didn't change him, he changed me. I've turned into a nagging bitch. I hate myself sometimes. But I love Eddie. He's a good kid. I think I've helped him, too."

She paused and then went on, her tone more confidential. "His real mother walked out on them a few years ago because of Jim's drinking. I couldn't believe anyone would just leave a husband and son, but I'm changing my mind on that one. If this treatment doesn't take, I'll tell you this, I'm not staying around any longer to put up with that kind of abuse."

Paul glanced around uneasily, wondering if Eddie heard her. "Don't worry about the kid," she said. "We've talked it all out. He knows exactly how I feel. He's old enough to take care of himself now. Hey, you never told me what kind of a doctor you are."

"I'm an OB-GYN," he said with pride. "Obstetrician and gynecologist."

Bonita threw her hand to her forehead and slid down in her chair. "Oh, God! One of those doctors who thinks every woman over forty is a neurotic wreck. I tell you, I finally had to find myself a woman doctor to get someone to take me seriously. I had this pain . . . ." She spent the rest of the time recounting her experiences with male doctors, and, while Paul found her to be an amusing person, he was exasperated, as he had been a thousand times in his adult life, at having his conversations always and inevitably turn to medical matters. Before he found out what the pain had been, Pat returned and asked the group to come into her office.

The room was large, sunny, and comfortable. Besides the desk, a bookshelf, and a small table containing several boxes of tissue, there were ten or twelve padded bucket swivel chairs on chrome roller frames. Eight of them were arranged in a circle. The group members hesitated, reluctant to choose their chairs. Paul took the lead and then wondered what Pat would conclude from the fact that none of his family chose to sit by him, even though any of them could have done so. He sat down, carefully centering himself on the chair, then shifted his position once, then twice, then again. Pat smiled at him, perhaps noting his nervousness. He locked himself in the least uncomfortable position, ankle across knee, arms across chest, and that was the way he remained.

During the next half hour the group members introduced their partners. Paul found out Connie was also from upstate New York, was divorced, had two other children, both older than the one who had gone through treatment. She worked in an insurance office and had refused to take off work while her daughter was here. But the judge had insisted she come, so she was using vacation time to comply. Other than the exasperation of being at the treatment center, she was, as she had told Beth, content with her life.

Eddie was a college freshman, had been involved in athletics, stayed in the dorm even though they lived only miles from the private college he attended in St. Paul, and rarely went home anymore. Paul noted he seemed ill at ease when Kris was talking about him, and he rarely looked at anyone.

Bonita and Connie both seemed surprised to hear Kris was only a high school junior. Paul looked at her with pride. She was lovely and had always been mature for her age, mothering both brothers even though she was younger than Tom and only thirteen months older than Rick. Before Rick was through introducing his sister, Paul interrupted. "I think the group ought to know you are a straight A student and president of your class."

"Dad, please," Kris responded in embarrassment.

"Well, we're proud of you, and I think it's an important part of your life."

Kris flushed.

"Did you want the group to know that, Kris?" Pat asked.

Kris answered with a shrug which Paul could not interpret, but it made him wish he hadn't said anything.

Then it was Bonita's turn to introduce Paul. She reached over and patted his knee. "This is Dr. Inghram. I guess half of you know him better than I do, but he seems like a pretty great guy . . . for a doctor." She laughed at her joke.

Paul grinned at Bonita and then at Beth, expecting she would be nodding affirmation, confirming he was a great guy. But she was looking at the floor, her face a blank. Paul rubbed his knee, then recrossed his legs as Bonita went on. "Paul delivers babies and tends to neurotic middle-aged women, and, as you all know, he's married and has three children. I guess that's it."

It amazed and angered Paul that his life could be so easily summarized. Realizing the group was waiting for him to introduce Bonita, he did so, but in the back of his mind he was thinking of what he should have told her, what he really wanted this group to know: professional accomplishments, his articles published in medical journals, the successes he had had with cases of infertility, the excellent reputation he had among his peers and at the hospital. He began planning in his mind the perfect introduction.

When his attention finally returned to the group, he realized Pat was talking about herself. "As is true of many of the staff here, I'm chemically dependent. Both my mother and stepfather were alcoholics and I vowed never to touch the stuff. And I didn't. But I touched pot and pills of all kinds and by the time I was in my twenties my life was a disaster. I went through a treatment center in California and have been drug free, now, for seven years. I worked at that center for several years and then heard about the advanced treatment programs in Minnesota, came here and took the training program at Hazelden, worked there first, and have been here for a couple of years."

She paused for a moment before going on. "If I seem a little distracted this week, I'm trying very hard to quit smoking. I was up to two to three packs a day and decided there was no point in being pill free if I was going to kill myself with nicotine, so please bear with me." She smiled, her eyes catching each person's eyes in the group except Eddie's. His head hung down, his eyes hidden.

As she passed out several sheets of paper, she told the group that the rest of the morning would be spent laying the groundwork so they would all begin with the same understanding of certain terms and with a broad view of all the feelings people can have.

Paul felt a yawn coming on and tried to stifle it. He glanced down the list of vocabulary words — words like *owning, controlling, stuffing, tough love, enabling, detachment*. He sighed. A new set of jargon to learn. They went around the room, each person reading a word and its definition. But when they got to *enabling,* Pat stopped the group. "We're going to be talking a lot about enabling this week and it's important you understand exactly what it means. The word is usually a positive word. An enabler is a person who helps another, enables another to do something the person could probably not have done alone.

"But, as we define it, it's a negative term. An enabler is someone who in one way or another makes it easier for an alcoholic to drink or a pill popper to pop pills or a pot head to smoke. I know none of you think of yourselves as enablers; none of you would deliberately help the person in your family who has the problem to continue using." Rick shifted in his chair as Pat went on. "But that doesn't alter the fact that you all, in one way or another, are enablers. It's not your fault you are. It's just one of those things that happens in families where one person is chemically dependent. We're going to be talking a lot more about that as the week goes on. But keep this thought in mind. All that an alcoholic needs is one enabler and a bottle of booze and he or she will never feel the need to begin recovery. There will always be booze around. It's our job to quit enabling."

Paul glanced at the members of his family and wondered, vaguely, what sorts of things they were doing that enabled Tom to use drugs. He, of course, wasn't around enough to be an enabler, but they must be doing something. Then he caught himself. He had almost fallen into the assumption that Tom was, in fact, hooked. The idea was absurd. Experimenting with drugs was, unfortunately, a way of life for teenagers these days. Tom just happened to get caught. That's all. Paul turned his chair slightly so he could see out the window. The view of the hospital across the street reminded him of home. He smiled, visualizing himself walking down the corridor in his white coat, a stethoscope hanging around his neck, the nurses nodding and smiling as he passes, the janitors stepping to the side.

"Are you hungry?" Pat was talking to him.

"What?"

"You smiled so broadly when I mentioned it was time for lunch I thought you must be hungry."

"Yes, yes. I guess I am." Paul got up, stretched, went over to Beth and put his arm around her. "Anxious to see Tom?" he asked. They had not seen him since he left for treatment three weeks earlier.

"Anxious about seeing him, I guess," she responded as they walked toward the lunchroom. "I have no idea what to expect. He was so angry when he left. He blamed me, you know. I don't think I can deal with that again. I should never have talked so openly to the probation officer. Then none of this would have happened."

"Hey, family, over here," a familiar but somehow altered voice called to them. Paul saw his oldest son standing with a group of men and women. Some looked older than Paul, others younger than Tom. Expecting to see the old Tom — the Tom with unkempt clothes; long, greasy hair; and dull, sullen eyes — Paul hardly recognized him. His blond hair was short and feathered back giving his face an open, vulnerable look. He seemed to take pride in his appearance — his polo shirt tucked in, jeans belted, and shoes tied. And he seemed taller, Paul realized, as they drew closer together. Could he have grown in three weeks? But, most surprising of all, he seemed relaxed and at home.

Kris got to Tom first and he gave her a big bear hug. "Little Sis, how goes it? What do you think of this place?" But before she could answer, he turned to Rick. "Hey, Bro." Rick shifted awkwardly, but Tom, who seemed eager to embrace his family, threw his arms around him, and the tension seemed to ease.

Then he turned to his mother and tears began streaming down his face. They hugged and wept and then laughed as they wiped their eyes. Finally it was Paul's turn. He stared at the floor and then at this son who had somehow become a stranger. Tom took a step forward and then hesitated. Paul wanted to put out his arms, ached to hold the boy as he had held him years ago, but he didn't, couldn't move, and the moment passed. Tom held out his hand and Paul took it, feeling a firm, adult grip. "Great to see you, Dad. How was the trip?"

"Not bad. A little rough, but not bad. Who are your friends?"

The group, which now surrounded them, relaxed and began to joke.

"Ah, they're just a bunch of drunks," Tom said, which struck everyone but Paul as extremely funny. Soon he was hearing names and shaking hands and hearing over and over again, "So glad you could come." "We've heard a lot about you." "That kid of yours is quite a guy . . . you should be proud of him." Paul felt as if he was being accepted into a family, a family of strangers, a family he had no desire to be a part of. He stepped back out of their circle and into the cafeteria line. After getting his food, Paul followed his family to a table in the corner where the members of the family program had gathered and sat down next to a man he took to be Bonita's husband.

"Hey, Doc. This is the guy I've been telling you about."

Paul extended his hand, embarrassed by her bluntness. But Jim just laughed and greeted Paul warmly.

"Believe everything she says. She couldn't possibly exaggerate about what a wonderful . . . ." He threw his arm over Bonita's shoulder. "Not the right word?"

"Not even close." She elbowed him in the ribs and he shrugged.

"I keep hoping."

Jim was a handsome man, gregarious and charming — qualities which led him into his career as a salesman and enabled him to rise quickly to sales manager of a company which did business all over the Midwest. Years of travel, taking clients out for a drink or entertaining where liquor, merchandising demonstrations, and sales were woven into a single fabric, had finally taken their toll. His judgments became questionable and his behavior inexcusable. After twenty years, his company told him either he quit drinking or he would lose his job.

"Is this your first trip to the Twin Cities?" Jim asked Paul, but before Paul could answer someone called for quiet and a young girl stood up. She couldn't have been more than fifteen or sixteen.

"I'm Kim, and I'm an alcoholic and cocaine addict," she said in a broad Texas accent, and everyone clapped and cheered. She giggled and did a little curtsy. "I want to tell you all I just found out I've been accepted at a halfway house in Austin, Minnesota, wherever that is, and so I'll be able to leave tomorrow." She smiled while everyone clapped, but as she sat down, her lips began to quiver, and the woman sitting next to her quickly put her arm around the girl young enough to be her child.

Then a young man stood up. He seemed nervous. "I'm Ben and I'm an alcoholic." When the group clapped he blushed and stared at his plate, a weak grin creeping across his face. "I have a bad attitude about myself. I also have a very poor self-image. I need the community to help me and support me." He started to sit down and then stood back up and said, so rapidly that it was hard to catch the words, "Also, I'm a worthwhile person and I like myself." During the loud cheering and clapping that followed, Tom turned around and slapped him on the back.

"Hey, you did it. It wasn't so bad was it?" Ben grinned and then laughed.

"What was that all about?" Rick asked Tom. Everyone in the family program stopped eating to listen.

"That girl, Kim, she's in my group. I think she's been here about four weeks, maybe more, but she didn't dare go home. Actually, she hardly has a home to go to. I think both her mother and father are alcoholics. She lived with her mother who had men around the house all the time. It was really bad . . . what they did to her." Paul looked past Tom and saw the girl's open, vulnerable face, trying to imagine what her life had been like. "You should have seen her a few weeks ago. She had so much makeup on that she looked like she was twenty-five."

Bonita laughed. "Do you suppose if I put on a little more, I'll look like I'm twenty-five?"

"Is that why you wear makeup?" Paul teased, "To look younger?"

"Boy, I tell you Doc, when you get close to forty you need all the help you can get." As she laughed loudly, Paul glanced at Beth sitting, as she so often did, with one finger pressed against the corner of her eye, and noticed for the first time the signs of age on her face. Deep creases spanned her forehead — worry lines beginning between her eyes and spreading, pinching temple to temple. The freckles that used to dot her nose giving her an impish look had faded, and the smile crinkles around her eyes that had once given her face a friendly, animated look, were now middle-aged wrinkles. When he had first met her, she was everything he wasn't: pert, spontaneous, flirtatious. He had fallen deeply in love with that Beth, but she had slipped away sometime during the past few years, quietly, imperceptibly.

"What about that kid?" Kris asked.

"Ben? He's one of the newer ones. You wouldn't believe the life he's had. But he's coming along. Just getting up and talking in front of the whole group is a good sign. He could hardly talk at all when he got here." Paul was fascinated by the authority and insight Tom displayed as he talked. He didn't remember ever hearing his son talk about anything substantive before.

As the conversation went on, Paul picked at his food, disgusted by the institutional wholesomeness of it. He noticed Bonita trying to compensate for Eddie's coolness toward his father by talking even louder than usual, joking first with one and then the other. Tom and Beth were sitting together at the end of the table, talking in that intimate way they had that always made him feel like an outsider. It had been that way from the beginning. He had stood helpless and watched as his wife endured what had seemed like endless labor. Then, another man delivered his son, handing him to Paul only after the cord had been severed and the first cry heard. At home, once again, he felt useless as his wife held the baby to her breast, giving him her energy.

In his office he cautioned expectant mothers about the problem, reminding them to be conscious of the feelings and needs of their husbands, but he had no idea if it did any good. Maybe it was inevitable, this feeling of isolation. Maybe that was the price men paid for being spared the pain of delivery.

The sounds of scraping chairs and clattering dishes indicated lunch was over. Tom left the table first, heading for the counter where they rinsed and stacked their dishes, and Rick hurried to catch up with him. Paul followed a short distance behind, and when he reached the boys, they quit talking. The feeling of isolation from his family, which had been forming all day, finally took hold and swept through him. He wanted to talk to the boys, to ask them what they had been talking about, what they were thinking, what they were feeling, but all he could say was, "Well, did you two get enough to eat?"

They looked embarrassed and fidgety. "Sure, Dad," Tom replied. "There's always plenty to eat here. In fact, they almost *make* you eat a balanced diet so your body will return to health."

"I didn't know your body was unhealthy," Paul said, but they didn't hear him.

Minutes later the group gathered in the meeting room again, this time for a film. Pat introduced it by saying that much of the time during the first days of the family treatment program would be spent learning about the disease of alcoholism. "I suspect," she said smiling, "there are more myths floating around about alcoholism than any other common disease. We want to dispel those myths and replace them with solid information. Today's movie has that as its purpose. You'll see many familiar movie stars and you'll hear a lot about the disease of alcoholism."

Paul settled back in his chair as Pat turned out the lights and started the machine. He recalled the alcoholism seminar he had had to take as a medical student. The films had shown the liver and brain damage of alcoholic indigents. He knew the American Medical Association recognized alcoholism as a disease. But he was one of many doctors who thought differently. He knew it was a problem, but important medically only because there were certain physical side effects. He wondered what scientific basis *these* people had for calling it a disease.

The speaker in the film was saying the abuse of alcohol is one of America's worst health problems. Damage done to many families by alcoholism and alcohol abuse causes enormous human suffering, and yet there is much we can do about it. That's what this program is all about.

Paul was surprised to see the familiar face of Ronald Reagan on the screen. But, when Foster Brooks came on acting like a drunk, Paul was repulsed. He had never thought the man was funny and couldn't imagine what he was doing in such a movie, but with him on the screen was a woman, and some of what she said caught Paul's attention.

The woman was going through a list of statistics. She said alcohol is responsible for forty percent of all snowmobile accidents, forty percent of all rape cases, sixty percent of all homicides, fifty percent of all traffic deaths, sixty-five percent of all domestic violence cases, seventy-three percent of all reported cases of child abuse, and seventy-three percent of all suicides. The statistics interested and impressed Paul, but when the film went on to another scene, his mind faded out. He slid down in his chair and didn't awaken until he heard the end of the film clicking against the projector as the back reel spun, waiting for someone to turn it off.

The group took a five minute break, then gathered in Pat's office, sitting in the same places they had taken in the morning. When everyone was settled, Pat held up a small book. "This book, *One Day at a Time in Al-Anon*, is a collection of thoughts put together by people like yourselves, people who have lived with alcoholics. There is one meditation for every day of the year and it's a great way to start your day. If you're interested in buying one, we have copies at the front desk."

She turned to a premarked page and then went on. "Each day we will be reading one of the meditations that strikes me as particularly appropriate. I'll go ahead and read today, and then tomorrow one of you can take a turn." She held up the book and began reading a portion of the meditation.

This day I will concentrate on the inner meaning of the Commandment "Thou shalt love thy neighbor as thyself." I will accept myself, for that is the primary condition under which the good in me can grow. Unless I am at peace with the child of God I am, I cannot love and help my neighbor . . . Condemning ourselves for mistakes we have made is just as bad as condemning others for theirs. We are not really equipped to make judgments, not even of ourselves.

When she had finished reading, she gently closed the book, set it on the floor beside her chair, and then asked for comments on the movie. Paul wondered if anyone had noticed he slept.

"What did ya think of the movie, Dad?" Rick asked in a way that was both teasing and cruel.

"Your father has had a very tough week, Erik," Beth explained, not for Rick but for Pat.

"Do you always feel the need to defend him?" Pat asked and Beth flushed. "How does it feel to have your wife run defense for you with your children?" Pat asked, looking directly at Paul.

"I guess I never noticed that she did before."

"How could you notice, you're never home," Rick said angrily.

"Erik, you seem angry that your father isn't home very often," Pat tried to draw him out.

"My name is Rick."

"Okay, Rick. You know, don't you, that your feelings are important, just as important as your father's? If it upsets you that he is never home, why don't you tell him?"

Rick looked at his father for a moment and then looked down. He rubbed his hands over his knees, then sat on them, and finally spoke. "He's home sometimes. I mean whenever he can be. Whenever he isn't working."

"But he works a lot of the time?" Pat asked.

Rick shrugged. "Ask him."

"Does it make you feel good when he is at home?"

Paul watched as his son shifted nervously again, avoiding his glance.

"It doesn't really make much difference whether he's home or not," Rick's voice had a tone of finality to it.

"Would you like to talk about that now?" Pat asked, but Rick shook his head no. "We'll be having private conferences later in the afternoon and tomorrow. Perhaps we can talk about this more then." Her eyes asked Rick if that was okay and he nodded brusquely, but when she looked at Paul, he couldn't meet her gaze.

Then, turning back to the group, she asked, "Well, what did you think of the movie?" her gaze skirting from Paul to the other members of the group.

"I liked the sports footage," Eddie spoke up, breaking the tension. "I don't know where I've been. I mean, I suppose it's been in the news, but I didn't know there were so many professional athletes recovering from alcohol and other drug abuse."

"I thought the part about the number of senior citizens who die alcoholics was haunting," Beth added. "Remember the line about how there's no generation gap when it comes to alcoholism? It can affect old or young or anyone in between." The members of the group nodded.

"The line I liked was the one about how a family that drinks together, sinks together. You wouldn't believe the number of people who've told me Jim wouldn't have had nearly the problem he had if I had just gone with him and drank with him." Bonita laughed as she thought about the absurdity of such advice. And then she said, "And there was another line that caught my attention, saying alcoholism, next to the common cold, is the most contagious disease in America. That's really true. It's incredible what living with an alcoholic has done to Eddie. God, the kid is so insecure and unsure of himself — "

Pat interrupted her, "Eddie will tell us what it has done to him when he's ready. What has it done to you?" Bonita was caught off guard but quickly recovered.

"Well, we've only been married for a couple of years, which is a little different from growing up with an alcoholic, but already I can feel my self-worth taking a nosedive. What I keep wondering is what there is about me that made me marry him in the first place. I've been going to therapy for half a year to try to figure that one out, and I still haven't come up with a good answer. I must be nuts." She laughed that loud, boisterous, infectious laugh and slapped Paul on the knee. "What do you say, Doc, am I nuts?" Paul laughed and was about to answer when Pat interrupted.

"Paul is here for the same reason the rest of you are here. He has been affected in an unhealthy way because he has been living with a chemically dependent person. In this setting he's not a doctor, he's one of the group. Perhaps it would help you to remember that if you'd call him Paul instead of Doc." As Pat was talking, Paul's eyes wandered from Bonita to Beth who was twisting a tissue nervously on her lap and on to Rick who was folding his arms across his chest and sliding down in his chair, with a sneer spreading across his face.

"I was the one who wanted to call you Paul in the first place, wasn't I?" said Bonita, undaunted. "What do you say, Paul, am I nuts?"

"Apparently we're all nuts," Paul responded.

"Wait a minute. You're not listening." Pat's voice had an exasperated edge. "What I said was that when you live in a family where one person is chemically dependent, the extreme behavior of that person tends to force everyone else into a kind of extremeness which is unhealthy, sometimes very unhealthy. The fact that you respond is not your fault any more than the chemically dependent person's behavior is your fault or his or her fault. It's just something that happens, and it always happens. You can count on it.

"I've been counseling for several years with families of alcoholics and drug abusers, and I've talked to colleagues who have been counseling for many more years, and none of us has ever come across a person who has lived with an alcoholic who has not been affected in very predictable ways. What we're here for is not to decide whether or not we're nuts but, to sort out the ways in which we have been affected, and then, realizing our response is our responsibility, to try to do something about it." By the time Pat had finished her lecture, which Paul took as directed solely toward him, he had unconsciously rolled his chair back three or four inches and was sitting in embarrassed silence.

Pat glanced at her watch. "Let me give you your assignments for tomorrow and then tell you what we're going to be doing for the rest of the day." As she handed out a sheet of paper, she went on. "Read through these goals. They're the things we will all be working on during this week. Then I want you to write out a personal goal or goals. Think about it carefully. What do you most want to get out of this week? I'll collect these sheets tomorrow and then Donna, another one of the family counselors, and I will consider what you've written and what we have observed about you. On Wednesday, we'll give you a list of goals that we think will be helpful for you.

"At two o'clock I'd like to meet with you, Paul, for a personal conference, and Beth, you will be meeting with Donna. The rest of you can gather in the cafeteria and talk about whatever you want to talk about. We strongly encourage the members of our groups to get together during free time. The better you get to know each other, the easier and more effective this process will be. There is much you can learn from each other.

"At three o'clock, Connie, you will be meeting with Donna, and we have scheduled a family conference for the Inghrams. Tom will be there with his counselor to talk to you about what he was and what he is. Take a break and I'll see you, Paul, in about five minutes."

Paul stood and stretched. The phone on Pat's desk reminded him of his office and he wondered if he had time to make a quick call to see how things were going. He was concerned about Mrs. Chenoweth. It was her first pregnancy and there had been problems from the beginning. She wasn't due for three weeks but you never knew, really. Perhaps he shouldn't have left town. He glanced at his watch, making a mental note to call early the next morning, went into the hall for a drink of water and then on into the men's room.

A few minutes later Paul and Pat sat down at her desk.

"You don't have a cigarette, do you?" Pat asked. "No, no. Don't give me one even if you do. Oh, help. This is as bad as kicking the pill habit." She laughed and Paul relaxed.

"How do you feel about things so far? I hope you're beginning to feel more comfortable."

"To tell you the truth, I'm not at all sure what the point of all this is. Sure, our family isn't perfect, but what family is? And Tom got into a bad crowd for some reason, but . . . you should hear some of the stories I hear in my office. Those are the people who need therapy."

"Maybe, Paul, if you didn't think of this as therapy, it would be a little easier for you. We don't think of it in that way. Our family program is designed to help people learn about chemical dependency and sort through their own feelings about the chemically dependent person in their lives and their feelings about themselves." Pat laughed, "You know, the term we use around here for people is *normally neurotic*. And I think most people for one reason or another would fall into that category. Certainly you and your family would fall within the bounds of normal."

Paul sat forward, knowing he had caught Pat in a trap. "If

that's true, then why is Tom here? Why is he being labeled? Why all this talk about disease?"

"Tom is a special case in your family," Pat started.

"He's not a 'special case.' He's no different from Erik or from hundreds of thousands of kids his age."

"One of the things we'll talk more about is the problem of denial. It happens in the family of any alcoholic or drug addict. Everyone works out an elaborate system of rationalizations and excuses so he or she won't have to see the real problem. This isn't exactly lying to yourself or deluding yourself, it's simply a means of protecting yourself from a truth that would be too painful to bear alone.

"Everybody does it, but we've noticed the problem is particularly evident in families of professional people, people who really have tried to be loving family members, people who have a need to understand what is happening. When they find they are living in a family where nothing makes sense, they begin building a network of defenses to protect themselves. Does that make sense to you?"

"It makes sense, but I still don't see how I fit into all this. I'm not even sure our family fits into the pattern. I can't believe Tom is addicted to anything. He was caught twice, well, three times, but one of those times he just happened to be in the wrong place at the wrong time. I don't really know that he has used any more than that."

"We'll be talking about that in an hour. Let's talk about you, now." Paul shifted in his chair and Pat fidgeted with her pen, holding it as one would hold a cigarette.

"How do you feel about your job? Do you like what you do?"

"Yes, very much. I always wanted to be a doctor and I feel very satisfied with my practice."

"Do you have a partner?"

"No, I like working alone. Some of those partnerships get really sticky. I just didn't want to be bothered with that. I have a good nurse and a secretary. That's all I need."

"Doesn't that demand a lot of your time, time away from your family?"

"I guess it does, but it also means I can provide very well for them."

"Does it seem to you that that is important to them?"

"Well, they certainly spend everything they get." His voice had a bitter edge.

"And they don't seem to appreciate you or the money."

"No, they don't." Paul felt the injustice of it all raging within him. "I don't know what's wrong with kids these days. If I had had half the opportunities they've had. . ."

"It just isn't fair."

"It's worse than unfair, it's . . . ." But before he could think of the right word, he was suddenly conscious both of her technique and of how inane he must sound, mouthing the universal frustrations of middle-aged parents. He breathed deeply and leaned back against his chair.

Pat waited a moment and then asked, "What made you quit talking, Paul?"

He adjusted his tie, first loosening it and then pulling it tight. "I just realized you must get sick of hearing parents rant about their ungrateful children."

Pat smiled and nodded. "I do hear it a lot, but it's almost never without cause. I'm younger than you and have no children. I guess that makes it a little difficult for me to understand or empathize with your feelings on some issues. But, on this issue I think I understand a little. I know the anger I have to fight in myself when dealing with young people who have everything I wanted or ever dreamed of having as a teenager, and they take it all totally for granted or toss it off like stale crackers. I know in my head it doesn't really matter how much you have or how many opportunities are open to you, life can still be miserable. But, still, I can't help but feel anger and envy when dealing with those kids."

She smiled at him when she was through, tossed her head in the air, and said, "Crazy, isn't it?"

Again Paul relaxed a bit. Perhaps it would be possible to regard her as a peer, not his counselor, but maybe a peer.

They sat in silence for a moment and then she asked, "Do you drink?"

"No."

"Never?"

He shook his head.

"Why not?"

Paul began fidgeting with his tie again, caught himself and self-consciously returned his hand to the arm of his chair. "Do I have to have a reason for not drinking?"

"No, it's just that drinking is very much a part of our culture. Usually if people don't drink, they have a specific reason. Are you religious?"

"Not particularly. My wife takes care of that for both of us." His tone was bitter. The silence that followed made Paul uneasy. He looked at Pat and then looked away, unable to meet her probing gaze.

"So, why don't you drink?" She asked.

"I simply choose not to."

"Never. You've never had a drink?"

"What is it with you people? You make people feel guilty if they drink and guilty if they don't drink." There was a pause during which Pat tapped her pencil as one would tap a cigarette to pack the end.

"Did your parents drink?"

"My mother drank wine occasionally."

"What about your father?"

Paul's movement caused his chair to roll back. "I don't know. He died when I was six."

"What do you remember about him?"

"Nothing. I don't remember anything."

Pat paused for a moment and then changed her tone. "One of the things we try to avoid in our program here is a concentration on the past. We're well aware of the fact that we're all products of our pasts, but our experience has taught us that talking about it a lot almost inevitably leads to blaming . . . it was my father's fault, it was my mother's fault. In dealing with Tom, we haven't allowed him to slide into that kind of thinking. His drug use is his responsibility and his problem. I asked you about your father, not because I want to psychoanalyze you, but because some of the things you said reminded me of a book I read recently called, *Adult Children of Alcoholics*. We have it down in our library. Why don't you glance through it in your spare time and see if anything rings true?"

"You mean because I don't drink you assume my father was a drunk. That makes a lot of sense."

Pat ignored the sarcasm and went on. "I'm not assuming anything. I'm just suggesting an avenue you might want to explore. What you do with that suggestion is your responsibility." Paul glanced at Pat for an instant and then his eyes wandered to the desk, to the floor, and finally to his watch.

"Weren't we supposed to have a family conference at three o'clock?"

"Before we get the others I want to say one more thing. I understand how difficult it is for someone who spends his whole life helping others to accept help himself. I hope as the week goes by you will get off the defensive and start seeing us as your advocates, not your judges. Trust the program, Paul. It works." She got up and went to the door, leaving him sitting alone, feeling exposed and angry. He got up, walked around, then picked out a book from her library and glanced through the table of contents. By the time the others arrived, he was in control.

Beth, Kris, and Rick came in and sat down. Then Tom came, followed by a tall, middle-aged man with a full beard and friendly, warm eyes. He walked straight to Paul and put out his hand. "Paul, I assume. I've had a chance to meet the rest of the family. Welcome to our center. I'm Dan, Tom's counselor." Paul shook his hand and smiled but quickly pulled away. The strength and energy of Dan's grasp made Paul feel, once again, weak, vulnerable.

They sat in a circle and Dan began the meeting. "During the family program, we generally have two family conferences. The first of these is usually a time for the family member who is chemically dependent, in this case, Tom, to explain to the family the seriousness of his illness. This is one of the things he's had a difficult time coming to grips with, but he now realizes how powerless he has been over chemicals and what a destructive effect they have had on his life.

"You have, perhaps, felt, at times, as if Tom had no sense of guilt, no conscience. In fact, you've probably tried many times to make him feel guilty so he would stop behaving in such a destructive way, so he would know how much he was hurting you.

"What you'll learn this week about people who are chemically dependent is that they know and feel guilt more than we can imagine. One of the reasons they keep using is to keep those feelings from becoming too painful. Tom is learning how to maturely accept responsibility for his behavior without blaming himself or others. It's a process you will all be involved in during the week. Another thing Tom needs to do is to start being honest with himself and with others. By the time people get to treatment for chemical dependency, they usually have been lying for so long that they need to learn how to be honest.

"I want to remind you again of the rules you discussed this morning. There will be no physical violence, and no one will leave the room until the meeting is over."

His speech sounded as if it had been delivered a hundred times. But then his tone changed, becoming personal and serious. "This meeting is going to begin differently from most such meetings because of a serious problem that just came up at our group this afternoon." Tom shifted uneasily and glanced at Rick. "Tom, why don't you go ahead and tell us what you told the group."

Tom turned to Rick, "Rick, I'm really sorry about this, but I just have to do it." Rick stared back at Tom, a look of dawning realization.

"A couple of weeks ago, not long after I got here, I called home and talked to Rick. I told him I just couldn't stand it here, that I was going crazy. I asked him to get me some ludes and bring them when he came. He gave them to me after lunch. I took them up to my room and sat on my bed staring at them. I wanted to take one so badly I could almost feel the sensation they give. But, somehow, I couldn't. I just couldn't betray all my friends here. So I flushed them down the toilet. Please don't blame Rick, he was just doing what I told him to do. I've always made him do that." Tom had hardly finished before Rick burst out angrily.

"What the hell has happened to you? You've turned into a goddamn redneck rat!"

"Erik, watch your language," Beth said quietly.

"Watch your language, watch your language. Is that all you can ever say? Why don't you just beat me on the head with that Bible of yours?"

"Whoa," Dan called out, holding up his hands. "I guess I forgot to caution you about verbal abuse toward each other. Let's try to avoid name calling or other kinds of verbal put-downs. Now, Rick, you seem pretty angry about this. Can you tell us why?"

But Paul, who had heard nothing of the last exchange, interrupted. "Wait a minute. I want to get this straight." Paul struggled for control as he addressed Rick. "You mean, you smuggled illegal drugs in here and gave them to your brother? Where on earth did you get that stuff?"

"I just took it out of Tom's supply at home. He's the big dealer, so get off my case."

"He's the what?" Paul stood, sending his chair crashing back into Pat's desk. Beth responded automatically, pulling her chair in front of Rick's, holding up her hand to calm her husband.

"Wait a minute," Dan interrupted forcefully. "Calm down. Let's not jump the gun here."

Paul pulled his chair back into the circle, embarrassed by his outburst at his son.

"Our first problem is the issue of smuggled drugs. Ordinarily a resident is immediately expelled from the program if there's any evidence of using any kind of mood-altering chemical. It was fairly clear to us that Tom hadn't taken any of the pills and that he had disposed of them, so he'll be allowed to stay.

"As the week goes on, you'll be talking a lot about enabling. Rick, I hope you'll pay particular attention to the discussion and try to think through all of the ways you've been sucked into contributing to your brother's illness. Now, Tom, why don't we get on with the real purpose of this meeting." Then Dan addressed the family, looking, it seemed to Paul, more often at him than at the others.

"Tom is going to be telling you a lot of things that you will likely find quite upsetting. I hope you understand Tom is describing symptoms of the disease he has. You didn't cause the disease, you can't control it, and you can't cure it, any more than he caused it or could cure himself. But you can help him in this most difficult process of recovering that he will be involved in all his life. You can help him by trying to be open and understanding. Go ahead, Tom."

"Mom, Dad," Tom looked from one parent to the other. "I have done so many bad things. I don't know where to start." He rubbed his hands on his knees and then leaned back, the pressure of his movement rolling his chair back, out of line with the group.

"Why don't you start at the beginning," Dan said softly.

Tom nodded. "I guess it really started in about sixth or seventh grade. The drinking and smoking, I mean. Before that I used to sometimes sneak cough medicine or sniff glue. You know, the kinds of stuff kids do. It always made me feel so good. You know?" Tom looked at his mother first and then at his father. Paul shook his head. No, he didn't know. Tom's eyes moved quickly to Dan who encouraged him to go on.

"At first it was just every once in a while, usually after baseball games. The guys would get together at someone's house, and we'd take booze from his parents' supply, sip a little, and act drunk. It was really pretty stupid, but that's how it started. I never liked the taste but I always liked the feeling. We would have little contests to see who could drink the most. I always won. It made me feel like a real big shot." He laughed, but no one joined him.

"Then, when I was in seventh grade, a couple of the ninth grade guys started talking to me, inviting me to join them during lunch. That was when I first tried marijuana. Man, was that great. Not just the feeling I had from smoking, but being able to be a part of that group. Those were the good years, all fun and no problems. But then things started to go bad. . . ."

Paul sat and looked at his oldest son hearing but unable to believe what seemed an unending story of drug and alcohol abuse — lies, cheating to get through school, stealing from home, shoplifting, robbery, senseless vandalism while under the influence of drugs, and finally, becoming a dealer in order to support his increasingly expensive habit. As Paul listened, his horror turned to rage toward Beth. Taking care of the home was her job. How could she have let all this happen? He shifted his glance from Tom to her and realized she was looking at him, her eyes filled with tears, the tears he had seen so often brimming in her eyes, tears somehow frozen in place.

Tom had stopped talking, and everyone was looking at him as he sat with hands locked between his knees and tears streaming down his face. "Mom and Dad," he went on, "I want you to know I never meant to hurt you. I hated myself for what I was doing but I couldn't stop. Sometimes I would lie in bed at night crying, thinking, what if you die before I have a chance to make it up to you?" The room was quiet, no one knowing how to respond.

"Tom, tell your folks what you need from them now," Dan's soft voice directed.

Paul watched as Tom turned his chair so he was facing him directly. Tom's eyes searched his face and Paul wondered what he was looking for, what he hoped to find. "Dad," he began and then looked back to Dan. He's afraid, Paul realized with incredulity, this boy who has always seemed so sure of himself, so arrogant, so independent, is afraid — afraid of me? How could he possibly be afraid of me? And then from deep within came blurred images of another father, of a son in terror, never knowing what to expect, always fearing the worst. Tears buried for 40 years took on new life as he listened to Tom. "Dad, I know I have no right to expect this. I have no right to expect anything, but I need to know you still love me." His voice cracked and then broke.

Without knowing how it happened, Paul found himself standing with his arms around the boy, feeling deep sobs against his chest. His? Tom's? He didn't know. It didn't matter. A minute, a lifetime, later, Paul sat down and reached for a box of tissue.

"How are you feeling, Tom?" Dan asked.

"Man, I feel great. I don't know why I was so worried about this. I should've known they'd understand. Some of the guys here have family members that just start screaming at them and won't listen, but you guys were just great."

"Would anyone else like to tell us what they're thinking? Feeling?" Pat looked at Beth as soon as she had finished the question.

Beth began slowly, "I don't know. I guess I'm having a hard time taking all this in. I just can't believe you were so heavily involved in drug use. I mean, I knew something was wrong, terribly wrong, and I didn't know what it was. But whenever we would talk, you'd always tell me you hated losing control, that you couldn't understand how some kids could stand acting like such fools. You told me you had experimented with drugs, but you just didn't like the feeling. Remember? When we would have those long talks? You told me you loved us too much to ruin your life on drugs." Her voice cracked as she looked at Tom with pleading eyes, appearing as if she wanted to be told all he had just said was untrue, needing to be reassured this drug abusing, delinquent Tom was not the child she had raised.

"Ah, Mom, you were such a fool," he said off-handedly. "I used to fill you full of so much bullshit, and you would just suck it in like some dumb guppy. God, you were a fool. You know,

Dad was the smart one. At least he had sense enough not to waste his time listening to me."

Paul wasn't sure he really deserved the compliment but enjoyed it, nonetheless. Then he looked at Beth and saw something in her eyes he had never seen before. Anguish? Anger? Hate? But, as quickly as it had come, the look was gone, and she sat, staring at the floor, her eyes glassy with tears that wouldn't flow.

"Beth, are you okay?" Pat asked.

"Yes, of course."

"Would you like to respond to Tom?" Beth shook her head no. "Perhaps we can talk about it tomorrow?" Beth shrugged.

Pat hesitated a minute and then said, "It's getting close to dinner time, so I think we'd better call it a day. Don't forget your homework for tomorrow. Get as much reading done as you can and then work on your personal goals. We have lots of work yet to do."

Later that evening Paul sat down in front of the TV in their hotel room to watch the 11:00 news which, in the Midwest, came on at 10:00. The evening had not gone well. Apparently he had been the only one in the group for whom the afternoon conference had been a good experience, and even his experience was beginning to dim as the memory of the closeness he had felt toward Tom was eclipsed by the memories of what Tom had said, what Tom had done.

He had decided to take the family to an expensive French restaurant he had heard about, but the kids had done nothing but complain about the slow service saying they would have been better off at McDonald's. Beth ate only a few bites of her dinner and then had the waiter take it away. Whenever he had tried to talk about the afternoon, no one would respond, as if they were somehow in league together against him. So he had talked about the weather and their horses back home and finally, he, too, stopped talking.

When they got back to the hotel, Rick and Kris had decided to go swimming, and Beth had taken her reading materials and gone to sit poolside, leaving him alone in the room. He had leafed through the packet of material and tried to read a pamphlet on grief. But he wasn't in the mood to read — particularly not about grief — so he put it down and picked up his goal sheet, trying to think of what he should write as his personal goals. As he considered his relationship with each of the people in his family, his mind locked on Erik and he thought for the first time since leaving the center about the pills Erik smuggled to Tom. Is that what they had been talking about after lunch when they had cut him off? He pounded the arm of the chair. Apparently Beth was unable to control either one of those boys. Well, now that he knew what was going on, he would get things straightened around. He flipped on the TV and waited for his family to return.

As the weatherman predicted warming temperatures with snow turning to freezing rain, Beth came in and Paul could hear Kris and Rick in the room next door.

"Beth, tell the kids I want to talk to them as soon as they get dressed."

"Tell them yourself," she retorted and went into the bathroom.

Paul sighed. Something had been eating at her for years, but long ago he had given up trying to figure it out. She usually wasn't rude, however. Oh well. He stood up and went to the door which connected the two rooms.

Tapping lightly on it, he said, "Erik, Kris, would you come in here when you're dressed?" There was no response.

Paul was tempted to open the door and demand his children come into his room immediately, but something stopped him. What if they said no? What then? How could he make them come? How could he make them do anything they didn't want to do? Just as a sense of powerlessness began sweeping over him, the door opened and they came in, wet hair combed back. His self-confidence returned.

"Sit down, kids. We need to do some talking." Paul turned off the TV as Kris sat on the edge of the bed and Rick took the only other chair in the room. Then Beth returned and Paul said, "Rick, give your mother your chair."

"Why don't you give her your chair?" His manner was cocky, baiting.

"Because I told you to — "

"It's okay," Beth cut in. "I'll sit on the bed with Kris."

"No, it's not okay. This young man needs to learn some manners among other things. What has happened to him?" He looked accusingly at Beth, as if it were her fault that Rick was so rude. She flushed but didn't respond. Paul, realizing there were more important things to talk about than manners, dropped the subject.

"I guess most of what I have to say doesn't involve you, Kris. Thank goodness we have one decent kid." She moved as if to leave. "No, I want you to stay. Maybe you can help me understand what is going on around here.

"Realizing I have one son who was a heavy drug user and another who would actually sneak drugs to him in treatment has been quite a shock to me. I don't understand what has been going on the past few years. Why did Tom get off on such a bad path?"

Paul spread out his arms, his fingers pointing downward, like a preacher describing descent into hell. But in the silence that followed, his dramatic gesture turned into a nervous tie adjustment.

Finally Rick sighed in exasperation and said, "Dad, for crying out loud, you make it sound like some sort of moral choice . . . a good path and a bad path. Where have you been, anyways? Everybody uses drugs these days."

"Kris, you?" Paul looked first at Kris for support, but she averted his glance, neither affirming nor denying. Then he looked at Rick. "You?"

"Of course I use drugs. I told you, everyone does." He looked at Kris, "Well, almost everyone."

"Why on earth would kids who have everything they could ever want, a good home, friends, every opportunity . . .?

What . . .? Why would they start messing up their lives with drugs? It makes no sense at all."

Paul had turned to Beth, and again his voice was accusing, as if she must know the answer, as if there had been some conspiracy between the three of them. This time she responded. "I've been trying to answer that for years. I can't believe you never thought to ask the question until now." Their eyes locked in mutual blame and Paul turned back to his son.

"Why, Erik?" Paul asked, almost pleading. Rick paused before responding, and a little of the defensiveness and hostility was gone from his voice.

"Because it's fun, I guess. Because it feels good. Because it makes life seem beautiful. Because it makes me feel important. Because it assures me of friends. Tom got a little carried away, I guess, but for most of us, it's just a good time. But, then, you wouldn't know about good times, would you Dad?"

Paul felt the anger return. "Don't you realize? Life's not meant to be all good times." Rick sat back with a smirk on his face, and Paul realized he had probably heard the lecture dozens of times before so he stopped. The dull roar of traffic from the crosstown freeway pressed on his brain and the wail of a siren seemed to be getting closer.

"But where do you get the money? That stuff must be expensive."

Rick laughed. "From you mostly." Paul was caught off guard. "I ask you for twenty bucks for a date. That's good for a few smokes. Or money for a school lunch ticket. That's enough to buy a bag. Then I can distribute enough to keep me happy for a while." Paul was dumbfounded.

"Both my sons are goddamn drug pushers!"

"Oh, knock off the self-righteous crap, Dad. Everyone knows you're the biggest Valium pusher in town. I've got friends who sell the stuff you prescribe for their mothers."

Paul was out of his chair. "How dare you equate what I do with illegal drug pushing on the street, you little punk!"

"Drugs are drugs. You push your way, and Tom pushes his." Rick laughed as Paul stepped toward him. "And he didn't have to go to school half his life to make a fortune either! You're the fool!"

Fury roared through Paul's head. The room blackened but for the taunting look on Rick's face.

"Paul, stop it!" Beth's shrill voice brought the room back into focus. The boy cowered in his chair, trying to escape his father's upraised hand. Paul stared at his son and then at his hand, a weapon somehow separate from him, out of his control. He stood for one terrifying moment poised to strike, and then turned, grabbed his coat, and fled out the door. Behind him he heard movement and then Kris' voice saying, "Let him go, Mom. It's better when he's not around."

Paul slammed the door shut and walked down the long hall of the hotel to the elevator, through the lobby, and out the front door. The canopy provided momentary protection, but then he felt the full blast of the Minnesota winter wind carrying with it sleet and snow. The icy rain stung his face, but anger kept him warm as he strode for blocks through the streets.

At first he hardly noticed others on the sidewalk, and then he became conscious of laughing couples coming from restaurants and groups heading toward bars. He felt like an alien in this world of night life, an alien by choice. It was nothing he had ever wanted to be a part of.

His rage toward his family turned to self-righteousness as he thought about his productive life. He had always made responsible decisions, even as a teenager. Why were his own children so different? Had his father been so much better an example to him than he was to his sons? He remembered Pat's probing questions about his father, and he tried to remember: What did he look like? smell like? talk about? Paul could remember nothing. Surely childhood memories must go back to the years before age six, but his mind was blank.

As Paul turned a corner, he ran headlong into a tall, bearded man with red eyes. "Get the hell out of the way!" The man shoved Paul toward the street. Paul tripped and fell, sprawling childlike on the icy street.

"Damn you!" Paul screamed after him. The man turned and sneered down at Paul before staggering around the corner. "Damn . . . damn . . . damn . . . " Paul uttered in almost sobs as he fought the impulse to chase after the man, to beat him, to hurt him as he had been hurt. But, he quickly regained control of himself, stood, brushed the snow and slush from his pants, and continued on. Eventually, however, cold set in, freezing the anger in his blood. He turned and headed back to the hotel.

As he entered the lobby, the sounds of music and laughter caught his attention. He turned away from the direction of the elevator toward the piano bar on the other side of the lobby. It was done in old pub decor and he could see through the wall of painted windows into the bar. The mood was festive. A gray-haired, elderly black man in a white shirt, black vest, and bow tie was playing old ragtime tunes on an upright piano. Black elastic bands held up his sleeves. There were couples at most of the small round tables and several men sat along the bar.

But then, you wouldn't know about good times, would you, Dad? The voice of Rick came back to him. *He's right,* Paul thought. *When have I ever had a good time? I was never invited to the parties in high school because I didn't drink, and in college and medical school I was too busy studying.* In a strange, twisted way, Paul found himself envying Rick's freedom, insolence, and fun.

Why have I been living like this? Paul wondered. *What value has it been for anyone? The money I make they use for drugs. My wife hardly talks to me anymore. And Kris, Kris, my little princess, thinks it's better when I'm not around.* Her words pricked his heart. *Let him go. Let him go.*

Feeling more alone than he had ever felt before, Paul walked through the open door of the bar and sat down awkwardly in front of an empty glass. The bartender stood in front of him, removed the glass, wiped the counter, and waited. Paul felt the pressure of his presence.

"A beer," Paul said, half expecting, half hoping, the bartender would argue, tell him he shouldn't drink, tell him to leave. But, in seconds a foaming glass was in front of him. It was so easy. So ordinary. So commonplace. But his hand shook as he lifted the glass to his mouth.

The smell of the beer turned his stomach. He breathed deeply. Relax. Have fun. But the heavy barroom smells, the pungent smells of alcohol and tobacco, made him nauseous. He gasped. Swallowed hard.

"Something wrong, mister?" The man next to him leaned toward him, leering, enveloping him in stinking, repulsive alcohol breath.

Paul gagged. Swallowed the acrid bile. Stumbled from the bar. Gasped for air.

The hostess at the door followed him out. "Are you okay, sir?"

Paul nodded and hurried through the lobby to the elevator, up to his floor, and then down the hall toward his room. When he reached the door, he stopped. *What if they're still up? What if they're talking and I interrupt something? What if the arguing starts again?* He stood for a moment, digging in his pocket for his key, wondering if he should actually go in. Then he realized he had nowhere else to go, so he quietly turned the lock and opened the door.

The room was dark except for the bathroom light Beth had left on for him, as was her custom. He quickly slipped out of his clothes, put on his pajamas, spent a few minutes in the bathroom, and then headed for the empty bed, his bed. But before turning back the covers, he turned and looked at Beth's sleeping form curled in the middle of her bed. He wondered if she was really asleep, if she would know if he crawled in beside her and wrapped his body around hers, feeling her warmth and strength, if she would remember all the nights they had slept like that. It hadn't been so long ago, two years, maybe three. What had changed things? What had gone wrong? He tried to remember. Was it the fights about how to discipline Tom? The behavior of the boys which had gotten so obnoxious he couldn't relax at home? Or her damn religious phase that made him feel she was substituting God for him? It wasn't that he didn't believe in God or recognize the value of church membership, but she had really gone off the deep end, going to little meetings at strange churches. She never said much, but he gathered she was praying for him and the boys. She should have been home disciplining those kids, not praying for them. He noticed the Gideon Bible sitting on her side of the nightstand, and the anger returned. He pulled back the covers on his own bed and crawled in.

Paul stretched out on the firm mattress and tried to relax. First the pillow wasn't right and then he realized the room wasn't absolutely dark. He got up and tried to spread the heavy drapes across the window, but one of them hung at an angle so that no matter how far he pulled it closed, there was always a triangular gap at the bottom which let the light in. He took the rack that held the suitcase and pulled it in front of the window, opened the suitcase and checked to see if the suitcase covered the curtain opening. It seemed to work so he went back to bed, tripping over someone's shoes on the way. Damn.

Lying in the darkness, he again tried to relax. He was exhausted, but something was nudging at his brain, some memory wanting to be recalled. He had trained himself to pay attention to those nudgings and as a consequence, rarely forgot meetings or messages or errands. But this one frightened him. There was nothing he needed to remember here, hundreds of miles from his practice. All he needed was sleep. He willed it away, rolled over, and began to plan what needed to be done to fix things in the family. Erik was right, he wasn't home enough. Apparently both boys needed a strong father's hand to get them back in line. And he would have to figure out some way to get Beth active outside the home. Perhaps she could volunteer at the hospital. A lot of women did that and seemed to enjoy it. Volunteering would give her something else to think about, something to do. Then, maybe, she would have a better perspective on her home. Appreciate it more. Take charge a little more effectively.

Then Paul remembered how embarrassed Kris had been when he had mentioned her grades. She needed more positive reinforcement, more encouragement to excel. And they would have to watch her carefully to be sure she didn't get influenced by her brothers.

Paul took a deep breath, thought through his plan one more time, and then nodded to himself. It would work. Things were going to be okay.

DAY TWO

Kris heard the wake-up call and sat up, expecting to see her room, to hear the voice of one of her friends. Then, remembering where she was, she picked up the phone, thanked the voice, and set it back in its cradle. Rick was in the bed next to hers, sound asleep. She would have to wake him, but she decided to wait until she was through in the bathroom.

Standing under the shower, Kris thought about the night before. The scene in her parents' room had deeply disturbed her and she wasn't sure why. She had witnessed dozens of screaming encounters between her mother and Tom during the past few years, but she couldn't remember any involving her father. It frightened her. It somehow upset a tenuous balance the rest of them had achieved. She didn't know what to expect from him.

But, now, she didn't know what to expect from Tom either. It was as if their whole family was coming unglued. Sitting and listening to Tom confess to their parents all the things he had been doing had been overwhelming. Some of it she knew, of course. Going to the same school she couldn't help knowing. But much of what he said came as a shock to her. And then when he started crying and he and her dad hugged, the surprise turned bitter. After all that he had done, all the times he had ridiculed their dad, lied to him, stolen from him, after all that, Tom was the one that Dad hugged.

The water turned cold. Reaching to readjust the knobs, Kris slipped and hit her ear on the shower head. Sharp, stinging pain. She struck back, hitting the shower head with her hand. Stupid. She held her hand under the water trying to ease the pain. Everything was so unfair. She had tried so hard to be good, to make her father proud, but she couldn't remember the last time he had paid any attention to her. And why did Tom need to know Dad loved him? It was Mom who had had to put up with him. It was Mom who had fought and pleaded with him, who had done everything she could to help him. And he just turned on her, calling her a fool. Kris had hated the old

Tom. She wondered briefly if she wasn't going to hate the new one too, but shrank from the thought.

She finished her shower, dried herself, and then blow-dried her short, wavy, auburn hair. "Rickie, you'd better get going," she called. "We're supposed to meet Mom and Dad for breakfast in about fifteen minutes." She heard mumblings and groanings from the room and began to get nervous. What if he wouldn't get up? They would blame her. She called again and he didn't answer.

She hated having all the responsibility and no authority. It seemed like it had always been that way. Even Tom, who was older, was her responsibility. When she was little she used to like it when her mother said things like, "What would I do without you?" or, "You're so mature and dependable." But now she hated it. Why did she always have to be the responsible one?

Kris shuddered as she remembered her father's comment about her grades the day before. Looking at herself in the mirror, she couldn't meet her own gaze. What if he discovered how things really are? Then what? How she only took the easiest courses so that she'd be assured of getting As. How she used term papers several times and borrowed book reports from friends if she thought hers weren't good enough. How she got so nervous before tests that she always felt nauseated, and how, sometimes, when her mind went blank, she had to glance at someone else's paper in order to get started. What would he think if he knew all that? There would be nothing left to love about her.

"Get up, Rick. Now."

By the time she got into the room, he was up and partially dressed.

"Kris, I hate this whole business," Rick said, reaching into his suitcase for a shirt. "Do you want to go? Couldn't we just pretend we're sick?" Sitting on the edge of the bed, shirtless and vulnerable, he looked like a little boy again.

"Dad would probably really blow if we tried to pull something like that. Come on, let's not make him mad by being late."

They got to the coffee shop first, and when their parents finally came, they seemed in unusually good spirits, especially their father. He didn't apologize or even bring up the subject of last night. He just seemed happy. Or, maybe not happy, but at least not upset. *Mom probably got him calmed down,* Kris thought. That's what moms are for.

By the time the family arrived at the treatment center after a frightening ride on icy freeways, the other three were there, waiting. As the Inghrams hung up their coats, Pat came in.

"The first thing on the agenda today will be a movie. We'll be focusing our attention today on the roles that family members fall into when one of them is chemically dependent," Pat began after everyone was settled.

"This sort of thing can happen in any high stress family, but it is a predictable occurrence in families of chemically dependent persons. The family structure described in the movie is one in which the parent is an alcoholic. For those of you with families where the addicted person is one of the children, the roles will be a little different, but there is still much you can learn from the film. Don't be too quick to say, 'There's no one in my family like that.' Think about it carefully, and then take what you can from the movie. Try to think about how your behavior has changed because of the stress in your family caused by the extreme behavior of the chemically dependent person." Pat clasped her hands together and smiled, signaling the end of her introduction.

Kris and Rick raced up the stairs, hoping to beat the others who took the elevator. They did, and chose places next to each other right in the center of the room. The movie was of a woman lecturing a group of people about chemical dependency. Kris glanced at Rick to see if he was as bored as she was, but he didn't look bored. In fact, no one looked bored. Kris listened.

The speaker said the person who becomes chemically dependent is affected emotionally. And everyone who loves the chemically dependent person has to deal with the emotional rejection that usually occurs. Family members get pulled into a family illness as they try to find a way to relate to the chemically dependent person who has rejected them.

Kris wondered if she had ever really loved Tom. She tried to think back to when they were little. All she could remember was how mean he had been, how he was always hitting and fighting, how he was never nice to her, how he always made fun of her and teased her. She hated him. Sometimes she would tell their mother what he was doing, but it never did any good. Mom was never able to stop him. She tried, but she never could make him behave.

The movie was now talking about the family member who loves the addicted person most. This person will be the first who is severely affected by the illness. And the reason the family member becomes affected is because he or she is trying to help the addicted person.

Kris wondered who that person in the family was. *It must be Mom, but how had she been affected?* The woman went on to describe this person as the "prime enabler." *Then it couldn't be Mom,* Kris thought. *She's the most normal one in the family. She's the one that holds everything together.*

But, when she glanced over at her mother sitting and listening intently to the movie, it wasn't love and respect she felt, it was anger. Anger toward her mother for all the times she had taken Kris for granted. It was as if she expected Kris to do everything, to be everything. But even when she did, even when she was, it was never enough. Her mother had never loved her as much as she loved Tom. No matter how hard Kris tried, no matter how well she did, it was Tom who got all the attention. It wasn't fair. Nothing was ever fair.

The woman in the movie caught Kris' attention again. She said all children bond to their parents through their emotions. When a child is unable to do this there isn't much feeling life going on in the family. So this child, often the oldest child, has no place to bond, and instead learns to live as the parents do, which is to keep feelings inside and learn to survive. The oldest child has a lot of problems with inadequacy and guilt. And the child needs to get his or her parents' approval because there is no emotional bonding. So, the child tries harder and harder to do well. And yet, the child can't do well enough to change the chemical dependency or the parent relationship.

These children also feel a lot of guilt. They work harder to make their lives better and feel guilty when they feel any happiness because the parents are still in pain. As small children they tend to be good kids, getting good report cards at school, accomplishing great things, making up for the lack of emotional closeness by working hard to get the approval of the parents and to have people notice them. And this need for approval becomes a trap.

Kris slid further down into her chair, feeling as if everyone in the room was staring at her. She wanted to leave but was afraid of what people would think. The voice in the movie droned on telling about the characteristics of other children in a chemically dependent family, but Kris wasn't listening. She felt exposed. She thought back on the early part of the film when the woman described a family where one parent was alcoholic. Sure, she kept saying that the same pattern applied to families where anyone was chemically dependent, but it had to be different. Her mother wasn't the neurotic person the woman described as the prime enabler. And where did her father fit into the description? Nowhere. And this person, the good one, was supposed to be the oldest child. Well, Tom was the oldest child and certainly he wasn't good. Kris quit thinking and tried to sleep.

When the movie was over, Kris sat staring at the empty screen. Her mother reached over and put her hand on Kris' shoulder. "You okay?"

Kris pulled away wondering what her mother was thinking. "Of course." Quickly she left the room and headed for the rest room hoping her mother wouldn't follow. By the time she returned, the group had gathered at the front of the meeting room. Pat was introducing the next speaker. He was a chaplain at the center and there was something grandfatherly about him which Kris responded to immediately. She slid into a chair and listened.

"Alcoholism is a disease of body, mind, emotions, and spirit, but mostly it is a feeling illness. Feelings are the first things to be affected and often the last to heal. We don't know everything about chemical dependency, in fact, we have very little factual information. We don't know what causes it, or why, but we do know what it does, and we do know what we have seen over and over again here and in other treatment centers around the country. What I am going to tell you is the best material available. It is dependable. You can lean on it. I can't prove it, but I can trust it. And so can you."

The man shoved his hands into the pockets of his baggy corduroy pants and smiled warmly at his audience, evoking the trust he had claimed. "You just saw a movie which showed you that alcoholism is a family disease, that everyone who lives with or associates closely with an alcoholic ends up affected in one way or another. We speak of chemical dependency as an addiction to alcohol and/or other drugs. But what we want to talk about today is another kind of addiction, or perhaps obsession is a better word. An addict thinks mostly of his or her drug . . . how to get it, when to use it, how to get away with excessive use. Those who live with an addict have the same kind of obsession, only theirs is with the addict's behavior . . . how to relate, how to control, how to cover up, how to survive. It's a slavery that keeps the whole family in bondage.

"You know, when I was a boy I had a wonderful father who would take me on his knee every night and read Bible stories to me. It seemed to me the Israelites were always having problems, but the worst was the problem they had when their enemies would conquer them and carry off all of the strongest people into slavery in an enemy land. Well, my friends, every generation has its problems, and the problem of this generation is every bit as great. Hundreds of thousands of our young people and adults are being carried off into slavery in the enemy land of alcoholism and addiction. And their families are being dragged along with them. Addiction is a national epidemic and tragedy. It is predicted that we will lose ten percent of this generation in one way or another to this kind of slavery. Not only is it costing our country billions of dollars a year, but alcohol and other drug abuse troubles one of every three U.S. families and is considered a major national problem by more than eighty percent of the population according to a Gallup Poll."

He pulled one hand from his pocket and began to gesture, emphasizing each important point. "The average city police officer spends at least half a workday dealing with alcohol and other drug-related problems. Our prisons are filled with people who did things while under the influence of alcohol or other drugs. Most murderers are drinking or using drugs at the time they take another's life. Industry loses several billion dollars a year because of absenteeism and work inefficiency related to alcohol and other drugs. We have in this country an estimated twenty-five thousand deaths a year from alcohol-related automobile accidents. And alcoholics are about three times more likely to be divorced than nonalcoholics. I could go on and on, but I think you get the picture. Our people are losing their freedom. They are becoming slaves in an enemy land."

He sounded like an evangelist as he paused for dramatic effect. "My dear friends, I hope, if you take nothing else back home with you from this week of treatment, you will take this thought: There is hope for our future. One by one people are returning from that enemy land. We have seen it happen hundreds of times. It happened to me, to my wife, and to most of the people you see working here. The road back is a difficult road filled with pain and pitfalls. Again, you will have to trust me when I tell you, freedom from the slavery of addiction is worth any price you have to pay. Stop feeling sorry for yourselves. You have a long way to go on your return trip. Get on with it." He looked from one person to the other, catching each pair of eyes.

Then he picked up his notes and began describing the four phases of drug use and the way a family responds to each phase.

Kris' attention wandered but came back when he said, "You know, the frightening thing about the rampant use of drugs by our young people is how quickly and easily a teenager can become hooked. These phases I'm describing, in adults who begin drinking heavily when they are in their twenties or early thirties, usually take about ten to eighteen years. Of course, that varies greatly from person to person. For some the time is much shorter. But, the point I'm trying to make is that it takes a certain length of time for adults to reach the stage where their using is really causing problems in their lives and their bodies demand the chemical. But with kids, with teenagers, whose body chemistry is in a state of flux anyway, the time frame changes and it only takes a year to eighteen months. That's how it happens that we had a twelve-year-old girl here going through withdrawal and a thirteen-year-old boy who is a junkie.

"Kids don't think about that much when they are out with their friends passing around a joint, do they?" He seemed to be looking at Rick who blushed. "There is no harmless mood-altering chemical, no matter what you hear or read. They all can be abused. They all can cause dependency."

"Surely you're not saying," Connie interrupted, "that every kid who messes around with drugs for a couple of years is going to get hooked, or every adult who drinks for ten or twenty years? That simply isn't true."

"I'm sorry. I didn't mean to imply that. Obviously not everyone who uses chemicals regularly for a given length of time is going to end up hooked. We don't know why some people seem able to maintain the ability to control their use and the ability to stop using while others lose that ability. There have been many studies done to try to determine whether people are born predisposed to chemical dependency, and there is some evidence that that is true. Other research ties dependency into early childhood experiences. That may also be true for some. There's some interesting research going on now linking alcoholism to nutrition. But, we just don't know. All we know is what we see, and what we see is an increasing number of teenagers and preteenagers whose lives have been nearly ruined through drug abuse. These people seem to have very little in common as far as family background, but one of the studies done here in Minnesota drew a profile of a typical alcoholic as being someone who is apt to be a perfectionist with above average intelligence and far-above-average sensitivity. For such people, a sober life is often painful almost beyond endurance.

"Nobody chooses to become an alcoholic. An alcoholic begins drinking, only something goes wrong. Whether that something happened genetically or through birth trauma or through later experience or through the body's chemical reaction to heavy, sustained doses of a foreign chemical, we don't know. All we know is that at some time that person loses the power of control . . . not through choice or moral weakness any more than a cancerous tumor grows because of choice or moral weakness. It just happens, and from that time on, the alcoholic and family are on a treacherous, downhill roller coaster ride from which no one can escape without help."

He spoke with a passion and intensity that commanded attention. And then he stopped, took a deep breath, glanced at his watch and said, "I've talked too much. We'll have to hurry on to the next assignment." He passed out two sheets of paper, explaining as he moved from person to person. "This first sheet is a synopsis of the movie. It shows the various roles people tend to fall into in a chemically dependent family and what will likely happen to each person if some intervention does not take place."

Kris quickly glanced down the sheet. None of the roles fit at all except the family hero role. She read across: *the family hero is the one with visible success who does what is right. Inside he or she feels inadequate. To the family, he or she represents self-worth, the person of whom the family can be proud. He or she is a high achiever.*

Then her eye caught the column "Possible future characteristics without help." *This person often becomes a workaholic, is never wrong, is responsible for everything and often marries a chemically dependent person.* Then she remembered the woman in the movie had also said that the family hero often has children who become chemically dependent because no one learns how to express feelings. Kris felt sick. She glanced over at Connie who seemed tight and withdrawn and remembered that she had both a husband and a daughter who were chemically dependent. Had Connie been the family hero? Is that the way Kris would look in twenty years? She shuddered.

"The second sheet," the chaplain went on, "is a questionnaire I want you to spend about fifteen minutes filling out and then we'll gather around that table and talk about what we've written." Kris took the paper and looked at the questions.

1. Do I really feel a need for help, and can I calm down enough to think? Kris quickly wrote *I don't know,* and went on to the next question.

2. Is there a family problem that I wish would change? (Describe the problem.) She thought for a minute and then wrote, *I hate it when Mom expects me to keep track of Rick and to tell her what he's doing. Why is that my job?*

The next two questions asked her to evaluate what part she played in the problem and what she could do differently. Kris thought a minute and then left them blank.

A few moments later the group gathered around the large table located at the front of the room. "Who would like to go first?" the chaplain asked.

"I'll go first," Bonita said with a chuckle. "Leave it to me to just jump in." She gave Rick a little poke with her elbow and everyone relaxed a bit.

"Do I feel the need for help? My God, do I feel the need for help! They let Jim go out for dinner with us last night, and before the evening was over, I was a blithering idiot. Why do I let him do that to me? And to Eddie? He's the one who's really being hurt. I know Jim's trying and we ought to be supporting him, but something happens when we're together. I don't know." She paused, sighed, picked up her pen, tapped the table, and then set it down across her paper. "I guess that's the problem, I just don't know. I don't know what happens and why or what I could do differently." She shrugged and looked down. The chaplain paused to be sure she was through and then asked who would like to go next. There was a long pause.

Kris heard her father clear his throat. Looking at him, she noticed a strange expression, one she had never seen before. He began. "It's hard to believe what has happened to me in one day. Yesterday at this time I thought Tom was a casual drug user who happened to get caught, and that Erik was a little mouthy but basically an okay kid, and that whatever was going on in the family wasn't really my fault or even my concern. I'd managed to convince myself that my role was to provide financially, and I certainly was doing that.

"But, last night, after becoming so angry that I nearly struck my son, I finally calmed down enough to think. This question didn't quite fit so I changed one of the words to make it more appropriate, 'Do I really feel the need *to* help?' and the answer to that is yes. I realize, now, how removed I've been from the family and how much things have deteriorated. I see one of my goals as reentering the family and helping Beth and the children with their problems."

"Now that you know what's wrong, you want to fix things," the chaplain responded, rephrasing Paul's comments.

"Yes, yes, of course." Paul set down his pen, glanced down the sheet and said, "I guess I've answered all the questions."

Kris felt a deep sense of relief after hearing her father talk. Maybe none of this would have happened if her father had been more involved before. Now, maybe, things would change. But, her relief was short-lived. Bonita spoke up.

"Boy, if this isn't *deja vu*. Hey, Doc, don't you remember me telling you how I married Jim to change him and to help Eddie, and all I ended up doing was changing myself? And not for the better!"

Paul shifted in his seat. "So, what you're saying is that I should ignore the problem? Go on living as I have been?" By the time he was through with his question, he was looking not at Bonita but at the chaplain.

"It seems to you that there are only two ways to respond to a problem, ignore it or fix it?" the chaplain asked. The long silence that followed made Kris uneasy.

"In my practice I never ignore problems," Paul said. "The only reason it seems as if I have ignored this one is because I didn't know it existed. Had I known, I wouldn't have ignored it." His tone was defensive.

"In your practice, have you ever come across a problem which you simply didn't have the power or knowledge to fix? Something that was out of your hands even though you were there and involved and truly cared?"

Paul cut him off before his last word was finished. "I see what you're getting at. I just refuse to accept the idea that I can't change . . . ." He stumbled on the word and quickly rephrased it, ". . . that I can't help the people in my own family."

"Paul, we work here with what is called a Twelve Step program. It was first designed by and for alcoholics and is now used by people for all kinds of addictions, including the kind of addiction people develop who live with a chemically dependent person. I think you talked about that yesterday. It sometimes involves the need to control another person's behavior, to fix things. The First Step is a recognition of our powerlessness over alcohol and over others. What I hear happening here is that you're moving from one unhealthy response, emotional withdrawal from the family, to another, fixing the family. We haven't time to talk about it now, but just let me suggest that you finish reading the information in your folder about letting go, about detachment with love. Okay?" Paul made no visible response.

"Who would like to go next?" The chaplain looked around the table and his eyes settled on Rick. "Did any of the roles discussed in the movie seem familiar?"

"I don't know. I slept through it." Kris knew he hadn't and wondered why he was lying.

"How do you feel about your family? Do you like being a part of it?" the chaplain persisted.

Rick stared at his paper on which he had written nothing and muttered, "I hate it."

"You hate your family, or you hate being part of it?"

He looked across the table at his mother and said, "Mom, I'm sorry, but I do. I hate being part of this family." And then he looked at the chaplain. "How would you feel if you were part of a family where everyone was better at everything than you?"

"How do you feel about it?"

"I told you, I hate it. I hate having a dad who's a doctor. God, I probably won't even get through high school. And Tom is always better at everything than me. Everything. There isn't one thing I can do better than him."

"But, what about the horses?" his mother interjected. "You're a much better horseman than Tom."

"But you bought them for him, to keep him out of trouble. You never cared whether I could ride or not. I heard you talking. I do know a few things. You thought if he got interested in horses he would quit hanging around with all his scummy friends. God, were you fools. He kept his stash out there. When you thought he was riding, he was stoned in the barn or selling dope."

"Rick," the chaplain's calm voice cut through the tension. "One of the very common responses of parents when they sense their child is out of control or has lost control, is to try to manipulate the environment. Sometimes that involves moving, buying a summer home, going on extended vacations, or sending the kid off to summer camp. More often it involves the purchase of something the parents think will divert the attention of the child toward something worthwhile. We've had other parents who have invested in horses. Some buy cars or drum sets or electric guitars or computers. It never works, of course, but it does give the parents a sense that they are trying."

He paused. "Do you understand what I'm saying?" Rick nodded. "Now, I want you to forget about Tom and think about yourself. How do you feel about the other people in your family?"

"Kris makes me sick, sometimes . . . always such a goody-goody. I hate the way she tries to take care of me and treats me like a baby."

"What about your mother?"

Rick paused, seeming unsure if he should say anything. "I don't know. She's okay I guess. But she always looks so sad. And all she ever thinks about is Tom. It's like nothing we ever do is good enough or bad enough to get her mind off him. Sometimes I just want to scream at her, 'Look at me! Listen to me!' But she never does. I mean she does, but it's like she's never all there. Like I don't really matter." Kris glanced down, unable to look at the pain in her brother's eyes. But his voice went on, sounding more normal, so she dared to look at him again.

"The thing I hate the most is that she's always on my case for doing things, but she never says anything to Tom for doing the same things. Like swearing. 'Watch your language. Watch your language.' But she never says anything to Tom, and he swears all the time. And she grounds me for coming in five minutes late when Tom stays out all night, and she never does anything to him."

"Do you think she should let you stay out all night, also?"

"I don't know. Probably not. But it just doesn't seem fair."

"Life isn't fair, kid," Bonita bubbled in, throwing her arm over his shoulders. "You might as well learn that now."

"Rick, is there a family problem that you wish you could change?"

"I don't know. Just get Tom out of there, I guess. These last weeks were kinda nice. If we didn't have him around things would be better."

Kris was surprised. "I always thought you liked Tom."

"I do. I mean . . . ." He stopped talking.

"You do and you don't?" the chaplain suggested. Rick nodded. The chaplain glanced quickly at his watch. "Sooner or later you'll probably have to live with Tom again. Why don't you spend some time this week thinking about how you can do that without allowing his behavior to affect you so deeply." The chaplain waited a moment for Rick to respond. When he didn't, he went on. "Who would like to read their responses next?" Kris quickly looked down, hoping she wouldn't be called on. "Connie?" Connie unfolded her paper but didn't look at it.

"I really resent the first question. It implies, as so much of what has gone on here implies, that somehow we are the ones who need treatment. I'm here because my daughter needed help, not because I need help. I went to a counselor for half a year after my divorce, and she helped me put my life in order. I'm content with myself and my job, and I really don't want to talk about myself." There was a tone of finality in her voice. The chaplain nodded and shifted his gaze to Eddie who was sitting next to Connie.

"I guess I need help trying to understand my father, why he drinks. I wish I could feel closer to him, but even now, when he's not drinking . . . I don't know. It's just that I guess I always wanted a father like some of my friends have, but there's always something . . . ." He shrugged, glanced at the chaplain, and then back to his paper. Kris wished he would go on talking so she could keep looking at him without him thinking she was staring. He was very good looking, and there was something so tender about him.

"So, you wish you could change your relationship with your father?" Eddie glanced at the chaplain and nodded. "Or maybe his relationship with you?"

Eddie looked puzzled for a minute and then said, "There is a difference, isn't there? I know what I really want is for him to change."

"Do you think Eddie can change Jim?" the chaplain asked.

"Well, no . . . ."

"What happens when people want something so badly, something they have no control over?"

"Okay," Bonita laughed. "I catch your point."

"What about you, Eddie? Do you see the difference? You can't change another person or his or her attitudes toward you. But you can change your attitudes and expectations of yourself." Eddie nodded.

"Well, Beth? Kris? Who's next?" Kris felt her mother look at her with questioning eyes. She quickly looked down and her mother began talking.

"I've known our family was in trouble for a long time, though I never realized how bad it was. But the one thing I thought was okay was my relationship with Kris. Then, this morning after the movie, I looked at her and she seemed troubled. I wondered if she was concerned about something she had heard, so I put my hand on her shoulder and asked her if she was okay. She just pulled away, cutting me off. I walked down the hall feeling so hurt and alone. Then I realized that through these bad years I had been leaning on her and counting on her but that I didn't really know her. We never really talked. I don't know how she thinks or feels. She always cuts me off when I get too close. Or maybe I don't want to get too close. Maybe I've been afraid that I'd find more trouble, and I just couldn't handle any more trouble. I want my relationship with Kris to change. That's what I wrote down. Now that I say it, it seems minor compared to everything else. I don't know. There's so much . . . ." Her voice trailed off and the room was quiet.

"What do you think you can do to change your relationship with her?"

"I don't know. Stop leaning on her so much, I guess. Start listening to her."

The chaplain smiled. "That's a good start."

"Kris, how about you?" Kris felt blood rising in her cheeks as everyone looked at her. She wanted to think about what her mother had just said, but there wasn't time.

"I didn't really know what to put for the first one. For the second one I just put that I hate the way Mom always expects me to keep track of Rick and tell her what he's doing. Why should that be my job?" She addressed the question to the chaplain.

"Why do you think you took it on?"

"I don't know." She shrugged and went on. "Dad was never around, and the boys were so mean."

"That explains why she needed help. It doesn't explain why you chose to be the helper."

"Somebody had to help her."

"Maybe or maybe not, but why did you choose to be the helper? What did you gain by taking on that role?" The chaplain watched her thoughtfully.

Kris didn't understand what he was getting at. "They lied to her all the time. Someone had to help her." He paused a moment and then picked up the new thread.

"Did you ever lie to her?" Kris' pink cheeks turned red.

"The boys would have killed me if I'd always told the truth. I hated being caught in the middle. Mom was counting on me, but they always threatened me. I had to lie." Kris wondered if she would ever be able to look at her mother again, and then as quickly as that feeling of guilt came, it was followed by resentment. Why should she have had to be the good one, anyway? She wasn't a parent. Why couldn't she just be mean like her brothers?

"Kris, one of the symptoms of a chemically dependent family is that people get caught in power struggles where they are almost forced into being dishonest in order to survive. That happens in other families too, but it almost always happens in chemically dependent families. Everyone in your family has been dishonest in one way or another. It goes with the territory." The chaplain paused a moment to let his words sink in.

"Well, people, we've gotten a good start here. But we're running late and the residents in the cafeteria are probably getting upset with us because they can't get their seconds until you go through the line. I probably won't be seeing you again. Good luck to all of you in your journey home." He looked from person to person, radiating a sense of encouragement and hope.

As the group headed toward the cafeteria, Kris walked slowly at first and then quickly so she would end up behind Eddie in the line. Her plan worked. The only place left at the table was the one on the end with Eddie on the right and Bonita on the left. At the opposite end of the table sat Rick with their mother and father on either side. They seemed to be in deep conversation. Even though it had been her choice, Kris felt alone and left out.

"What are you thinking about?" Eddie was looking at her with concern.

"Nothing, really," she responded. "How about you? What did you think of the morning?"

"I don't know. Everything seems so confusing right now. I was thinking after your father spoke that I would like to have rewritten that first question, also, to, 'Do I really feel the need for hope?' Then I could have answered with a resounding yes."

"You don't think there's hope for you?"

Eddie paused a moment. "I guess it must be hard for you to imagine what it's like having a drunk for a father. You've always had a father you could be proud of. I've often thought that if only I could be proud of my dad, maybe I would feel better about myself."

Kris thought about what he had said as she drank part of her milk. "I'm proud of my father, I guess, and yet I feel terrible about myself. It's funny, until you said it, I had never thought of being proud of your father as something important." Eddie shook his head in disbelief.

"It's everything. You can't imagine what it's like to live someplace where everyone looks down on you because of your father, where people won't let their kids come to your house and don't even want their kids playing with you. I dropped out of sports, everything, because I was afraid my father would come to one of my events drunk and embarrass me." His hands started shaking as he talked, and he quickly put down his cup of coffee.

Bonita, who had been talking to Connie, picked up the end of the conversation and jumped in. "And he did, too, didn't he? Remember the sports banquet?" Eddie started to laugh that kind of laugh which is a substitute for rage. Bonita turned to

Kris. "It was incredible. He was loud and obnoxious all night, and then, when Eddie went up for his letter, Jim jumped up on his chair and started cheering and shouting, 'That's my boy.' Everybody laughed but it wasn't very funny for us, I can tell you. That was before we got married. I should have seen the handwriting on the wall. But no. Not me. I just jumped in thinking I could save the family."

Kris finished eating as Bonita talked, glancing from time to time at her family at the other end of the table. They were still talking. She tried to hear what they were talking about, but couldn't.

After lunch the group gathered in Pat's office. Kris sat down in a chair, between two empty chairs hoping Eddie would sit by her, but her mother sat in one and then, before Eddie had chosen a seat, Pat sat in the other.

"Did you have a good lunch?" her mother asked.

"It was fine." Kris wanted to ask what they had been talking about, but somehow couldn't.

Pat took a small book from her desk as she waited for everyone to get settled and then opened it to a premarked page. "This is a Christmas gift I received this year. It's a book of daily meditations called *The Promise of a New Day*. It was written by people involved in Twelve Step living, and the reading for today was so meaningful for me as I read it this morning that I wanted to share it with you." She cleared her throat and read a small passage.

> *Retrospect offers us what no one moment, in the present, is capable of doing. There is a pattern to the events of our lives, and even what appear as the most inconsequential occurrences are contributing their input to the larger picture that's developing. There is no question but that every event has meaning. No experience is without its impact. Time will reveal the reason for the baffling or troubling situations that have dogged our paths along the way.*

Pat paused for a moment before beginning the session to give everyone a chance to think about what she had read, then she began. "First a little business. When this meeting is over at about two-thirty, I'll meet with Kris for a personal conference and Donna will meet with Rick. Then, at three-thirty I'll meet with Eddie, and Donna will meet with Bonita. Again, I encourage you to make plans to get together for dinner or in the evenings. The better you get to know each other, the more beneficial this week will be." Kris glanced at Eddie. He was looking at her. Maybe she should talk to Bonita and see if they could come to the hotel that night. As this thought occurred to her, Pat went on, "Now, why don't you fill me in on what went on this morning?"

Connie stubbed out her cigarette, cleared her throat, and began. "I had a hard time understanding how the roles described in the movie are any different from the roles you can read about in any child psychology book. Children in families tend not to compete with each other for the same space. My daughters are all very different, but so are the children in almost every family I know."

"You're still resisting the idea that alcoholism affects the whole family," Pat responded.

"I'm not saying people are not affected, anything that happens in a family affects everyone. It just seems to me that you people are trying to justify your own existence by insisting that people in families need treatment." Connie held Pat's eyes for a moment and then reached into her purse for another cigarette.

Pat seemed unperturbed. "I don't know if this is a question of general interest or not, but let me give you a little background on family treatment and then if you have further questions, perhaps we can talk about it later.

"As you probably know, treatment for alcoholism and drug dependency has been going on for many years. As time went on, it became increasingly apparent that no matter how effective the treatment was, sending an alcoholic back to his or her family was almost always counterproductive. The family system had adjusted to accommodate the extreme behavior of the alcoholic. When the alcoholic's behavior becomes less extreme, everyone else is thrown out of balance again. It seems as if the family members might subconsciously want the alcoholic to drink again, even though, rationally, of course, they don't. You see what I mean? If the alcoholic goes back to extreme behavior, then the family system will be in balance again without anyone else having to change. It's often more comfortable to hold onto old problems than to risk change.

"We began working with families in order to increase the chances for sobriety of those who went through our program. It didn't take long, however, to realize that other family members had been deeply hurt and changed by the behavior of the addicted person. They needed help for their own sake, first to recognize those changes, and then to work toward becoming healthy people themselves, people who could, in turn, work toward achieving a more healthy family system. Does that make sense?"

Connie shrugged noncommitally and Pat looked at the others. "Other comments about this morning?" She waited and then went on. "If not, I'd like to do a little exercise this afternoon. Recall the problem you spoke of this morning or some other problem you want to talk about, and then try to think of two or three options you might have for dealing with this problem. Then we'll take a look at those options and see how workable they are." She waited for a time and then said, "Who would like to go first?"

"I will." Kris looked across the circle, surprised to hear Eddie's voice. "This isn't what I talked about this morning, but I thought about it during lunch. My biggest problem right now is that somehow I can't believe anything is really going to change. I don't want to be that way, but it's hard for me to have hope."

"You've had your hope dashed too many times?"

"I guess."

"What do you think your options are?" Pat continued.

"I don't know. Maybe if Dad stays sober for a year or so, I would feel better."

"Do you really want to give him the power to determine how you look at life?" Eddie looked confused. Pat went on, "You're saying that if someone else does something, you'll feel better. In Al-Anon, we always stress things that we can do to help ourselves so others don't have that kind of power over us."

"You mean I have to figure out how to be hopeful even if Dad never quits drinking?"

Pat nodded. "Can you think of how you might be able to do that?" Eddie shook his head. "Do you want to ask for help from the group?"

"No. I just need to think." He leaned back in his chair and slid down on his spine. As Kris watched, wanting to reach out in some way, his eyes darkened and she felt shut off.

"Who would like to go next?"

"I guess I could," Beth spoke up. "I talked this morning about a problem I had relating to Kris. I realized after listening to her what a difficult position I have put her in and I understand why she is resentful." She paused.

"Why do you think you put her in that position?"

"It hasn't always been that way, you know."

"Of course it hasn't, Beth, and no one is blaming you for it. I just think it would be helpful if you thought through what has happened to you in the past few years."

"I don't know. It was like I ran out of ideas, ran out of energy. Things were getting worse and worse no matter what I did."

"You were trying to control your children and it wasn't working."

"It wasn't working with the boys."

"But you could control Kris."

Beth thought for a moment before answering. "I never thought about it in those terms, but I guess you're right. It felt good to have some power some place. But, more than that, I thought, or hoped, she could get through to her brothers. She had always been so good with them."

"So, when you lost direct control of the boys, you tried to control them through Kris."

Beth pressed her finger to her temple. "There was no one else to turn to. I felt like a single parent."

Kris quickly shifted her gaze from her mother to her father. He was fidgeting in his chair, muttering something about how all that was going to change now.

"You seem angry over your powerlessness." Pat said, but Beth didn't respond. "Beth," Pat went on, "I'd like to have you read a handout we have on the difference between being a 'good' parent, as it is usually defined, and being a responsible parent. Also, pay particular attention to discussions about letting go and detachment with love. Okay?" Beth nodded.

"We need to move on. Who would like to go next? Rick?"

Rick sat up in his chair and leaned forward. "I don't know. This morning I was talking about how I was going to live with Tom again, but listening to all this talk about Mom and Kris got me started thinking about Dad. I don't know. Maybe living with him is going to be difficult now, too."

"In what way?" Pat asked.

"This sounds so stupid, like I'm never satisfied, but, well, I don't know. It seems so weird. I hated Dad for so long because it seemed as if he never paid any attention to me. He would come home and sit in his big chair and read the paper. When I would think of Dad, all I would see were knees and hands and a newspaper. Sometimes I wanted to just rip the paper out of his hands and say, 'I'm here. Look at me. Talk to me.' But last night when he started getting involved, I just wanted him to get out of our lives. And then, today, at lunch, we were talking about how things used to be, and I remembered how he would play with us and read to us and how proud I was of him. I don't know. I'm just confused. How did things change so much?"

Kris didn't hear the response to that question, if, in fact there was one. She, too, began remembering the way things used to be. She had never liked Tom. He had always been mean. But they had had fun — the whole family together. She remembered the trip they took to Disneyland and how her dad had held her on his lap when they went on the pirate's ride. Everyone else was scared and screaming but she had felt safe, secure. And the times when Mom would go out at night and Dad would be home taking care of them. He always let them stay up later than usual, and then, when he put them to bed, he would tell them funny stories about a little creature named Schloopy. Schloopy was invisible sometimes and could turn himself into anything. He was a wonderful friend and would always help children out of their problems.

Suddenly it occurred to Kris how her mother's God was like her father's Schloopy. Her mother's stories weren't funny, but they were always about a God who helped people out of their problems. For a long time Kris had believed that there was such a God. But the problems had just gotten worse. Doubt had crept into her, chipping away at her core until finally there was no Schloopy, and there was no God.

"Kris, you seem to be a hundred miles away," Pat's voice broke in on her thoughts.

"No, I was listening. You were talking about the way things used to be."

"That was fifteen minutes ago," Pat said with a grin. Kris flushed. Then Pat reached down and picked up from the floor two stacks of papers. "Time for your homework assignment." She started one of the sheets around the circle. "The first sheet is called 'Enabling Behaviors.' It lists some of the general kinds of behaviors which, in fact, enable the chemically dependent person in your family to continue abusing drugs. It also gives examples of specific behaviors.

"For instance, one common enabling behavior, particularly for fathers, is to get very busy with their jobs, to withdraw from the family physically and emotionally. By doing so, fathers are unable to see how serious the problem is, and therefore apt to excuse obvious problem behavior with such cliches as, 'Boys will be boys,' or, 'Let them sow their wild oats,' or, 'Better now than later,' and so on.

"Spouses of chemically dependent people often become super workers, providing financially for the family and then assuming all the domestic responsibilities covering for the failure of their spouse."

"But, someone has to do it!" Bonita interrupted.

"I admit it's a double bind." Pat went on, "But if a chemically dependent person can get anyone . . . boss, spouse, parent, child, anyone . . . to cover for him or her, it postpones the day of reckoning when the person finally accepts help. Chemical dependency is a progressive, fatal disease, and anything that postpones treatment is a negative thing."

"You mean we're supposed to just leave the bills unpaid?" Bonita asked.

"Or let your son end up in reform school?" Beth added.

"We're often faced with some very difficult choices, but the important thing to keep in mind is that any time we protect an addicted person from the consequences of his or her behavior, we prolong the disease." Pat scanned the group, asking with her eyes if there were any more questions, and then went on.

"Of more importance, however, is that these enabling behaviors are hurting you, hurting your chances of living a full, free life. In Al-Anon we talk a lot about changing all those things we can change, accepting those things we cannot change, and figuring out how to tell the difference."

"Like the prayer up there?" Bonita interrupted, pointing to a large plaque on the wall.

"Yes, that Serenity Prayer has become deeply meaningful to members of A.A. and Al-Anon all over the world. I hope it's one of the things you will take home with you. At any rate, what it boils down to is that all you can really change are your own behaviors and attitudes, and if trying to fix things has left you feeling helpless or angry or frustrated or feeling like a failure, then maybe it's time to let go, both for your own sake and for the other person's sake."

Pat paused for a moment, as if something she had said had triggered thoughts about her own life. Then, she shook her head and directed her attention back to the group. "Another enabling behavior is to take on responsibility and guilt for the chemically dependent person's behavior. Such people tear themselves apart with 'Why did I . . .' and 'If only I hadn't . . . .' Whenever chemically dependent people can find someone to feel guilty, then they don't need to take responsibility for their own behavior. If a husband tells his wife that it's her nagging that is causing him to drink, and she believes him and takes on the guilt, not only will he have found a needed scapegoat, but she will be miserable.

"Families of chemically dependent people cover up for them, lie for them, bail them out of legal and financial problems, hide their bottles or drugs, or try to buy their love by buying them booze.

"All of you, in one way or another, have gotten caught up in enabling behaviors. What I want you to do for tomorrow is to read through this list and talk it over among yourselves so you understand what each item is about. Then," as she spoke, she began to pass the second sheet around the circle, "then I want you to spend some serious time filling in this 'First Step' sheet. We call it the First Step sheet because it brings you to the point of realizing that your lives have become unmanageable because of chemical abuse and that you are powerless over it. This, as you have heard before, is the First Step in the Twelve Steps of Alcoholics Anonymous, Al-Anon, and Alateen. Because what has happened to you through living with a chemically dependent person is so like what happens to that person, we have discovered the same Steps to recovery used by the residents here are also helpful for the families. Tomorrow morning after our film, we'll share what we have learned about ourselves through working on this sheet." She glanced at her watch.

"Well, it's two-thirty. Take a break, Kris, and then I'll meet you here. Rick, you're scheduled to meet with Donna."

Kris grabbed her purse and ran down the two flights of stairs to the pop machine in the basement. As she waited for the diet cola to drop she heard steps behind her. Connie came up to the machines checking to see what was available. "You'd think they would have something a little more nutritious in these machines," she complained, "I thought this place was supposed to emphasize physical health." She pulled a cigarette out of its pack and searched for some change. Then she looked at Kris. "I can't believe we're going to have to sit through three more days of this. You look about as bored as I feel."

Kris felt she was expected to respond affirmatively so she did. "It really is a drag, but I think my father is being helped." Connie didn't respond. Kris popped open her can, waited a moment wondering if she should say anything else, and then ran back up the stairs.

Alone in the office with Pat, she felt nervous. Pat seemed able to read her mind.

"Well, Kris, how are you feeling about things so far?" Her voice was kind and concerned.

"It's okay, I guess." Her voice trailed off.

"Would you like to tell me what you were thinking about this afternoon? I was watching your face. Your expression went from one of joy to one of real pain."

"It was nothing. I was just thinking about the stories Dad used to tell us when we were little."

"What were they about?"

"Well, they were about this little creature named Schloopy. The people in the stories always got into some problem, but Schloopy would get them out."

"Sort of a guardian angel?"

Kris smiled. "Yes, I guess that's what he was. I was thinking of him as being like the God our mother told us about in her stories. He always helped people, too."

"Do you believe there is such a God?"

Kris looked at the floor and then out the window. "There's nobody that takes care of anything."

"What do you mean?" Pat asked.

"Dad's never around and Mom tries, but nobody listens to her. I used to pray, but God didn't listen to me. It's like I'm the one." Her voice kept rising. "People expect me to fix things and everyone blames me when things go wrong."

"And just once in a while, you'd like to have someone take care of you, someone you could lean on."

Kris felt tears flooding into her eyes. "I hate it. I hate being the one."

Pat reached over and took hold of her hand. "It's okay to cry, Kris. You don't have to be strong here." Kris felt her nose starting to run, but before she had a chance to be embarrassed, there was a tissue in her hand. She wiped her nose and dried her eyes and felt in control again.

"Tell me how you feel about your mother."

Kris tried to think about how she felt toward her mother.

"She's really great. I mean, she's had to put up with so much from those boys and she's always there . . . ."

"But, if she's always there, why do you feel so alone, as if all of the responsibility were yours?"

"I don't know."

"Do you ever talk to your mother about your feelings?" Kris shook her head. "Do you ever tell her about your problems in school or with your friends?" Again the answer was no. "Why do you think you feel the need to be the strong, problemless person in the family?"

"Is that wrong, to be strong? To not have problems?" Kris responded defensively.

"It's not a question of right or wrong, it's a question of what's helpful and what isn't. Has it been helpful to you to play this perfect child role in the family?"

Kris began tearing the tissue into little shreds. She felt Pat waiting for her to respond. Finally she shrugged, hoping Pat would go on to something else. She glanced at her watch. Ten more minutes.

"Kris, I noticed you wrote down as your personal goal that you wanted to feel better about yourself. To any outside observer that would seem an absurd goal. After all, why would an attractive, bright, talented girl like you not feel good about herself?"

Kris shrugged. "I don't know why. Maybe nobody really feels good about themselves. I know none of my friends do."

Pat laughed. "Well, I will admit that being a teenager makes one highly susceptible to a low self-image, but I think with you there are some special causes. What do you think would make you feel good about yourself?"

Kris thought for a moment. "I don't know. I just wish Tom would be different and Mom would be happier."

"So you tried to change Tom and do things to please your mother." Kris nodded. "Has it worked?" Kris knew no answer was necessary. "How does that make you feel?" Once again Kris felt tears filling her eyes, but she forced them back. "Guilty? Angry? Powerless?" Kris nodded.

Pat sat back in her chair. "Kris, how would it change your feelings about yourself if you could really believe that Tom's behavior is not your responsibility, and neither is your mother's happiness? Those are their problems. You don't have to take them on. Will you think about that?" Kris gave no indication that she had heard the question, but she was thinking, thinking about what it would be like not to have to worry about Tom, not to have to feel responsible for him. She smiled to herself and then listened again to what Pat was saying.

"We haven't much time left, but I wanted to say one more thing to you. Kris, you're only sixteen years old. You don't need to be forty. It's okay to be a kid, to do foolish things, to make mistakes. The behavior of your brothers is not your problem. And the way your parents feel about you is not your problem either. They love you as much as they can, right now. They're going to be able to love you more, eventually. But, in the meantime, it's important that you learn to let yourself be human regardless of what others expect. It's okay to be yourself. Can you believe that?" She paused.

"Kris, look at me." Kris felt blood rising in her cheeks as her eyes moved from the floor to Pat's probing eyes. "Can you believe that?"

Again her eyes filled with tears. "I don't know." She looked quickly away, out the window this time. It was beginning to snow.

"I hope that by the end of the week, if nothing else, you will trust yourself and your parents enough to be open with them. Work together on sorting out which problems belong to whom. That will be a good start for you."

Pat stood up and Kris followed. Then Kris saw Pat step forward. "Can I give you a hug?" Kris nodded, but felt awkward and stiff and pulled away quickly. Then she immediately felt guilty. She didn't want to hurt Pat's feelings.

"What are your plans for the evening?" Pat's voice was casual and friendly. Kris relaxed.

"I don't know if we have any yet, probably just dinner and swimming, the usual. The pool at our hotel is great."

"Have you made any effort to get together with the others in the group? That might be fun."

Kris grinned, "Yes, that might be." Pat caught the implication. They giggled over their shared secret as Kris opened the door and went out to find her family. Rounding the corner into the hall, she almost ran into Eddie who was waiting for his appointment. She blushed, wondering if he'd heard what she had said.

"I guess we'll be seeing you later on tonight," he said.

"What?" She wasn't sure she had heard him correctly.

"We were just talking to your folks. They invited us over to your hotel tonight. I don't think Connie is coming, but Bonita and I will be there."

"Great. Bring your swimming suit." Kris couldn't believe her parents had actually thought of inviting them over.

Later, when Kris and Erik were resting in their room before dinner, Rick asked, "Have you thought about that enabling stuff, yet?" Kris rolled over so she could see Rick's form in the darkening room.

"Not much. I can't really think of anything. Why?"

"I did things all the time. I'd have to write a book. Did you know I used to hide his stuff in my room or sometimes in your room so Mom wouldn't find it when she would search his room? And I would lie for him all the time, always saying I didn't know where he was, or saying he was somewhere when I knew he wasn't. It was like I was his right-hand man. How was I supposed to know he was hooked?"

"What would you have done if you had known?"

"I don't know. Probably nothing. He had me so twisted around his finger. It was like anything he wanted, I would do. I wanted his approval so badly I would do anything, be anything. I don't have any idea who I am." He paused for a moment and then went on. "Kris, can you keep a secret? Mom and Dad would die if they knew this."

Kris rolled to her back. Another secret. Another thing she would have to keep inside. But his voice was so tender, so plaintive, that she said, "Sure, of course."

"When I was talking to that other counselor this afternoon, she asked me about my own drug use. Kris, I've been thinking, ever since we came here, that maybe I'm hooked, too. She wants me to take the assessment for chemical dependency. Do you think I should?"

"What assessment?"

"I don't know. I guess there's someone here who asks you a bunch of questions and they can tell if you have a problem or not. Do you think I should?"

"I don't know. If you want to." They lay in silence for a few minutes and then Kris began talking. "At my conference we talked about God, some. Do you ever think about God anymore? I've been thinking about Him more and more since we got here. Maybe there really is a God. What do you think?" Without waiting for a response, she went on. "Do you remember the stories about Schloopy that Dad used to tell us? I told Pat about them and she . . . ." Kris was suddenly conscious of the sounds of deep breathing from the opposite bed and realized Rick had fallen asleep. She sighed and rolled on her side, pulling the spread over her legs. The next thing she heard was a loud knocking at their door.

"Did you kids fall asleep? It's time to go to dinner." Kris called out something so her mother would know they were awake and then tried to shake the sleep from her head. She turned on the light and gave Rick a nudge. Within a few minutes they were ready.

Dinner was pleasant and uneventful. Everyone, apparently, had slept that deep, late afternoon sleep that leaves a person feeling groggy for hours and then not able to sleep at night. They were just finishing dessert when they heard a familiar voice.

"There you are. We thought we might find you here." Bonita and Eddie pulled up chairs and joined them at their table as they all exchanged greetings.

"Don't let us interfere with your dessert. We'll just sit here and drool." Kris thought how great it would be to have someone like Bonita for a mother, someone who was always so cheerful and funny.

As they were leaving the restaurant, Paul suggested it might be a good time to do homework. Later they could swim. Having decided to do their work poolside, the group split, the adults gathering around one small, round, glass table, and the teenagers around another.

Kris pulled the worksheet out of her purse and found extra pens. Silently, they read through the introductory statement, *Your primary goal in Phase I is to recognize and accept on a feeling level your powerlessness over addiction, dependency, and an addicted, dependent person . . . that in your attempts to control the addiction and addicted person you were powerless and your life was unmanageable . . . . Please give specific examples of your behavior for each of the following:*

Kris read the first question and then turned to Eddie. "In what ways have you been preoccupied with your father?"

"I don't know. In what ways have you been preoccupied with Tom?"

"I haven't. I just try to forget he exists."

"But, isn't that preoccupation?" He asked with a grin, raising one eyebrow. Embarrassed that she hadn't thought of something so obvious, Kris quickly looked down and made a note on her paper.

"What about you, Rick?" Eddie shifted in his chair so he could face him. Kris, too, looked at her younger brother, wondering if he would talk about all the ways in which he had been affected by Tom. Rick seemed unusually thoughtful.

"I think about him all the time. I really do. I'm always wondering what kind of a mood he will be in and what he will think of me. Whenever I do something new, I always wonder if he will approve. Like the horses. I loved riding. But whenever he was out there, he just made fun of me and would always want me to come in the barn and smoke with him."

"Is that why you quit riding?" Kris felt more sympathy for Rick than she ever had. She had never seen him so vulnerable.

"I've quit everything. I was just thinking about it today. I can't do a damn thing well. And now Tom is going to come sailing back home, sober, and he'll be able to do everything he tries to do. He's always been able to."

"So, get with it, Kid. You're only fifteen. Stop being such a quitter." Eddie's voice was harsh, and Rick responded with anger.

"You're telling me you never quit anything? You've had a drunk for a father and you haven't been affected?"

Kris watched Eddie pull back into his chair, a sulking look on his face. But Rick wouldn't shut up.

"What are you going to do, leave the sheet blank? Come into the group tomorrow and say, 'Look, gang, I'm perfect'?"

"Rick, knock it off." Kris stopped him before he had a chance to go on. "Forget about him," she said, turning to Eddie. "He's nothing but a brat."

They sat in awkward silence for a time and then Eddie sat up, leaned forward looking down at his sheet and said, "Sorry I got on your case like that. I just didn't want you to end up like me.

Of course I've been affected. I used to knock myself out trying to get his approval. Big jock. Captain of the team. It never worked. He would brag about me to other people when he was drunk, but I never felt as if he really gave a shit what I did. So I quit." He looked down and Kris wondered if he was through. "I got my first semester grades today. Three *C*s and a *D*. Cripes, I used to get straight *A*s in high school." He stopped talking and began writing on his sheet.

"Look at the next question," he went on. " 'How have I tried to control his use of chemicals or his behavior?' I used to lie awake at night thinking up plans to keep him from drinking so much, like watering down his wine, or hiding the liquor, or insisting that he help me with things so he wouldn't have time to drink." He paused for a moment sighing deeply. "But the stupid thing was, when he would ask me to drive him to the liquor store I would do it. It was the only time he was nice to me. We would talk and laugh all the way over. But once he got the stuff, it was like I didn't exist again."

"You must have really hated him," Kris said sympathetically.

Eddie pulled back into himself. "I didn't hate him. I just felt sorry for him. He was missing so much. It didn't really matter to me. Years ago I found other men who treated me like a son. I just started spending most of my time at the homes of friends."

"You kids going swimming?" Bonita's voice broke in.

Kris looked from Eddie to Rick and then back to Eddie. He seemed hesitant.

"I don't care what you two do, I'm going swimming." Rick left the table heading for their room.

"What do you want to do?" Eddie asked.

Kris shrugged.

"It's really beautiful out, and warm. Would you rather take a walk?"

Kris folded her paper once, then again and again. She had never been on a date and felt awkward around boys other than her brothers. But Eddie was mature and kind and seemed to understand her. "Sure. I have to get my coat. I'll be right back."

Minutes later they were walking on Nicollet Avenue toward downtown Minneapolis. Snow was falling in huge, wet flakes through balmy air.

"I love downtown Minneapolis," Eddie said as Kris felt him put his arm around her shoulders. "My old gang from high school used to hang out down here a lot. There's a bar down a couple of blocks that never carded anyone. I guess we all looked like we were nineteen. Or maybe they just didn't care. I heard they got busted a few weeks ago for selling to minors. Too bad."

Kris was upset by what he was saying and wondered if she should say anything. They walked in silence for half a block, and finally she worked up the nerve.

"It seems funny to me that you like to drink when you have a father who is an alcoholic. It would seem to me that you'd hate the stuff." She felt his grip on her shoulder loosen.

"I used to feel that way, but someone told me the worst thing you can be is a fanatic. What you have to do is to learn to drink responsibly. Besides, it'll never happen to me. I've lived with that too long to ever fall into that trap." He paused and then looked at her quizzically, "Don't you ever drink?" Kris felt like a ten-year-old as she shook her head no. "You really are a goody-goody, aren't you?" Before she had a chance to get angry, he grinned and winked and snuggled her a little closer.

Just as they reached an intersection, a car squealed to a stop in front of them. A head popped out of the back seat window yelling, "Eddie? Is that you?"

"Toad, you old turd, what are you up to?"

"Hey, pile in. We're on our way to a party."

Eddie looked at Kris questioningly but before she had time to object, he was pushing her into the already crowded back seat of an old car.

Once inside, Kris realized she was sitting on the lap of a creepy looking boy whose breath reeked of beer. She heard a can pop and everyone shifted to avoid the foam pouring over the edge.

"Here, Ed. You might as well get started. Just a sec, I'll get one for your broad."

"She'll share with me," Eddie responded to the faceless voice, "and knock off the broad business." Kris was so grateful that she forgot he was the one who got her into the situation in the first place.

Within minutes they pulled up in front of a large, old house which had been turned into apartments.

"Who lives here?" Eddie asked.

"Skid's old man threw him out a few weeks ago so he got an apartment. It's a perfect place for parties."

As they walked up the outside stairway to the second floor apartment, Kris caught Eddie's attention.

"I don't think we should be doing this. One of the rules for the week was that we weren't supposed to use any mood-altering chemicals. Why don't we go back to the hotel?"

"You've got to learn to relax, kiddo," he said in the same tone that had made her embarrassed before. "We'll get someone to drive us back in a few minutes. I really want you to meet my friends."

They threw their coats on top of a mound of jackets and boots near the door, and then Eddie reached in his pocket and handed a guy sitting near the door some money.

"What are you doing? We have to pay to go to a party?" Kris whispered.

"You just pay for the glass. Then you can drink all you want. That way one person doesn't get stuck with the whole cost of a party. Sometimes you can even make money throwing a party."

"But I don't want to drink," Kris protested as Eddie handed her a glass.

"You don't have to." His voice sounded fatherly. "The best thing to do is to fill your glass and then just sip slowly all night. That way people will stay off your back. Here." He took her glass, filled it from a keg sitting on the kitchen counter, and handed it back to her. "Now, just keep sipping."

Kris took a sip, getting a mouthful of foam, and grimaced at the taste.

"The first taste is always the worst. After that it doesn't taste so bad." Eddie took a long, slow drink and then another, almost emptying his glass. "Try it, just drink a little more," he said as he went back to refill his glass.

There was something wrong about all this, but Kris couldn't think clearly enough to sort it through. And besides, Eddie was older and had been around. He ought to know. She drank some more of her beer.

"Atta girl," he said encouragingly. "Here, I'll fill up your glass and we'll go into the other room." He led her into the living room and began introducing her to the people he knew. He told them she was an old friend from New York who was visiting for a week. With those credentials she was accepted into the group in a way she had never felt accepted before. There was a couple of pillows along the wall and Eddie led her to them, pulled her down next to him, and, once again, put his arm around her shoulder. She felt his body twitch to the loud rock beat and his hand on her shoulder move sometimes to the music, sometimes slowly, tenderly, up and down her arm.

Kris sipped some more of her beer. The hand patted her shoulder approvingly. She realized, with some concern, that Eddie had finished his second glass and had sent someone into the kitchen to get him a refill. Looking at his face, she saw the change. All the tension that had been present during the day was gone. He seemed relaxed and content. His eyes, usually so deep, so shadowed, were open, beckoning. He saw her looking at him and grinned, pulling her closer. "This isn't so bad, is it?" Just then his friend returned with his glass. Eddie took it, set it on the floor and reached over, taking Kris' half full glass and handing it to the girl. "Here, freshen hers up a bit, too, would you?" Kris began to protest but he stopped her. "You don't need to drink it, you know."

Moments later, Kris was relaxed against the wall, holding a full, cold glass. She sipped again, and this time it tasted good. Eddie seemed not to be noticing what she was doing, but when her glass was half empty, he signaled someone who came and filled both their glasses again. The music turned mellow and couples were dancing in front of them. Almost involuntarily, Kris curled toward Eddie and felt his arm drop from her shoulder down around her waist, his fingers moving along her lower ribs. He put his glass down and reached for something. She felt his chest expand as he inhaled deeply.

"Want to try a little of this?" he whispered into her hair. She lifted her head and saw that he was holding a skinny, poorly wrapped cigarette. He must have felt her body stiffen because he passed it quickly on and began stroking her back. "You worry too much. Can't you just relax?" His voice was tender this time, almost loving, and Kris wanted to please him. "Come on, let's dance."

He stood up and reached down to help her. As she stood, her head turned to liquid. Eddie held her around the waist and led her to a darkened corner of the room.

"You dance very well," he said after a few moments.

Kris giggled. "Are you surprised that I can do anything?" He held her closer.

"I'm sure you could do anything you wanted to," he said as they swayed to the music, hardly moving from their spot in the corner. Kris had never felt so content, so at peace. As the record changed, they stood for a moment without separating and then began dancing again.

Suddenly Kris became conscious of something hard pressing against her stomach. She pulled back, unsure, frightened. "Hey, don't do that." Eddie's voice was reproachful as his hand slipped down to her lower back, pulling her close to him again. He didn't seem to notice or care that she was no longer dancing. "Come on," he said, "I think the bedroom's empty."

Sour panic rose in Kris' throat. She swallowed hard and pulled away. Grabbing her arm, he turned toward the bedroom. She pulled away again, her back to the wall.

He looked at her with disgust. "I should have known you'd be a waste of time," he said as he quickly made his way through the crowd.

She hesitated for only as long as it took her eyes to adjust, and then, terrified at being alone in this dark room filled with strangers, she followed him. Trying to keep him in sight, she didn't notice the couple dancing next to her, and she bumped heavily into the girl.

"I'm sorry," Kris apologized.

"It's okay," the girl responded and held out her arm to block Kris from going farther. "Don't worry, he'll be back in a minute." It was the girl who had been filling their glasses. "I'm glad you didn't give in to him. When I first saw you, I thought you'd be another poor sucker." She danced off and Kris leaned back against the wall, hurt and angry.

A few minutes later he was back, acting as if nothing had happened. "I found us a ride back to the hotel. Are you ready to go?" Without responding, Kris followed him across the room to the pile of coats and then out the door.

The car they got into was a new sports car driven by a boy Kris had not noticed at the party. Before taking off, he handed a half-smoked joint back to Eddie telling him to hold it or finish it, it didn't seem to matter to him one way or the other. Then he shifted into reverse and the car bulleted out of the driveway, skidded on the snow-covered street, and headed around a curve toward a busy thoroughfare.

Kris sat on the edge of the seat, fighting nausea as she watched them pass car after car.

"Relax, kid, we'll be there in a minute," she heard Eddie say in a tone devoid of affection or concern. Moments later they pulled up under the canopy of the hotel and skidded to a halt. As they entered the lobby, they were met by a delegation of angry parents.

"Where have you been?" Bonita glared at Eddie.

"What's all the fuss about?" Eddie was calm, in control. "We just stopped at a little cafe and got to talking." Kris felt the eyes of her parents on her, and she couldn't look at them.

"Well, young man, you gave us quite a scare. We were ready to call the police." Kris grimaced, amazed that Bonita had believed the story. "Come on, let's get out of here so these folks can get to bed." She patted Eddie affectionately on the shoulder as they began walking toward the door. "See you all at eight-thirty," she called to the Inghrams as the door closed behind them.

"From you we want the truth," her mother said as they got on the elevator. The tone of her voice combined with the upward movement of the elevator sent a woozy feeling sweeping through Kris. She grabbed the handrail and swallowed, trying to look normal. Her father, who was standing closest to her, leaned down and breathed deeply.

"Kris, you've been drinking." Kris couldn't stand the hurt in his voice. She turned toward the wall grabbing the handrail with both hands as the elevator came to a stop.

"She looks like she's going to be sick," she heard her mother say in a faraway voice. "Quick, get her to her room. Erik, run ahead and open the door."

Half pushing, half carrying, her father maneuvered her down the hall. The sour contents of her stomach moved into her throat. She swallowed it back. Once more it came, and again she forced it down. Then, with the bathroom in sight, it came again. She lunged forward, grasping her mouth, warm, acrid fluid filling her hand and pouring out onto the bathroom floor. She crumbled to her knees as her stomach convulsed again and again, spurting vomit onto white tile.

Gasping for air, Kris sat up and wiped her mouth. From behind she heard the voice of her brother. "I'm not sleeping in here tonight. It stinks."

"Get your things, you can sleep on the floor in our room." Then the voice of her father was closer, harder. "Clean up your mess and then get to bed. We'll talk about this in the morning." Kris thought she heard her mother crying as the door closed, leaving her alone.

Not knowing where to begin, Kris sat back on her heels, wiped first her eyes, and then her mouth with the back of her hand. The smell was so bad she thought she was going to be sick again. Then she took one of the snowy white washcloths from the counter, sopped up what she could, and rinsed it in the toilet — over and over until all that remained were spatters on the wall.

Trying to avoid looking in the mirror, she brushed her teeth, spitting again and again. But when she fell into bed, fully clothed, the sour taste was still there.

DAY THREE

Cold and stiff after a night on the floor in his parents' hotel room, Rick opened his eyes and stretched. Morning light trimmed the curtain edges, and the incessant, rumbling sounds of traffic along the freeway signaled the beginning of the early rush hour. Wrapping himself in the spread from his father's bed, he sat up and leaned back against the bureau wondering why his parents weren't up yet and if he should wake them. Being in their room and seeing them asleep in their separate beds made him feel awkward, embarrassed, like an intruder in a private world.

Memories flashed back of other times years ago. At the first signs of dawn, he and Tom and Kris would crawl out of their own beds and race for their parents' room, bounding into their bed laughing and tussling. Then the dog would come, leaping on top of the pile, licking faces, trying to crawl under the covers. His parents would lie on each side of the bed, snuggling the closest child, tickling another.

He heard the phone ringing in the next room — twice, three times, four and five times. He jumped up, gathered his clothes in one arm, and went through the door connecting the two rooms. He picked up the phone, thanked the voice, and seconds later heard the phone ringing in his parents' room.

The dull smell of vomit hanging in the room reminded him of the night before. He sat down on the edge of the bed and gave Kris a nudge. "Kris." She moaned and rolled over. "Hey, Kris, wake up." Gradually she lifted her head and turned, staring at him as if she had never seen him before. "It's me, Rick, your brother. Remember? Boy, you must have really gotten trashed last night." Without saying a word, she got out of bed and went into the bathroom.

Rick pulled on his pants, rummaged through his suitcase for a clean shirt, slipped it on and was buttoning it when there was a light tap on the door. "Are you kids up?"

Rick didn't respond at first, expecting Kris to, as she always had, but when no acknowledgment came from the bathroom, he said, "Sure, Mom. We'll be ready in a little while."

The door opened a few inches. "Erik, where's Kris?" Hearing the water running in the bathroom, Beth didn't wait for a response. "How is she?"

"I don't know. Crabby. She didn't talk to me." Rick noticed how deeply sad and tired his mother looked. He went over to the door and said, "Don't worry, she'll be okay." His mother's smile was so grateful that it made him feel both proud and guilty at the same time.

A few minutes later Kris came out of the bathroom and sat down on the edge of the bed to take off her shoes so she could change her clothes. "Rick, you've got to help me. What am I going to say? They're going to kill me."

Rick thought of the countless times he had heard Tom say the same thing. But, somehow that was different. He didn't want to help Kris. She shouldn't have gotten herself into the situation in the first place. It just wasn't the way things were supposed to be. He shrugged, "You got into it, now you can get out of it," and then ducked quickly as a shoe came flying at him.

"After all . . ." she began but didn't finish. "Just get out of here so I can get dressed."

He went into the bathroom and took as long as he could washing up, hoping their folks would come in so he wouldn't have to face her again, alone. When he heard voices he opened the door just as his father was saying, "Do you want to tell us about last night?" He didn't hear her response, but he saw Kris turn away from them and brush her hair vigorously.

After a strained breakfast, the family arrived at the treatment center where they were greeted with a friendly good morning by Bonita and Connie. Eddie appeared not to notice that they had arrived. Rick looked from him to Kris, who was standing with a sullen face behind their parents, and back again to Eddie. He was becoming increasingly curious as to what had gone on between them the night before. Perhaps he should have been nicer to Kris when she tried to talk to him. Maybe she would have told him.

Before they had a chance to sit down, Pat came bubbling in. "Well, I want you all to know I made it through the whole evening without a cigarette. That's two days now." No one responded very enthusiastically. "So, did you all have a good evening?" Rick looked around wondering if anyone would respond.

"Sure, great," he answered after an awkward pause. "I went swimming and did my homework," his voice trailed off as Pat glanced quizzically from person to person.

"Well, perhaps there are things we can talk about later. Right now, we have another movie. This is by a recovering alcoholic who has done a series of films on facets of the illness. We don't agree with all of his ideas. In fact, we strongly disagree with some. But still, he has much to say, and he says it in a way that almost anyone would find interesting."

"What things don't you agree with?" Paul asked.

"Well, for instance, you'll hear him say all family members are made sick by the behavior of the alcoholic. That simply isn't true. There's a difference between being affected, even affected adversely, and being made sick. We can talk about some of these things after the movie, but just let me caution you that whenever you hear an absolute statement made by him, or by anyone else in the field, substitute words like *most* or *often* or *probably*, and then you won't be misled."

The group followed her up the two flights of stairs to the meeting room and spread out in the room, no one sitting next to anyone else. As the lights were turned off, Rick slid down in his chair, suddenly feeling very tired. But the warm, friendly face of the man on the screen caught his attention and he listened. The man was saying alcoholism is more than just personal involvement of family members when one member is alcoholic. Other family members become affected and need treatment, too.

Rick looked away from the soft, penetrating eyes of the speaker who seemed so sure of himself, so knowledgeable. Yet, here they were at treatment, and things were not getting better, they were getting worse. Kris had never gone out drinking before. And Mom seemed quieter and sadder than ever. It was true something had happened to make their father start getting involved with the family, but now that it had finally happened, Rick wasn't at all sure it was a good thing. And when he thought about himself, he realized he was more confused than ever.

The speaker also said the alcoholic is addicted to a drug and his whole life revolves around that. He winds up frustrated and isolated. The frustration is so acute that the alcoholic often commits suicide.

Rick thought of Tom sitting alone out in the barn, often for hours, sometimes overnight. He had always thought of Tom as having all kinds of friends. Maybe they weren't real friends. He remembered the time he had come out to feed the horses early one morning and found Tom lying behind one of the stalls, his head in a pile of horse shit and his clothes soaked with piss. It was a miracle he hadn't been kicked or stomped. As Rick pulled him away, Tom came to and started to cry, pleading with Rick not to leave him. And then, before Rick had a chance to respond, Tom turned on him, calling him a gutless fag.

The movie caught Rick's attention again. The man said all we know about the alcoholic, and all he knows about himself, is what he does, and people are judged by what they do. Don't try to appeal to an alcoholic's sense of shame, he knows shame you have never heard of. He knows guilt you've never read of. The only thing that helps is the drug that's destroying him. The insanity of the alcoholic is not what he does when he's drunk, it's when he's perfectly sober and he picks up that first drink.

People are judged by what they do . . . the insanity . . . picks up that first drink . . . it's insane . . . . Sweat began to soak Rick's armpits. He heard the counselor's voice quietly recommending to him that he take the assessment for chemical dependency. Could it be that he, too, was hooked? He used all the same drugs Tom used. Probably not as much, but he didn't really know how much Tom used. He thought of his mother. She couldn't stand it, knowing both her sons were junkies. He knew she couldn't stand it.

The movie said the alcoholic is the greatest manipulator on earth and you can't live with such a person and not have it rub off on you. Rick wondered, *what had rubbed off?* That was the question. Rick listened to see if the man on the screen would answer it for him, but he was talking about how a drunk man physically abuses his wife and children. Then he started talking about how wives of alcoholics often turn to God and become fanatic, or they turn away from God after years of unanswered prayers, bitter and disillusioned. Again he thought of his mother. Was it because of Tom that she had gotten so religious?

Rick heard a chair scrape against the floor and turned around and saw Eddie shifting uncomfortably from one position to another. The speaker said that in families that are really not functioning, you will find alcohol in four out of five cases. And in students with bad disciplinary problems in school, you will find the bottle at home in about four out of five cases. *But how did that apply to their home,* Rick wondered, *where it was the kids, not the parents who drank, where it was the kids, not the parents who had the problems? It didn't make sense.* Rick glanced back at the projector and saw the film was almost over.

The man said the family must get well together. Whether the alcoholic gets well or not, the family is affected and needs help. Some alcoholics die, but the family must still live and solve its own problems. With that, the movie was over.

Pat entered the room and asked Eddie to turn on the lights while she shut off the machine. He got up slowly, grudgingly, and walked to the switch on the wall.

"Take a quick break," she said, "and then we'll meet in my office to discuss the movie and your First Step worksheets."

Rick got up, stretched, and then walked over to the window, looking out at nothing until he felt an arm on his shoulder. He was startled at first and then surprised as his father gently squeezed him and said, "Well, son, do you think the movie is right?"

"About what?"

"Do you think we really will find happiness in all this mess?"

Rick wanted to say something hopeful, something that would keep the conversation going, but he didn't know what to say. As he stood staring straight ahead, his father's hand slipped from his shoulder. Rick couldn't look at him, but as they walked together toward Pat's office, he sensed a bond with this man he hardly knew, a bond of uncertainty and fear, a shared dread of the future, a mutual perception of life as a giant puzzle whose pieces never quite fit together.

His father sat down and Rick, after a moment's hesitation, sat next to him. His father looked at him and smiled, as if thankful for this small favor. Again Rick didn't know how to respond, it was so strange, so new.

"Well," said Pat as she joined the group which had finally gotten seated, "what did you think of the movie this morning?" She waited.

"I liked this film," Bonita responded. "It seemed relevant, to the point."

"What seemed relevant?" Pat asked.

"I don't know. I guess all the talk about what happens in families, especially to spouses. I could really see myself ending up like that if something doesn't change."

"Ending up like what?"

"You know, the part about how the wife becomes the martyr who thinks of herself as the good one, the responsible one, the one who holds everything together; and her husband is the bad one. I'm already starting to think like that, and we've only been married two years!" Her laugh this time was edged with bitterness.

"Any other comments or reactions?" There was a long pause. Rick glanced around the group wondering if anyone else was going to talk. No one seemed interested so he spoke up.

"I liked the movie. I mean, he was good and funny and all that. But I kept thinking it didn't really apply to our family. He kept talking about all the terrible things that happen in a family when one of the parents is an alcoholic, but in our family, it's one of the kids. How did the kids get so screwed up if the parents were okay?"

"Maybe they weren't okay," his mother responded, and Rick wished he hadn't asked the question.

"Now wait a minute," Pat jumped in before anyone else had a chance to say anything. "Don't be so quick to heap guilt on yourself." She looked directly at Beth. "I get the impression that you do that a lot, but we'll talk about that more when we start on our First Step sheets. In answer to your question, Rick, all I can say is that we don't know why it happens. All we know is that we're seeing it happen more often. Of course, no parent is perfect. But in many of these cases, the problems with the children go so far beyond anything that would ordinarily be expected from a given home, that there must be some other explanation.

"Not everyone in the field agrees with this, but my theory is that some people are born predisposed to chemical dependency. Because the use and abuse of chemicals has become so popular in our country among young people, those persons so disposed become hooked while they're still living in their parents' home, and therefore it's the parents who become affected by the disease rather than the other way around.

"I heard a speaker once who referred to a verse from the Bible that said, 'The parents ate the sour grapes, but the children got the sour taste.' He said we're living in a time where everything has become topsy-turvy, and now it would be true to say, 'The children ate the sour grapes, but the parents got the sour taste.' " Rick wasn't sure what eating grapes had to do with anything, but the first part of what she had said made sense.

"Any other comments about the movie?" No one responded so Pat went on. "Then, why don't you all take out your First Step sheets and we'll talk about what you learned about yourselves from answering those questions. I think it works best to take one question at a time and have everyone share his or her answer before going on to the next question. So . . . ," she said as everyone shuffled through their folders finding the right paper, "who wants to start?"

Rick felt his father move forward and then say, "I guess I can. When I first read the question, I couldn't think of any way in which I was preoccupied with Tom. I couldn't even remember thinking about him much over the past few years. And then it occurred to me that that wasn't normal. It's not normal to never think of your own son. As I thought about it, I realized my preoccupation with Tom was a preoccupation with avoiding him. That included avoiding talk about him also, which meant I had to cut off my wife too."

Rick watched as his father and mother looked at each other across the room. It had never occurred to him that his mother and father didn't talk about everything. He had always thought of them as some kind of all-seeing, all-knowing unit.

Paul went on. "I'm really sorry, Beth, that I haven't been more support to you. I wanted to talk to you about it last night, but then we got distracted." There was a long awkward pause. Pat looked from one person to the other, but let it drop.

"Who wants to go next?" Beth nodded and opened up her sheet.

"I hardly knew where to begin. I thought about Tom all the time. I couldn't sleep at night because I was so worried. My dreams often were about him. My prayers were always about him. I know how boring I must have been to everyone because I talked about him constantly. The crazy thing was that after pouring out all my troubles onto my friends, if they didn't respond right, I would cut them off."

"What was a right response?" Pat asked.

"I don't know . . . just listen, I guess. I know what the wrong responses were. I got so paranoid, my antennas so finely tuned, that I could tell in a minute if the person blamed me or thought I was at fault in any way. I thought I was to blame, but I couldn't stand to hear it from anyone else. And, I guess, everyone, somewhere in their thinking, blames parents when things go wrong with kids. Soon there was no one left.

"Then I pretty much stayed home, thinking and thinking, spinning my wheels, trying to figure out what I had done wrong.

I had to figure it out so I could fix it somehow." Rick looked away as tears flooded her eyes. There was a long pause and then Bonita spoke up.

"I had some of the same things on my list, though, Lord knows, I didn't spend a lot of time praying. I can understand how a mother would think everything was her fault, would spend a lot of time trying to figure out what she had done wrong, but I did the same thing and, my God, the guy was an alcoholic when I met him. Why should I have thought it was my fault? And yet, every time he drank heavily, I tore myself apart trying to figure out what I had done to trigger it."

"Do you realize, now, how counterproductive that was?" Pat asked.

"Counterproductive? I realize it didn't do any good. I never could figure anything out."

"And, how did that make you feel?"

"Angry, I guess. Guilty."

"If you assumed the guilt for Jim's drinking, what did that do for him?"

"I know, I know. My therapist told me that a thousand times. If I took on the guilt, then Jim didn't need to be responsible for his own behavior."

"So, why do you think you held onto that guilt?" Pat addressed her question to both Beth and Bonita.

"I don't know," Bonita responded.

"What does guilt imply?"

"That you've done something wrong," Kris broke in.

"Not necessarily," Pat responded. "Let me put it this way. Say a man comes home, walks in the door, and is hit with full volume rock music from the kid's stereo. The first person he sees is his wife. He yells at her, she bursts into tears, runs upstairs, and locks herself in her room. So, he sits down to watch the news and begins to feel guilty. Why is he feeling guilty?"

"Because he yelled at his wife," Bonita answered the obvious question.

"And because she started to cry," Kris added.

"Which is more important, do you think?" Pat asked.

"If she had laughed and told him to go shut it off, he wouldn't have felt guilty," Kris concluded.

"So, guilt, at least some of the time, is a feeling we get when we do something which produces certain negative effects." Everyone nodded, following her logic so far. "Guilt, then, at least in some cases, is based on the assumption that we have the power to hurt or influence another person. Right?" Again the group nodded.

"Now, what do you think the man is planning as he sits there in front of the TV?"

Paul cleared his throat. "He's probably thinking of ways to make amends so she'll stop crying."

"So, if he holds onto the assumption that he hurt her, he can hold onto the assumption that he can help her."

"But, in this case, he did hurt her," Connie interjected.

"Maybe and maybe not. What if she had just received a phone call telling her that her father had been killed in an automobile accident, and she was so stunned she hardly noticed her husband?"

"Then her sadness wasn't his fault," Bonita concluded.

"And?" Pat pressed.

"And?" Bonita thought. "Oh, and he can't fix things by apologizing or making amends."

"Do you see what I'm getting at? As long as people hold onto guilt, they're also holding onto the assumption of power. They had the power to cause something, and, therefore, they have the power to cure it." Pat checked to see if people were following her and then went on.

"If, for instance, as a parent, you did something at some point in your child's life to cause the chemical dependency, then by some reverse action, you might be able to undo it, to fix things, to cure. Beth mentioned being obsessed with figuring out what she had done wrong so she could fix it. She thought she had power over Tom. People hold onto that guilt because to let go of the guilt is to let go of the belief that you have power. The truth of the matter is that in the area of chemical dependency no one has the power to either cause it, control it, or cure it." Even though it was Bonita who had raised the issue, by the time Pat quit talking, everyone was looking at Beth.

"I had never thought of that, but I guess it's true. I've had a thousand plans over the years for solving the 'Tom problem.' I guess I always did believe I caused it and could therefore cure it. I don't like to think I don't have that power." She laughed a little at herself and then another voice was heard. Everyone turned to Connie, surprised to hear her speak up.

"I think parents, particularly mothers, are in a terrible double bind. On the one hand, we're told we're the major determining factor in the lives of our children. All of society seems to hold us responsible. If there's a problem with the child, the automatic assumption is that there's a problem in the home, particularly with the mother. Even the movie this morning talked about how one can assume there is a problem in the home whenever there are discipline problems at school. And now you tell us that, in fact, we are not to blame. How can parents be both responsible and not responsible, both all powerful and without power? It doesn't make any sense."

Everyone turned to Pat, expecting an answer. She paused for a time and then said, "It's a paradox. Both statements are true, even though they seem to cancel each other out. We've observed that chemically dependent teenagers come out of all kinds of homes, from the most loving and supportive to the most abusive and destructive. There doesn't seem to be any causal relationship between a particular problem in a home and chemical dependency among the children, except that children of alcoholics tend to have a higher risk factor than other children. Whether that is genetic or environmental or both, we don't know.

"We've also observed that when parents or spouses tear themselves apart with guilt, they are totally unable to move forward toward health. Whether they are at fault or not, whether they at some time did something that might have been a causative factor or not, it does no good to accentuate that guilt. At this point, what people need is release from guilt and the self-confidence to move on." She paused again, looking from person to person.

"Now, I'm afraid I've made it sound like a whitewash, like maybe you really are to blame, that we're just telling you you aren't so you'll feel better. That isn't true. When I think back on my childhood and try to figure out why I became chemically dependent, I could say it was because my parents were alcoholics, and certainly that may have had something to do with it. But my sister and brother grew up in the same home, and they have led more or less normal adult lives. Certainly not all children who have alcoholic parents become chemically dependent. I could say it was because I was raped by my stepfather when I was twelve, but sexual abuse of children is more common than anyone would like to admit, and, while it surely leaves deep scars on all victims, they don't all become drug abusers. When questions of cause come up, because we know so little, we have found it the best policy to try to relieve guilt and not affix blame."

Rick found it difficult to listen carefully as Pat talked. His mind wandered back to the conference he had had the day before. Would his mother feel guilty about his drug use, also? He tried to think of anything she had ever done that might have influenced his drug use one way or the other and he could think of nothing. He grinned to himself. It was funny, actually, when you thought about it, that parents think they have any influence over teenagers at all. His attention refocused on the group. Eddie was talking.

". . . Then when he'd ask me to take him to the liquor store, that was after he lost his license, I would do it." He shook his head as if unable to believe his own actions.

"Why do you think you'd help him get liquor when you hated so much what it did to him?" Paul asked.

"I don't know. It was just that he was so nice to me when he needed me. I remember the line in the movie about what manipulators alcoholics are. I guess that's really true. At least he was always able to manipulate me."

"Why do you think you let him do that?" Pat asked.

"I don't know." Eddie sighed deeply. "What was I supposed to do?"

"You could have refused," Connie said sharply. Eddie's face turned angry and defensive.

Pat quickly intervened. "She's right. You could have refused. That was one of the options open to you. But, you didn't. At this point it's much more helpful to ask yourself why you didn't than to beat yourself with 'should haves.' What was the trade-off? What did you get out of it?"

Rick remembered the conversation the night before when Eddie had mentioned how he and his father would talk and laugh all the way to the liquor store. Then his mind drifted off again, this time thinking about all of the times Tom had gotten him to do things for him. Like the time Tom had come to him one Saturday evening. He'd said he was grounded and really needed a big favor. "One of my friends has some pills that he'll sell to me. It's all legal, don't worry. I just need you to go to the corner by Jack's store. He'll be there. Just give him this money and bring the stuff home." When Rick hesitated, Tom had patted him on the back and told him what a great brother he was, and how he didn't know what he would do without him, and how if it weren't for their uptight parents, he would never have asked Rick to do it. Rick couldn't remember if Tom had been grounded and wondered vaguely why grounding was stopping him this time when it had never stopped him before. But he had felt so flattered to be asked, so pleased to be accepted that he had taken the money and walked to the corner.

When he arrived, he recognized one of Tom's friends standing against the wall. It was a corner where kids hung out all the time so there were people all around. Rick walked over to the kid who appeared very nervous. "You Tom's brother?" he asked. Rick nodded. "Here, take this and get out of here fast." They made a quick exchange and Rick hurried on down the street. He thought he heard steps behind him. Turning, he saw two men gaining on him. He began to run. They followed. Quickly he turned a corner, tossed the package into the open window of a parked car, and kept running. When they finally caught up with him and frisked him, they found nothing. But they had taken him to the police station for questioning. Who was he? How did he know the boy on the street? Why had he run? What had he done with the stuff? Rick had acted totally bewildered and finally, when he started to cry, they let him go. On the way home he had gone back to the street, but the car was gone, and all he could think about was how he had failed Tom and how angry Tom was going to be with him.

For the first time, as Rick sat there in his swivel chair, he realized Tom had used him, that he had known it might be dangerous, that he hadn't really been grounded, that he had deliberately gotten Rick into trouble. Rick wondered how many other times he had been lied to and manipulated like that. He had always thought he was the one Tom liked, the one Tom could trust. It made him feel good about himself to think he was, somehow, special. But Tom didn't like him or trust him. He used him.

"Rick?" Pat's voice pulled him back. Everyone was looking at him. "Have you been off in another world?" Rick covered his embarrassment with a laugh.

"I was just thinking about how Tom used to get me to do stuff for him. I always thought it was because he liked me and needed me. But he was just using me. Cripes. It makes me mad." He dropped his foot to the floor and sat forward.

"Mad at Tom for using you or mad at yourself for letting him?"

"I don't know. Both I guess. I just feel so stupid for not catching on. How could I have been so dumb?"

"Don't be so hard on yourself, honey," his mother said. "I'm an adult and I let him use me all the time and never caught on to what was really happening."

"You're both being too hard on yourselves," Pat interjected. "You have to realize that an addict's whole way of life is dependent on getting drugs, and to do that they often have to manipulate others. They become absolute masters of the art. It's difficult for people to see when they're being used, maybe because they really don't want to. It hurts to think someone you love is using you. That's why we so strongly encourage families to get involved in Al-Anon and Alateen. Someone else who has been through it will be able to pick out manipulation in your life in a minute, manipulation that you might never see yourselves." Pat glanced around the room, focused on Eddie, and then returned to Rick and Beth.

"But before we leave the subject, let me ask you the same question I asked Eddie. What was the trade-off? What did you get out of it? What personal needs were being met by the manipulative situation? When you've figured that out, you should be able to come up with healthier ways of taking care of your own needs."

Pat glanced at her watch. "Well, we never seem to have enough time. I hope in your spare time you'll get together and share your answers to the rest of the questions. Talk about ways you've tried to punish the dependent person. Think of things you've done and said that go against your own value systems. For instance, almost everyone who lives with an alcoholic takes on lying as a way of life. It's almost necessary for survival in that situation, and yet most people hate having to lie, and feel guilty for doing so. Also, talk about how this situation has affected you emotionally . . . mood swings, depression, irrational anger at others in the family, temper flare-ups, crying jags, and so on. Many people also develop physical symptoms . . . nervous tics; shortness of breath; excessive tiredness, or the opposite, the inability to sleep; chest pains; intestinal or digestive problems; arthritis; high blood pressure; all the stress-related physical problems. It's important to realize how so many of the parts of your personality that you couldn't explain and didn't like were simply responses to the situation. Any questions?" She waited a moment and then went on.

"Donna and I have worked together formulating goals for each of you, goals we'd like you to accomplish before the week is over. We base these goals on what you listed as your personal goal, information about you we gathered from our personal interviews, and other things we've observed during the past two days."

She looked at the names on the paper. "Okay. First, the Inghrams. We want you all to spend as much time as possible writing out the things that you see as blocks in your relationship with Tom. Those blocks might be resentments you feel toward him because of things he has said or done. They might be fears or anxieties you have, or feelings of guilt or shame. They might have to do with your sense of responsibility for Tom which has fostered feelings of failure or inadequacy. Try not to edit yourselves as you go along. If the thought or feeling or memory comes to you, it's important. Write it down. There will be more than enough problems in the present to deal with when you get home. We don't want you to be carrying home any of the baggage from the past. Any questions about that?" Pat looked at each of the Inghrams, and they each, in turn, indicated understanding.

"Then I'd like Paul and Beth to do what we call a dyadic encounter. We assume, here, that any time a family has gone through what you have gone through, the marriage relationship has suffered. This encounter is a way of beginning to rebuild the bonds you once had. The instructions are on the top of the page. And then I want you both to read the book, *Why Am I Afraid to Tell You Who I Am?* You can take a copy out from the library downstairs, or buy a copy at the desk. Any questions?" She handed Paul a copy of the goals. He took it, read it as if it were a prescription, and then folded it and put it in his inner suit coat pocket.

"Looks like you're next, kiddo," Pat said with a grin, turning to Rick. Rick clasped his hands between his knees and couldn't look at her. "You're to work on a list of blocks toward Tom, also. Try to be specific. For instance, don't say simply, 'He used me,' or 'He manipulated me.' Mention specific situations when you let him use you, or hurt you, or set you against your parents or Kris. Then I want you to write letters to both of your parents telling them anything you feel important, maybe that you're sorry about certain things, or maybe angers you have toward them, and then tell them what you want and need from them. What kind of a relationship do you want to have with them when you go home? Finally, as you and Donna talked about in your interview, we want you to take the assessment for chemical dependency." Rick felt hot blood surging up his neck into his face.

"All of you young people," Pat went on, looking at Kris and then Eddie and finally Rick, "are high risks because of the situation you have been living in. Don't let that frighten you unduly. I mention it only so you'll be cautious, and, if you feel you need help, you won't be afraid to get it." She paused, and then said to Rick, "We've set up an appointment for you today after our afternoon session. Okay?" Rick nodded without looking up.

The meeting went on for some time as Pat explained goals to the other people in the group, but Rick didn't hear what she said, so concerned was he about the assessment he had to take. He wondered if he should lie, tell them he didn't use drugs often, cover up the trouble he had been in. But what was the point? He really wanted to know about himself. And if he didn't tell the truth, how could he ever know? He wondered what kind of questions they would ask, and whether they would be able to tell right away or if it would take them some time to figure him out. He looked down and realized he had made jagged tears all along the edge of his goal sheet. He folded the paper quickly, hoping no one had noticed.

The morning meeting was over and the group hurried down the two flights of stairs to the dining room. As they walked down the hall leading to the dining room, Rick heard Eddie's voice behind him say, "I'm really sorry about last night." Thinking he was being spoken to, Rick turned around but quickly realized Eddie was talking to Kris. "Were your folks really mad at you?" Rick tried to hear her response, but the noise from the dining room covered her answer if, in fact, she answered at all.

Eddie's father, Jim, and Tom greeted them at the door and joined them as they picked up their food and gathered around the corner table. Jim sat at one end with Eddie and Bonita on either side of him. Rick took the spot next to Eddie after noticing that Kris was moving toward the opposite end of the table. Tom sat across from him.

"How was your morning group?" Jim opened the conversation, looking at Eddie who was taking a bite out of a large chili dog. Bonita answered for him.

"We talked about those enabling sheets I told you about. And we learned about what manipulators you guys are, right?" she said, looking at Eddie first and then at Rick.

"I'd like to be a mouse in a corner at one of your meetings," Jim joked.

"Oh, don't worry, you'll find out all our complaints. We're meeting with you late this afternoon. Boy, is my list a mile long," she laughed, poking him in the arm with her fork.

"Well, I don't think anything you could say would spoil my day," he responded good-naturedly. And then, directing his comments to Tom, he went on. "I took my Fifth Step this morning. Man, is that something. I feel like a new person. I think I know what Christians mean when they talk about being born again. Have you done yours yet?"

Tom shook his head no, as he chewed a mouthful of food, and then he responded. "I decided to wait until after our next family conference. I guess that's going to be tomorrow. It was really weird, when I sat down to try to think of all the ways I had hurt people and wronged people, I really couldn't think of much. I guess I was high so much of the time that I really didn't realize what I was doing was hurting anyone." He scanned his family with his eyes. "I'm counting on you to refresh my memory."

Everyone else at the table was wondering, but it was Paul who finally asked, "What's a Fifth Step?"

"The Twelve Steps are printed over there," Jim responded, and everyone turned and tried to read the large plaque on the wall. "It's simply admitting to God, to ourselves, and to another human being all of our wrongs. Of course, before you can do that, you have to remember what they are. That's the Fourth Step. Actually, the Fourth Step is taking a moral inventory that includes both your liabilities and assets. For instance, you write down all the times you can remember when you've been dishonest with yourself or with others, and then you think of those times when you've been honest. I have to admit that my negative list was a bit longer than the positive one, but there were a few things on the positive side." Jim chuckled and grinned, first at Bonita who responded in kind and then at Eddie who kept his eyes fastened on his plate.

"If that's the Fourth Step, then what is the Fifth Step?" Paul continued his query.

"After you've finished writing everything down, you find someone to hear your list. Often the person is a member of the clergy, but it doesn't have to be that way. It should be someone who'll keep it confidential and who knows something about chemical dependency and the Fifth Step. Then you sit and talk with the person, telling everything about your behavior that has kept you from living a happy, worthwhile life."

He paused, finished the last of his coffee, and then went on, his tone more personal, more intense. "You know, even though I had written down all those things, it wasn't until I sat with a chaplain and told him that I really admitted them to myself and to God."

"But what about people who aren't Christian or who don't believe in God?" Connie asked.

"Well, in the first place, you don't have to be a Christian to believe in a God or a Higher Power. We just talk about 'God as we understand Him.' Jews believe in God, and so do Muslims and even agnostics. But, you'll see if you look over the Twelve Steps that in order to get to the Fifth Step, you have to get past the Second Step. That Step involves believing there's a Power greater than ourselves that can restore our sanity. Some of the people here have real trouble with that one because they've gotten so turned off by religious people who have laid the big sin trip on them. But counselors and chaplains help you work through that here because, for the program to work, chemically dependent people have to admit their own powerlessness and turn their lives over to a Higher Power, some sort of spiritual force in their lives." There was a pause, the only sound being the clicking of forks against plates and cups against plastic trays.

Then Bonita spoke up. "So, if you decide to be an atheist, you'd better make sure you're not an alcoholic."

Jim pondered that one for a moment and then said, "There's a difference between religion and spirituality. I don't really understand it, but they say a person can be spiritual without being religious in the usual sense of the term. Also, there are other kinds of treatment programs for alcoholics that don't depend on recognition of a Higher Power, but for some reason they're not nearly as effective."

"After you've told the chaplain about all you've done, what does he do? I mean . . . does he forgive you?" Beth asked.

Jim seemed confused at first by the question. "I don't remember that he really did anything, but I felt this enormous burden falling from my shoulders. I felt so light, I thought I was going to levitate on up to the ceiling." He looked up, gesturing and laughing, as he tried to explain what had happened to him. "And then, it was the strangest thing. I haven't been to mass since I was a kid. I think I quit going when I was fourteen or fifteen, about the time I started drinking. But all of a sudden it was important to me again so I asked the priest if I could have the sacrament. We left his office and went to a little meditation room. As he handed me the bread, I felt a kind of peace I didn't know was possible. I'm really able to start over." His eyes filled with tears. Bonita reached over and hugged him as Eddie picked angrily at the food remaining on his plate.

Tom glanced at the clock on the wall, shoved his chair back, picked up his tray, carefully put his chair back under the table, and came around the corner to where Jim was sitting. Patting his shoulder affectionately, he said, "Let's go, buddy. We're going to be late for our group." After the two left, an introspective silence fell over the group. It wasn't until Pat came, joking about how somber they all looked, that they seemed to come to. She sat down in Jim's chair, directing her comments to Eddie.

"Your father had quite an experience this morning, I hear."

"Yeah. That's really great for him." Everyone at the table noticed his hand shake as he put his cup down. Then he picked up his tray, and left the table.

"Something's really eating at that kid," Bonita said softly to Pat. "What can we do to help him?"

"Just leave him alone. He's coming along fine. When you protect people from the pain they need to go through, you rob them of the experiences they need to return to health."

Rick looked at Kris and noticed her eyes followed Eddie as he left the dining room, but the expression on her face was a mystery to him.

A few minutes later the group reassembled in Pat's office. Pat handed the open Al-Anon book to Paul and asked him to read. He glanced down the page and then began.

> *One source of frustration we seldom recognize is in* expecting *too much of others, or* expecting *too specifically what we feel they ought to be, say, give or do.*
>
> *If I* expect *another person to react in a certain way to a given situation, and he or she fails to meet my expectation, have I the right to be disappointed or angry?*

Paul closed the book and handed it back to Pat. She opened the meeting by mentioning that Bonita and Eddie were going to be meeting with Jim that afternoon. "I talked to both of you early in the week about writing down all those fears, hurts, resentments, and guilts that are a part of the wall that separates you from Jim. You'll be able to share them with Jim later. I'd like to have you share them with us, now, if you don't mind." She looked first at Bonita and then Eddie.

"I didn't have time to get mine done," he said. "I thought there would be an hour or so after our group this afternoon — "

Paul cut him off. "If you hadn't taken our daughter out drinking last night, you might have had time to get your work done." The group tensed. Pat, with raised eyebrows, looked from Eddie to Kris.

"Drinking?" Bonita exploded. "Is that what you were doing all that time?"

"Kris was so sick she puked all over the bathroom floor." Rick couldn't resist throwing in the comment, plus an imitation of Kris gagging.

"Shut up. Do you think you're perfect?" The eyes of the group focused on Kris. She turned to Pat. "I hate this. It wasn't my fault. But everyone is treating me like an outcast."

"Do you want to tell us what happened?" Pat asked.

Kris looked first at Eddie and then down. "Why don't you ask him?" she muttered.

"I'd like to have you tell me," Pat persisted, but Kris, crossing her arms across her chest, refused to look up. Beth reached over and patted Kris' shoulder, trying to console her saying they hadn't meant to treat her like an outcast.

Paul said to the group, "I think Eddie should tell us what happened. Kris has never done anything like this before, and I'm sure she wouldn't have last night if it hadn't been for him."

"You're excusing her and keeping her trapped in the hero role," Pat responded giving him a penetrating look. And then she turned to Kris again. "You don't need to tell us about last night if you don't want to, but I want you to notice what just happened. You've gotten very good at using silent withdrawal to manipulate people. You did it to me during our conference, and I suspect you do it to your parents and perhaps your friends regularly. Your parents were, apparently, quite upset about your behavior last night, but all you had to do to turn them around was to wrap yourself in a shield of hurt, self-pitying silence." Kris appeared to withdraw further and further into herself.

Pat continued to focus on Kris. "Who are you angry with, Kris?" Pat kept up the pressure. "Your parents?" She paused waiting for a response. "Eddie? Yourself?"

"I told you it wasn't my fault!" Kris almost screamed at Pat and then immediately closed herself off again.

Rick glanced at Eddie, wondering if he would speak up, if he would contradict her or verify what she was saying. But he was staring at his shoes.

"What if it had been your fault?" Pat went on. "Would that have been so bad? You don't need to be perfect, you know." Kris didn't respond.

"How did it feel to be blamed, to be the one everyone was angry with, the one your parents were disappointed with?" Kris turned her chair slightly and pushed it back.

"Did you feel your parents loved you less?" Kris looked at Pat, her silence now the silence of assent.

"How could she think that way when she accused me of loving Tom the most, and I was angry with him all the time?" Beth addressed her question to Pat.

"Why don't you ask her?" Beth hesitated and then turned to Kris.

"Honey, how could you . . . we never . . . I mean, I didn't want . . . ." Rick had never seen his mother at such a loss for words. He wished Kris would say something instead of just sitting there in silence. It made him furious when she did that. "I was rebellious when I was young. I never really expected . . . . It's not that I wanted you to . . . . We never stopped loving the boys. Why would you think we'd stop loving you?" She reached over again and put her arm around Kris' shoulder, but Kris wouldn't look up.

Pat waited a moment and then turned back to Eddie. "Are you going to give us the silent treatment too?"

Without looking up, Eddie shrugged and said, "It was nothing. We just ran into some of my old friends and went to a party, that's all."

"A drinking party," Pat said.

"Is there any other kind?" Eddie joked, but no one laughed.

"During your personal conference, did you talk to Donna about your drinking habits?" Pat asked.

"She asked, but I told her I didn't drink much. I don't. God. What kind of a fool do you think I am? I'm not going to turn into a drunk like my father."

Pat hesitated a moment and then said, "I want you to take out your goal sheet and add two things. I want you to do one of them, for sure. The other I can only suggest. You have to make the decision." Eddie reached into his folder and got out his goal sheet.

"I want you to read the book *It Will Never Happen to Me*. With an attitude like you have, you're a sitting duck. And then, I would strongly urge you to take the assessment for chemical dependency. Let me know what you decide so I can set up an appointment." Eddie sat with pencil in hand as if he were going to add the new goals to his sheet, but he wrote nothing, put his goal sheet back in the folder, and dropped the folder to the floor. He looked at Pat defiantly. She held his gaze until he looked away.

"Now, where were we? Oh yes. Did you get your list finished, Bonita?" Bonita nodded and took it out.

It appeared as though she were going to begin reading and then she stopped. "You know, I feel really foolish about all these things, now, after listening to Jim this noon. I mean, he's feeling so good, and I come along and dump on him."

"Don't worry about Jim," Pat said. "He can handle it. He's got a lot of support here, and, if you don't get it out now, it'll eat away at you and come out in irrational ways."

Bonita looked at her paper again and this time began reading. "Dear Jim, I love you so much, at least I think I love you. But you've done so many things that have hurt me and Eddie that I can hardly think about you or look at you without feeling angry. I hated the way your moods would swing so we never knew what to expect. Sometimes you were so loving and kind, but it seemed as if the times we needed you the most, you were either distant or cruel or just not home — "

"Bonita, can I interrupt a minute? You're writing this for you, not for you and Eddie. I want you to change all of the 'We's' to 'I.' Eddie is going to have to work out his own list." Bonita nodded, looked back to her list, seemed confused for a moment, then shrugged and went on.

"I remember the time you promised Eddie you would go with him to Parents' Day at college, and then you called me with some excuse I was supposed to give him. I knew you were lying. I always knew when you were lying." Then she paused and looked at the group, "At least I thought I knew when he was lying." She sighed and went back to her list. "I hated you for lying to me, and it made me feel so guilty when I lied for you. I know I could have refused, but each time I thought, 'Okay, just this once, never again.' But, I kept doing it. And then, at night, when you would come to bed drunk." She paused again, not sure she should go on. Pat gave her an encouraging nod. "Jim, I needed you to touch me, to love me, so badly, but when you did, it was sometimes so terrible." Again, she looked up, apparently feeling the need to defend Jim to the group. "I know he didn't know what he was doing, but when he hurt me, I wanted to kill him. And he usually couldn't even . . . ." Her voice began to break. Rick felt embarrassed. He leaned forward and put his forehead on his hands so he wouldn't have to look at her. The voice went on.

"But the worst thing of all, the thing I don't know if I can ever forgive you for . . . ." Rick looked up and noticed Bonita's shoulders beginning to shake. Tears were streaming down her face. She looked at Pat. "I can't even say it."

"Of course you can." The silence in the room was broken only by the rustling sounds of Bonita's paper as she curled and uncurled one corner.

"After all I did for you, after all I put up with, after all the help I gave you with Eddie, you turned around and had an . . . had . . . had an affair with that girl across the street. My God, she is only two years older than your own son." Her voice had an hysterical edge. "And you didn't even have the decency to be discreet about it. Everyone in the neighborhood was talking about it. Laughing at me. What a fool I was. What a fool I am." Her last remark was addressed to the group and followed by a loud laugh.

"Bonita, you don't need to laugh when you feel like screaming or crying."

Bonita stopped laughing, but she didn't scream or cry either. The moment had passed, the emotion was released. Then a voice came from the other side of the circle and everyone pivoted their chairs to look at Eddie.

"It pisses me to hell to think of my dad sitting down there glowing with all that relief and religion after what he has done to her. Isn't she the one he ought to be confessing to, not God?"

"What about you? What ought he be confessing to you?" Pat's voice was firm, directing. Eddie didn't answer.

"Think of how your father's behavior has affected you." Still no response.

"Eddie. It was probably because of his drinking that your mother left. Eddie, you've been deeply hurt. You lost a mother who loved you very much."

"Loved me? That's a crock of shit. If she had loved me, she wouldn't have gone. She would've taken me with her." His face was red and his hands shook with rage. "They can both burn in hell for all I care. I don't need either one." He shifted in his chair, first leaning forward, elbows on knees, and then sliding back and crossing his arms across his chest.

Pat's voice was soft and caring, "Eddie, how old were you when your mother left?"

"Twelve." His voice stammered on the T.

"What do you remember about her . . . I mean, when you were younger?" The pause was so long everyone thought he hadn't heard or wouldn't answer.

"She hardly ever got dressed." His voice was bitter.

"And that bothered you?" He thought for a few moments.

"When I was little it didn't. I would come home from school and she would always be there. Her housecoat was pink and soft. I think she spent her whole day waiting for me to come home. I would tell her everything that had happened at school, and she would help me with my homework. She smelled like hand lotion." He brusquely wiped away tears that had spilled onto his cheeks.

"When did it start to bother you that she never got dressed?"

He thought back. "Sometimes my friends would stop over after school, especially after we started playing sports in fifth and sixth grade. She would always want to hug me right in front of them as if they weren't there. And then one time one of them asked me if my mother ever got dressed. I had never thought about it before. After that, I never wanted anyone to come over, but our house was right on the way from school, and sometimes they would just stop there. I hated it. God, you'd think she could have at least gotten dressed."

"How did you react when you came home with your friends and your mother was in her housecoat and tried to hug you?"

"What was I supposed to do? Nobody else's mother acted that way."

"What did you do?"

"Nothing."

"You just stood there and let her hug you?" Eddie's hands began to shake uncontrollably. "I didn't mean it. God knows I didn't mean it."

"Didn't mean what?" Eddie didn't respond. "Did you tell her how you felt?" Again, no response. "What did you say, Eddie?"

At first the words wouldn't come out, and then they came out in a whisper.

"I didn't hear you, Eddie. What did you tell your mother?"

"I told her to . . . ." The words seemed caught in his throat like fish hooks that would tear out his insides if forced.

"Louder, Eddie. What did you say?"

"I told her to f . . . ." His voice was a whisper, the words inaudible.

"I can't hear you."

"I told her to fuck off!" He shouted the words at Pat and then dropped his head into his quivering hands. "God," he said, shaking his head back and forth, "I told my own mother to fuck off."

"And it was shortly after that when she left?" His back and shoulders shook with convulsive spasms and then from deep within came a grief-filled wail — pain, long-buried under guilt — pain over the loss of softness and love. The depth of his mourning was too painful to watch. The other members of the group stared at their hands or their feet or at a spot in the rug somewhere in the center of the floor as they waited for the sobbing to subside. When all that could be heard was the sound of occasional sniffles, Pat spoke up.

"How are you feeling?" Eddie's arms and hands rested calmly on his lap, and his eyes, red and puffy, had an openness and softness that the group had never seen. He shrugged and grinned a little.

"I haven't thought about her for a long time."

"Do you understand, now, why she was the way she was and why she left?"

He didn't seem to understand the question.

"Your mother was living with an alcoholic. All that we've learned about what happens to people who love an alcoholic had happened to her. Her way of coping, or surviving, was to withdraw from life. I suspect she slept most of the time when you were gone. And then she turned to you for all her love and support. No child should have to bear that burden. You reacted in a very predictable way. I'm sure what you said hurt your mother a great deal, but it also forced her to face things in a way that she had been avoiding for years. The way she chose to cope with such a painful situation was to leave. It wasn't your fault, Eddie." She paused as tears ran freely from Eddie's eyes.

"You still love her very much, don't you?" He nodded. "Maybe you should try to get in touch with her, let her know you're beginning to understand what happened. I'm sure she needs to know that as much as you need to tell her.

"And you'll probably find that one of the by-products of this experience is that you'll be able to relate to girls in a more mature, positive way. You've been carrying around a lot of anger and guilt toward women in general, I would guess."

Eddie looked at Kris, causing everyone in the group to shift their gaze to her. She blushed but seemed less hostile, less defensive.

"Is there anything anyone would like to say? Any questions?" Pat glanced from person to person, looking for any indication of concerns or problems. Then she went on, "Eddie, you have a little over an hour. I want you to go someplace by yourself and really work on a list of problems in your relationship with your father. Recall all the things you've said this afternoon beginning with your anger about his Fifth Step and then go all the way back to everything you can remember about his relationship to you as a child and to your mother.

"Rick, you have your appointment downstairs in about five minutes, and the rest of you can visit or begin work on your goals. This might be a good time for you to start your dyadic encounter, Paul and Beth. Have a good evening."

As they were walking out, Rick felt a hand on his shoulder. Before he had a chance to turn to see who it was he heard his father's voice, "Are you really concerned about your own drug use?" The tone was concerned, but all Rick could do was shrug. "We're pleased you're going ahead with the test."

"Mom, too?" Rick asked, surprised.

"We were talking a little about it last night, hoping you'd have a chance to take a closer look at yourself."

"I thought you'd be really upset thinking you might have two sons who are hooked."

Patting Rick's shoulder, Paul responded, "Everything about this week has been upsetting, but I guess there's no point in leaving any stone unturned. We're going to get to the bottom of this and get things taken care of." By that time they had descended the stairs to the first floor. Rick turned, feeling relieved as his father's hand dropped from his shoulder. Rick had made the choice to do this himself, but suddenly he felt like a three-year-old, again, doing what his father wanted. Something in him wanted to keep going, to run out the back door and never return, but when he came to the office he had been told to go to, he walked in.

A man he had never seen before was there bent over his desk, working on some forms. Intuition more than sound alerted him to Rick's presence, and he looked up, smiled warmly, and signaled Rick to a chair next to his desk.

"So, you're concerned about your drug use?" Rick nodded. "Was it mostly Pat's idea that you come or mostly yours?"

"Mostly mine, I guess. I mean, I brought up the subject and then she told me about the assessment and wondered if I would like to take it."

"Good. Then we won't have to worry about your not being absolutely honest. Right?" The man grinned and Rick began to relax.

"The easy questions come first. We need to know your name and age, the names of your brothers and sisters, their ages, and where you live." As Rick gave him the information he filled in a form. Then he pushed the form away, took out a blank sheet of paper, sat back in his chair, and asked, "Do your parents drink?"

Rick thought for a minute, trying to remember. "Mom does once in awhile, but Dad never does."

"What was the attitude in your home toward alcohol and other drugs? Were you told it was wrong?"

"No, I think they just wanted us to be responsible. I can't remember Dad ever saying anything, but with Mom, it was like she knew we would probably be exposed to stuff so she would say things like, 'Don't be afraid to say no,' and 'All things in moderation,' that kind of stuff."

"Did you listen to her?"

Rick grinned. "Does anybody listen to parents?"

"Tell me about the first time you used a drug illegally."

"You mean real drugs or just beer?"

"Beer is a real drug. In fact, it's the most abused of all drugs." Rick was embarrassed. He knew that, of course. He had heard it a dozen times since coming to this place, but it was hard to change the way he had always thought.

"The first time I drank was when I was in seventh grade. Mom and Dad were gone one night, and Tom had some of his friends over. They brought a case of beer."

"Did you want to drink?"

"No. In fact, I wasn't even going to stay at home, but when I went through the family room Tom handed me a beer and said, 'Hey, kid, join the fun.' When I shook my head, he called me a pussy and all the guys started laughing. I hate it when people laugh at me. So I took the beer and started drinking."

"Did you like the taste?"

"No. But everyone was watching me to see how I would react, so I acted like it was great."

"Did you drink with Tom and his friends often after that?"

"I tried to avoid them, but then he started making friends with my friends, getting them to drink and smoke pot. Pretty soon I hardly had any friends left . . . he had taken them all. And they thought he was so great. It made me sick."

"So, you joined the crowd?"

"Yeah, I guess that's what happened."

"Tell me about the kinds of drugs you use now and how often."

"We always drink on weekends, and, of course, there's always pot. We usually go out during study hall to the john or outside and smoke. Last summer things got pretty crazy. There were all kinds of pills around, and once in a while we would get cocaine. Tom and his friends were doing acid too."

"Did you ever try that?"

"I don't know why, but that scared me. Nothing else really scared me . . . I mean, I had taken all the drug education junk they have at school, and I knew about all the effects of all the different drugs, but I didn't worry about any of the other ones, only acid." The man wrote rapidly, trying to catch everything Rick said.

"Did you ever sell drugs?"

"No, Tom did. And sometimes I would take stuff to people and he would give me some in return, or I would sell off a bag to my friends, but I never really got involved in the business."

"Did your drug use ever interfere with your school work?"

"I'm sure it didn't help, but I was never very good in school anyway."

"Really? You seem like a very bright, articulate young man."

"Ever since grade school teachers have told me that, but I don't know, I just always like to horse around. I was always in trouble. Really, it was sort of fun, you know? Always smarting off to teachers. The kids would cheer for me when I would get the teacher to lose her cool."

"Sounds to me like you did a lot of things to get the approval of your peers."

"I guess I did. I don't know. It seemed like Tom always had all the friends. They were just there. But I always had to work so hard at it."

"Talk to Tom about that sometime. You'll probably find out he was even more insecure about friendships than you were."

"Tom?"

The counselor nodded. "Most addicts are what we call 'people pleasers.' For whatever reason, and usually it has nothing to do with the reality of things, they feel very insecure and will do anything to gain the approval and acceptance of their peers." Rick tried to absorb what he was saying, but it seemed so out of tune with his image of Tom.

"Describe for me exactly how drugs make you feel."

"Which drugs?"

"Whichever ones you like the best."

"Cocaine is great, but it's so expensive. But, I like pot too. It makes me feel, I don't know, mellow, friendly, like everything is okay. I don't worry about things so much."

"Do you ever get a wonderful sense of release?"

Rick thought a minute. "No, not really. It's just, I don't know," he grinned, "nice."

"Since you've been here, have you wanted to drink or smoke pot?"

"No, I guess I never thought about it. At least not until last night. My sister, who's always been such a goody-goody, went out with one of the guys in the program. They went to a beer party and she came home and threw up all over the bathroom floor. God, what a mess."

"Did it make you wish you had been with them?"

"No, it made me sick. I couldn't believe she would do that."

Then the counselor went on asking questions which became increasingly probing, increasingly harsh. Exactly how much do you use? When? Where? With whom? How do you get it? What trouble have you been in because of your drug use? Fights? Arrests? Trouble at home? And then the same questions over and over again.

Rick was about to lose his temper, or cry, when the counselor stopped, sat for a few minutes making notes, and then leaned back in his chair so far Rick thought he was going to tip over.

"I'm sure you've learned, since coming here, that we believe some people are predisposed, for whatever reason, to chemical dependency. Based on what you've told me, I don't think you fall into that category. But, drugs are addicting. Anyone can become dependent on drugs if their body chemistry is subjected to regular, heavy doses over a period of time. What regular and heavy means varies from person to person." He paused. "What I'm saying, Rick, is that you've been involved in regular drug use for a period of time now. You could walk into dependency very quickly if you're not careful. You're going to have to make some very mature choices about your friends, and you're going to have to develop the ability to say no, even if it means you'll be ridiculed or left out. If you don't, you could find yourself in some real trouble."

Rick listened closely, trying to catch everything the man was saying. "You mean, you don't think I'm hooked?"

"My guess is that when you get back to New York, if Tom stays sober, you both will gradually find yourselves a whole new set of friends, friends who don't use drugs. But, if Tom doesn't stay sober, he's going to put a lot of pressure on you to join him in his drug use. That's when your strength is going to be tested." A huge smile spread across Rick's face. He hadn't even heard the part about the possibility of Tom not staying sober, so relieved was he to hear he was okay.

The counselor stood up, signaling the end of the interview. Rick walked to the door and then turned to thank the man.

"Take care of yourself, kid. I don't want to see you back here." He patted Rick on the back and closed the door behind him.

Rick walked buoyantly down the hall and into the reception area where his family was waiting for him.

"Well, what's the news?" His father stood up as he entered.

Rick grinned first at his mother who was looking at him with questioning eyes.

"Are we going to have to leave you here, too?" his father went on.

Rick pulled up a chair and sat down. "The guy was really nice . . . it was like he knew me almost before I said anything. I told him about when I got started and how much I used. I really thought when I told him about how often we snuck out of school to smoke pot during the day that he'd think I was hooked. But he just told me I'd have to be careful and try to choose better friends, friends who don't use drugs. Do you think there are any people like that around?" He directed his question to Kris.

She shrugged and grinned, not minding the gentle tease. "You'll have to look hard."

"Is it really so impossible to be around kids who use drugs and not get involved?" Beth asked. "Can't you just say, 'no thanks'?"

"I had always thought you could until last night," Kris responded. Everyone looked at her, wondering if she was finally going to talk about it. She hesitated for a moment and then went on. "I really didn't want to even get in the car last night, and when we got to the party I didn't want to go in, and I really didn't want to drink. But he told me to just hold the glass and take a sip now and then and that would keep people off my back. It made sense, so I did it. But he kept refilling my glass and, I don't know, I didn't intend to, but I just kept sipping. I don't know if everyone else who was there wanted to drink, but there wasn't anyone who wasn't."

"And, you've got to realize, Mom," Rick added, "that at our age, everything we do with drugs is illegal. It's not safe to have people around who know what's going on but aren't involved. They might rat. So kids really do have to choose between using drugs or being left out."

Paul sighed deeply. "It seems incredible to me that I've been living in the same house with you kids for all these years and have been so unaware of how complicated your lives are, how difficult your choices are."

Rick felt a closeness with his family he hadn't felt since he was little. He wondered why it had never occurred to him before that he could talk to them, that they might understand.

His father went on, "I'm almost afraid to go home." His voice slid away and he seemed unable to finish his thought.

Just then the door from the stairway opened and Tom's counselor came in. "Tom tells me he wants to go out to dinner with you tonight."

"Yes, we were wondering if that would be possible," Paul responded.

"He has to be back no later than seven, so you probably better not go too far away. Have you tried either of the restaurants across the street? They're not too bad." Without waiting for a response, he went on. "Tom will be down in a minute. Have a nice dinner."

Half an hour later they were sitting in a booth in a pleasant restaurant waiting for their order of cheeseburgers and steak sandwiches.

"How did your group go this afternoon?" Tom asked.

"Boy, you should have seen Eddie fall apart," Rick responded.

"Well, he has every right to. His father has done some things to him that hurt very much."

"But, it wasn't his father that he was mostly upset about. It was his mother," Rick went on. "She left them when he was —"

"Wait a minute," Paul cut in. "Are we supposed to be talking about this to people outside of the group?" Everyone remembered the confidentiality pledge they had signed, but couldn't remember if it excluded people like Tom who were almost a part of the situation. They suspected that it did, but the conversation was too interesting to let it drop.

"I keep thinking," Beth said, "about a comment Pat made to Eddie about how his attitude toward his mother had probably affected his relationships with girls. I wonder if last night had been tonight, would he have been so insistent that you go along with him . . . ." Beth was talking to Kris, but Tom, who knew little about the situation, jumped in.

"You mean, Eddie came on to you last night?" Before Beth had a chance to correct his interpretation, the blush on Kris' face answered his question.

"Boy, that guy works fast!" Rick exclaimed. "He must have taken lessons from you," he said to Tom, jokingly.

"Is that the way you are with girls?" There was a catch in Beth's voice as she looked from one son to the other, and Rick wished he hadn't brought up the subject.

"Don't worry, Mom, that was the old me. The new Tom Inghram is going to treat every girl with ultimate respect, keeping his hands to himself, and his lips to himself . . . ."

"And his . . . ." Rick added, and both boys broke into bawdy laughter.

"You're crude," Kris commented, wrinkling her nose, and then joining in their laughter.

"All right, that's enough," Paul cut them off as Beth stabbed a tomato with her fork and swirled it around the bottom of her salad bowl.

The family ate as Tom rambled on, telling story after story about his former escapades. Then Rick, who always finished his food first, spoke up. "Tom, I've been wondering about something the guy who tested me for chemical dependency said." The clinking of forks and dishes stopped.

"I was telling him about how I always had such a hard time making friends and how it seemed to be so easy for you. You always seemed to have all the friends anyone could ever want. He said you probably felt as insecure as I did, but that I should ask you about that."

Everyone waited for Tom to finish chewing his food. "Did he talk to you about people pleasing?" Rick nodded. "I was the ultimate people pleaser."

"That apparently didn't include your family," Paul interjected with uncharacteristic bitterness.

"Well, you can't please everyone," Tom responded with a laugh and a shrug and then went on. "No one is sure whether it's a cause of the disease or a symptom or maybe both, but nearly all chemically dependent people have terrible self-images. Remember that kid you saw the first day at lunch who stood up and talked? He still can hardly think, much less say anything good about himself. A lot of the people at treatment were like me . . . they seemed popular . . . and others, like Trisha, Connie's daughter, were real loners, but we all thought of ourselves as alone, as inadequate."

"You never seemed to have a poor self-image. In fact, you were always good at everything you did." Paul seemed puzzled.

"But, Dad, the point is, it doesn't matter what you are or what you can do or how others see you. The fact is, you feel miserable about yourself. I could never get enough encouragement or praise. And all I ever thought about was myself . . . I mean, it would never have occurred to me to encourage or support someone else or even think about their feelings. All I thought about was getting attention for myself."

Rick looked at his older brother who, in so many ways, was changed. All of the toughness and bitterness and anger was gone, yet in other ways he wasn't different at all. He could sit and talk about how he used to be conceited, how he used to demand all the attention. Yet, since they had left the treatment center for dinner, he had possessively held onto the attention of the family. Everything still had to be his way, it was just a different way now.

Tom was still talking. "I guess it must have seemed as if I had plenty of friends, but I never felt they were really friends. I always thought I had to do something for them, be something for them in order to be accepted. It was great when I was selling drugs because then everyone needed me. But even that wasn't enough. I just never felt good about myself."

"Didn't you ever feel guilty about selling?" Beth's voice had a pleading quality. "Didn't you know it was wrong?"

"Wrong?" The word seemed to have little meaning to Tom. "Well, sure, I guess if I'd thought about it I knew it was wrong. . . I just never thought about it. I never thought about much of anything except getting drugs and keeping people off my back."

Rick tried to imagine Tom as insecure, as feeling inadequate, as needing friends, but the image just didn't ring true. It was too different from the way he had always seen him. And even now, Tom could sit and talk about these things, but the authoritative way he talked, the confident way he gestured with his fork for emphasis, seemed to contradict his words.

"So, what's going to happen when you get back to Rochester?" Paul asked. "How are you going to find and keep new friends?"

Tom paused before answering, "Haven't they talked to you yet about that?"

"About what?" Paul asked.

Tom seemed suddenly nervous and unsure of himself. "About whether I should go home or not?"

"Whether you should go home or not! Of course you're going home. You can't stay in treatment all your life."

"Where would you go?" Beth added.

Tom held up his hand to calm them down. "Most of the kids don't go home right after leaving treatment. It's just too easy to fall back into the old roles, to get back in with the old gang.

Dad, they have halfway houses all over. People go there and live for a few months after treatment . . . it's like a home where people work and support themselves, but they also try to emotionally support each other. They say that the chances of staying sober are much greater if people go to a halfway house first, before trying to live at home. I thought they would have talked to you about that . . . ." His voice trailed off.

"But, you have to finish high school," Beth argued.

"That's the least of my worries. I could take the test and graduate anytime. Academically, I'm way ahead of most of the kids here. They have tutors here, you know, who keep all of the high school kids going on their school work. I don't worry about that. My biggest problem is going to be staying clean."

"When do we have to make the decision?" Paul asked.

"If I'm going to get into a halfway house, I have to get my name on a waiting list right away or there might not be an opening when I get out of here." Their waitress cut the conversation short by stopping at the table and asking if anyone wanted dessert. No one was hungry.

Paul checked his watch and noted it was almost 7:00. "Time for you to get back to the center, young man," he said to Tom.

"Relax, Dad. I can handle my own life now," Tom responded in a good-natured, but pointed way.

Paul pulled his shirt sleeve down over his watch, picked up the check, and pulled out a credit card. Minutes later, the Inghrams stood in the entryway to the restaurant watching Tom as he jogged to the corner, stood and waited at the red light for the traffic to break, and then jogged on across the wide avenue paying no heed to the light which was still red.

Back at the hotel, Kris and Rick sat in their room trying to decide whether they should go swimming or not.

"Maybe we should just watch TV and work on our goals," Kris suggested. "We have to at least get the list of our problems with Tom finished before tomorrow."

"What else do you have to do?" Rick asked.

"I have to write letters to Mom and Dad and read part of this book." She held up a copy of *Why Am I Afraid to Tell You Who I Am?*

"Do you have some extra paper?" Rick asked. "I think I'll get my list done. Do you know what my first one is going to be?" Kris said nothing, seeming to wait for a response. "I resent how he's always the center of attention . . . no matter what he's doing, or where he is, he's always the center of attention."

"Or, at least it seems that way to you," Kris commented.

"Well, doesn't it to you?"

"I always thought the center of attention was one or the other of you, but never me."

"You thought *I* got attention?" Rick was amazed.

"It's really funny, isn't it?" Kris commented after a pause. "I bet everyone in the family thought someone else was getting all the attention. I wonder if it's that way in every family. Guess what my first resentment is going to be."

"What?"

"I resent him so much for all the times teachers would come up to me and say things about him or somehow imply that they were surprised anyone in the family was worth anything. I wanted to change my name so many times or go to a different school or move to a different town. I hated having to spend half my life, actually all my life, in places where everyone knew Tom." She paused. "And I resent so much how he would always hurt Mom. I've always hated him for that," she added.

"I can remember one night," Rick said, having had his thoughts turned toward their mother, "I was sleeping, but I woke up when I heard shouting by the back door. Mom and Tom were really going at it. It must have been three or four in the morning, and I suppose Tom was really high. He was cursing and swearing and calling her all sorts of names. And then she must have slapped him because he said, 'You ever touch me again and I'll pound the shit out of you.' I hated him so much and was so afraid he would hurt her. I wanted to go up and protect her. But I just lay there, and then the next day Tom came into my room, and he was so nice to me that, it was like I switched back to his side again.

"I guess that's one of the things I really resent about him. He always made me feel like I had to take sides, and if I was on his side I felt guilty towards Mom and Dad, and if I wasn't he was so mean that I couldn't stand it. I never felt good about myself, no matter what I did."

Kris stopped him, "Don't you remember Pat telling us that no one can make us feel anything? People do things to us, but we choose what our response will be." Rick looked confused, so she said, "You just said, 'He always made me feel — ' "

"Well, he did make me feel . . ." Rick interrupted defensively.

"You chose to respond that way," Kris corrected him.

"Oh, shut up," he laughed good-naturedly. "You're not a counselor."

The two sat in silence for a time and then began working on their lists so intently they didn't notice the ringing of the phone in their parents' room. Soon there was a tap on the door.

"You kids sleeping?" It was their father. Both parents came in, Paul heading for the chair, but Beth staying by the door, caught between an empty room and a room filled with family, torn between escape and a sense of responsibility.

"How are your lists going?" Paul asked.

"We've both got a few things," Kris responded.

"That was Bonita on the phone," he went on, changing the subject.

"Are they coming over?" Kris asked somewhat apprehensively.

"No, I don't think so. She just needed to talk. She was almost hysterical." Kris and Rick put their pens down, waiting for an explanation.

"You know, they had their family conference this afternoon. Well, she just clammed up. She couldn't say anything. She tried to read the list she had prepared, but she just couldn't face him with her feelings. Now she really thinks she's crazy. And she's tearing herself apart, wondering what it is about her that makes her so unable to control her life."

"What did you tell her?" Kris asked.

"I guess I mostly just listened."

"Your father did very well," Beth added, falling back into her old habit of explaining Paul to the children. "He said all the right things."

"But how can you ever know what's right in a situation like that? I just wanted to make her feel better, but maybe that kind of pain and questioning is a good thing to go through. I don't know."

"She doesn't seem crazy. I mean, she's so funny and seems so strong," Kris commented thoughtfully. "But it really is strange that she would choose to marry an alcoholic. She knew what she was getting into, but she did it anyway."

"Who knows?" Paul sighed. "As we were talking, I was just thinking about how being here this week has answered so many questions for me and made so many things make sense that never made sense before. At the same time, it has opened up a thousand new questions about humans and why they do what they do, questions that'll probably never be answered. It's frustrating. As a doctor, I like to think there are answers and cures."

Though Rick had said nothing, he felt as if he were a part of an adult conversation, as if he were struggling with deep, adult questions. He liked the feeling and was disappointed when his mother said they had better get back to their homework, and she and Paul left.

Yawning loudly, Rick asked Kris what time it was.

"A little after nine. I can't believe how tired I am."

"That's what a wild night life does to you," Rick teased and got a pillow in his face. "Sorry. I don't know why you're so uptight. What you did is nothing compared to what Tom or I've done over the years."

"So, why don't you just shut up about it?" Rick wasn't sure if she was really mad or not, but he didn't have the energy to pursue the subject. After standing up and stretching dramatically, he went to the bathroom, put on his pajamas, and got ready for bed. Then he turned on the bed light and curled up under the covers, trying to focus his thoughts on Tom and all the things about their relationship that bothered him.

But, the first thing that came to mind was not a resentment. It was a time when Tom had practically saved his life. It was at one of the big parties last summer out by the river. Everyone was doing drugs of one kind or another. A shipment of angel dust had come, so some were trying that, others were taking acid or coke. Most of the kids were older — Tom's age and older. Rick had felt out of place, but once he was there he didn't have a way to get home. He had smoked a joint and was feeling pretty mellow when a huge, tough-looking guy came by and tripped on his foot. Before Rick realized what had happened, the guy grabbed him by the jacket, pulled him up, slammed him against a tree and started hitting him. He was wild, animal-like. Rick thought he was going to die after the second punch in the stomach when, from out of nowhere, Tom leaped on the guy, knocking him to the ground and holding him there while others came and helped. After it was over, Rick had thrown his arms around Tom telling him over and over that he was the greatest brother a guy could have.

Suddenly as Rick lay in the motel room in Minneapolis, hundreds of miles away from his home, feeling gratitude toward his brother, it occurred to him that if it hadn't been for Tom, he would never have been at the party in the first place. It had always been Tom that got him involved in everything he did that turned out bad. Rick wrote that down as a resentment and put in parentheses "party where someone beat me up."

Then, after thinking a little longer, he added more events to the list. *The time you hid all your porno magazines in my room and Mom found them and thought they were mine. The time you told me to just walk out the night Mom tried to keep me in, saying Mom couldn't do anything about it anyway. All the times you convinced me to skip school with you. All the times you beat me up when we were little and made me run errands for you and made me do your jobs.* The more Rick thought about it, the angrier he got. Tom had been dumping on him all his life, and he had never realized it. He had been so flattered to receive any attention that he could never see through it to what was really going on.

Rick rolled over, wondering how Kris was doing on her list and noticed that she had fallen asleep, pencil in her hand. Quietly he got up, put her pencil and paper on the table, pulled the spread over her, and then, after turning out the lights, crawled back into bed and was asleep in minutes.

DAY FOUR

Gasping for breath, Beth bolted upright in her bed, sweat pouring down her back. She breathed deeply as her eyes adjusted to the early morning light. Paul stirred on his bed and opened his eyes.

"Are you okay?" he asked.

"It was nothing, just a dream." She lay back down, facing her husband. "I was being crushed. I couldn't breathe. Have you ever had a dream like that?"

"I never remember my dreams. What was crushing you?"

"It was a tiger. My tiger. He was beautiful. We were sitting on our old couch, you know, the one we had in the living room in our old house, and everything was so peaceful. At least I was peaceful. He was dreaming; I could tell by the way his legs twitched. I stroked him to calm his legs, to change the dream, but he woke up and started moving onto me. I tried to push him off, but he was too heavy, too big. I screamed and screamed, but no sound came. He sat on my chest, Paul. That huge tiger sat on me crushing my breasts and ribs." She gasped for breath, feeling again the pressing weight. "I couldn't breathe and no one came to help. I was dying and no one cared." Her voice rose with each phrase, edging on hysteria.

Before Paul had a chance to respond, the phone rang and the desk clerk told him it was 6:30. "Why did we have to get up so early?" he asked as he hung up the phone.

Dropping her head back on the pillow, Beth tried to remember. "I didn't finish my list for the family conference today." She began to feel in control again as she turned on the light over her bed, breathed deeply, and picked up the notebook she had left on the table which separated their beds.

"Wake me in about a half hour," Paul said as he rolled over and pulled the covers over his head to block out the light.

Beth read through the list of things she had written the night before and they all seemed so petty, so unfair. It wasn't, after all, Tom's fault that he was the way he was, and, now that he was getting so much better, it wasn't right to pour all this on him. She went back to the beginning of the list and read the first statement — *I resent you for the way you used language . . . the poor grammar and all the obscenities . . . . It seemed like a deliberate attempt on your part to irritate me.* She began to scratch it from her list. It was embarrassing to think she had let such a little thing make her so angry over the years. She had always thought parents who got so upset over length of hair or manner of dress were foolish, yet she had let something equally as unimportant become a major focus of conflict. But then she remembered Pat's warning not to be her own editor. Pat had said feelings were neither right nor wrong, good nor bad, they just were, and if you had the feeling, it is important, so write it down.

She read on. *I resent you for destroying all of my theories on child rearing and totally undermining my self-confidence in dealing with the other children.* Into Beth's mind flashed the books and journals and magazines filled with the advice of experts; the lectures of professors who had spent a lifetime studying the behavior of children; the hospital nursery where she had learned to care for babies long before she had her own; but nothing she had learned, nothing she had experienced, had prepared her for what had happened in her own family. Nothing she had read over the years had helped her understand or deal with the deterioration happening all around and within her.

The recollection of their first encounter with professional counseling still infuriated her. Tom was four, incorrigible, defiant, with an unending supply of energy, as if someone wound him tight in the morning, sending him charging through each day, undaunted, undeterred.

When they arrived for their appointment with Tom in hand the secretary had looked surprised. "Weren't you told to come alone?"

"The appointment is for Tom," Paul explained.

"Oh well, never mind," she responded with exasperation. "We'll watch him while you take the tests."

As the morning wore on and Paul and Beth were put through a battery of psychological tests, it became painfully apparent that the assumption was they were the problem, not Tom. The psychologist had emitted a tired sigh as he talked about professional parents who had lost their common sense and tended to intellectualize experiences rather than responding directly. As a result, they ended up with troubled children searching for guidelines. "Go home," he said. "Be firm and consistent. There's nothing wrong with Tom that a little strong discipline won't cure."

They drove home feeling guilty, chastised, determined to try harder, to do better. But Tom always was able to match every firm resolve with firmer resistance, every strong discipline with a more obnoxious, more destructive counterattack. Their home became a battleground with only losers.

They kept searching for answers. Together they had taken Parent Effectiveness Training and learned a whole new set of techniques, techniques which worked beautifully with their other children but didn't faze Tom. There were the school counselors, teachers, principals, everyone with advice, everyone assuming that Beth and Paul, as parents, were at fault. Beth had accepted the guilt handed her from every direction, accepted it and absorbed it, and had ended up weak and in despair.

She picked up her pencil and added a resentment to the bottom of the list. *I resent you for the fact that I feel like a failure at the only important thing I have done in my life.* She read what she had written once, and then again, and then with angry lines, she scratched out the words, *feel like* and added *am*.

Hearing the phone ring in the room next door, she reached over and shook her husband, and then went into the bathroom to get ready for the day. A few minutes later Paul came in naked and hugged her from behind, rubbing his stubbly chin on her neck as she stood at the sink trying to fluff out her hair. She tried to return his smile in the mirror, tried to respond to his warmth, tried to savor his touch, but her body froze. Another expectation. Another demand. Another need she couldn't meet.

"Are Kris and Rick up?" she asked, pulling away and going quickly into the room to get dressed.

At breakfast, Beth tried to make amends by being cheerful. "Did you all sleep well? Anyone else not done with their homework? Do you suppose we'll flunk the course if we come unprepared?" But there was something wrong with her voice, she knew, because her children couldn't look at her and her husband's look was professional.

Finally he said, "Beth, are you okay? Would you rather not go today?"

"I can't just not go," she responded, surprised that he would suggest it. She felt him touch her shoulder with one hand as he signaled for the bill with the other. The pancakes she had for breakfast began expanding, swelling into her lungs, pressing against her heart, threatening to explode like some angry volcano. She grabbed her glass of water and drank, cool liquid forcing down hot lava.

Some time later, the group gathered in the dining room and listened to Pat. "The movie for this morning is my favorite. Every time I see it, it brings tears to my eyes and also a new sense of hope. It's called *One Day* and it's about a huge gathering that took place here in Minnesota a few years ago, a gathering of alcoholics and their families to celebrate sobriety. You'll probably recognize Dick Van Dyke and Gary Moore, both of whom are recovering alcoholics. There are also several political figures who make appearances near the end, Hubert Humphrey, Walter Mondale, and other Minnesota politicians. But note particularly Harold Hughes, former senator from Iowa. He's a recovering alcoholic and has led a fascinating life. The rest of the movie gives background sketches of some of the people who attended the festival. Their stories are as diverse as they are filled with hope. Enough said. Let's go on up."

As they walked down the hall from the dining room to the stairs, Beth noticed one of the doors was open. Glancing in, she saw the chaplain, who had spoken to them the second day, sitting with his feet up, a book on his lap. He looked up and grinned as she walked by.

The rest of the group was ahead of her, and she noticed the camaraderie each person seemed to have with someone. Kris, Eddie, and Rick led the way, joking as they climbed the steps two at a time. Pat was explaining something to Connie. And Bonita was talking to Paul, telling him her troubles, no doubt. It had always amazed Beth to see how easily other women were able to talk to her husband and how attentively he listened. It was his job, she knew, what he had been trained to do, yet it had never stopped irritating her. She thought, when she saw him talking to someone else in that way, how wonderful it would be if he would ever be so attentive to her, but when he did listen to her in that way, it filled her with rage. After all, he was her husband, not her counselor.

When they arrived in the meeting room, she took a place by herself near the back of the room and watched as the film began. It showed a giant tailgating party at a stadium parking lot near Minneapolis. There was a carnival-like atmosphere — clowns, rides, hot dog stands — and everywhere, everywhere there were happy, smiling people, all of them recovering alcoholics or addicts and their families.

Her stomach began churning again and without thinking about what she was doing, Beth got up and walked out. She stopped in the bathroom and tried to gag herself but nothing would come up. And then, unable to face those happy people again, she wandered down the stairs and found herself in front of the chaplain's open door. He glanced up, the questioning look on his face turning immediately to recognition and concern.

"Come in, sit down," he said as he ushered her into his office, pointed to an easy chair by his desk, and returned to his seat. Beth hesitated.

"It's okay. I haven't a thing to do all morning. I'd love to have someone keep me company." She relaxed.

"So, tell me about your week. How have things been going since the last time we talked?"

"I don't know. Fine, I guess."

"So, why do you feel so miserable?" His manner was so gentle, so caring, that Beth was disarmed.

"I don't know. I don't know what's wrong with me. I couldn't stand to sit in the same room with them this morning. And the movie. Have you seen it? All those people in a giant parking lot laughing and talking. I felt like I was going to throw up. Maybe I'm just getting the flu or something." She paused, waiting for him to respond. When he didn't, she felt awkward and kept talking.

"Do you have a family?" she asked. He nodded. "Have you ever wanted to run away? To never see them again?" Again he nodded and she was surprised. "This week was supposed to bring us all together, and I feel more alienated from my family than ever." She stumbled over *alienated* and couldn't look at him when she was through. He didn't respond and finally she had to look up. He was calmly waiting. "Can you understand what I'm saying? After all these years, I don't care anymore. I really don't care. I don't love them. I don't want to see them or talk to them or be near them. I'm the wife and mother and I don't care. What in God's name is wrong with me?"

"Wives and mothers are supposed to be sources of unending, unconditional love, God's emissaries here on earth," he baited her.

"Yes, yes they are." But even as she voiced agreement, she recognized the absurdity of the statement. There was a long pause.

"Tell me, Beth, have you ever had these feelings of not caring before toward anyone in your family?" Beth shifted in her chair.

"Never toward Erik or Kris."

"What about Tom? How did it feel to have a son who took all the love you gave him and shoved it back down your throat? What was it like being used and manipulated and abused, being played for a sucker over and over?"

"I hated it." Her voice was a whisper.

"You hated it, or you hated him?"

"I loved him. It was myself I hated. I was the one who was to blame. Don't you see? I gave birth to a beautiful, innocent baby and I turned him into a monster. I know they keep saying it wasn't my fault, but I can't stop thinking about what he's done. Did you know he was selling drugs? My son was a drug pusher! I had always thought those people should be taken out and hanged. But it was my own son!"

"What did you say when he told you about what he had been doing?"

Beth tried to remember. "Nothing, I guess." The chaplain sat forward in his chair and looked at her intently.

"Think back to the past few months when Tom was getting into all kinds of trouble, when he was getting arrested, when you were having to go to the police station to pick him up, when you had to sit and listen to him have his rights read to him, when you had to appear in family court, how did you feel about him then? What did you think about when you were lying in bed at night unable to sleep?"

"I don't know. I can't remember."

"Of course you can remember."

She paused, trying to control her thoughts, edit her words. "I kept trying to think of ways to solve the problem. Sometimes I would think of sending him to live with my parents, or putting him in a foster home, or telling the probation officer all the ways he was breaking probation so they would put him in reform school. But I knew none of those things would help, they would just make things worse."

"So then what did you think about, wish for?"

The heavy pressure on her chest made her gasp for air in short, erratic breaths.

She looked up at the chaplain and knew that he knew, knew that he had read in her mind the secret she had kept from everyone, the secret she was too ashamed to even admit to herself.

"Sometimes . . . ." Her voice faded off. He waited. "Sometimes when I was almost asleep, when I wasn't really thinking about what I was thinking, sometimes, then, I would imagine he was dead." She looked at him, pleading for understanding, and saw no hint of judgment in his eyes.

"I'd lie in bed and imagine the funeral. Sometimes I'd be giving a beautiful eulogy for him. I remember the last line of one of them, 'May he find the peace in death that he never found in life.' But, don't you see, it was I who wanted the peace. I who needed the peace of not having him around, of never having to worry about him or fight with him or be afraid of him. Ever again." Again she hesitated, checking to see if the man understood. "I didn't want to think that, I didn't mean to, but, can you understand . . . he was destroying everything. I hated him for what he was doing to our family, especially Erik. All I ever wanted was an ordinary family with ordinary problems and he was ruining everything." The pitch of her voice rose with every phrase.

"And so you hoped for what seemed like the only solution."

"It wasn't that I hadn't tried. For years I tried everything I could think of. I talked to everyone who knew anything about raising children. I read every book. We even took him to counseling when he was younger but nothing ever worked. Do you realize what that's like? To try everything you can think of and have nothing work? To have things keep getting worse and worse? Can you possibly understand what it is to live like that for years?"

"Yes, as a matter of fact I can. My son was an addict. He died of a drug overdose before we could even get him into treatment." Beth stared at the gentle eyes and was aware, for the first time, of the deep pain and sadness etched into the lines around those eyes.

"When he died, my wife and I had to deal with grief at the loss of our son but also with overwhelming guilt because we had wished him dead. The only thing that helped us was getting involved in Al-Anon and realizing that those death wishes are as common as escape fantasies. Hardly anyone can live with a drug abuser without wanting to run away, wanting to be dead, or wanting the other person dead. In a way it's what keeps you sane while living through an insane situation. It gives you hope. It provides a solution." He looked at Beth and smiled. "Does it make you feel better getting that off your chest?" She nodded.

"You can't imagine," he continued, "how hard it was for me to finally admit those thoughts to another person. Here I was, an ordained clergyman, a person who was supposed to be some sort of model, have some sort of direct source of strength, and I was wishing my own son would die."

"It really is hard, isn't it, being the person everyone else thinks of as religious?"

"Is that the position you're in?" he asked.

"The whole thing is absurd," Beth complained. "You turn to God for help and not only does He not give any, but all of a sudden everybody is forcing you into this perfect, religious person role. I couldn't even lose my temper or swear without someone pointing a finger, as if Christians were never supposed to think an unloving thought."

"How do the people in your family respond when you tell them how you feel?" The question hung in the air.

"I guess I never do," Beth finally answered. During the long silence that followed, Beth began to realize the impact of what she had just said. But how could she be honest when her thoughts were so terrible?

"What church do you attend?"

"We were, I guess still are, Episcopalian. But a couple of years ago I started going to a little gospel church. They seemed to have the answer to everything and everyone looked so happy and joyful. Every meeting someone would tell a wonderful story about a miracle that had happened to someone. I kept thinking if I did what they did, if I praised the Lord and sang gospel songs, if I prayed for a miracle, one would come. So I sang and I prayed but things only got worse." She sighed a deep, despairing sigh. "I've lost everything. I can't love anymore and I no longer believe. Everything that was important to me is gone."

"You've been sucked dry." Beth nodded and then her eyes got a faraway look.

"Even when he was a baby I couldn't satisfy him. I could never hold him long enough or walk him long enough to make him happy. And when I nursed him he sucked and sucked until my breasts were empty and then he would bite my nipples in anger. I drank a lot of liquids, and sometimes I'd massage my breasts waiting for that tingly feeling that meant they were filling with milk so I could feed him some more. It always came back, then. Sooner or later they would swell and milk would soak the front of my shirt." Then her voice changed, losing its nostalgic tone, turning bitter, "But those days are over, gone."

"And now you feel empty, dry, like you have nothing left to give."

Yes. Yes. Stop. Don't say it. God, what did I do that was so bad, so wrong, that you have stripped me and left me alone, with nothing. I wish I were dead.

She pounded the desk with clenched fist over and over, sobbing curses she had never thought before, railing at the injustice of a God who was supposed to be just, mourning the loss of love and hope.

And then, spent, truly and deeply empty, she crumpled back into her chair. The chaplain waited for the compulsive, gasping breaths to ease and then, as he handed her some tissue, he said, "The milk is going to flow again, Beth. Trust me when I tell you that. It will flow again." She cried again, tears of relief and release pouring from her eyes.

The moment was shattered by the ringing of the phone. Beth sat back in her chair, put the used tissues in her purse, and took out a handkerchief as the chaplain answered the phone. "Yes, she's down here. Yes, I'll tell her."

"The group meeting is starting upstairs, but don't feel you have to leave." Beth was unsure about what to do. She clamped the purse shut and set it down on her lap.

"How can I thank you for — " But he wouldn't let her finish. He began saying something, stopped, as if searching for a better way, and then began again.

"Remember how you used to drink liquids and massage your breasts to get the milk to come?" She nodded. "You knew you needed to feed yourself, to take care of yourself, in order to be able to feed your baby." Again she nodded. He paused. "I would guess that for the past few years you've forgotten about taking care of your own needs. You've let the people you love suck you dry, and then you've accepted their right to be angry with you, but never your right to be angry with them. We call that 'stuffing anger.' And pretty soon a person who stuffs anger gets so packed there isn't room for anything else. You've got to start being honest with your family about how you feel."

"I'm supposed to tell Tom I wished he were dead? A mother can't say that to her own child!"

"Tom can handle it. He's heard enough around here that nothing's going to be much of a shock to him. And it would probably be good for him to know that you, too, have been enslaved and are returning to freedom. That you, too, are human. No one is perfect, you know." Beth laughed that a statement so trite could be so meaningful.

The chaplain went on. "Human nature is a fascinating thing. I sometimes think of a human as being on a continuum between beast and angel, never all one or the other, always caught somewhere in between. And I think there's something about being parents that brings out both the worst and the best in us, sends us sliding from one extreme to the other."

His chair creaked as he leaned back, putting one foot on the edge of his desk. "Parents who are given an addictive child are dealt a very difficult hand to play. Some play it better than others. I've gotten to know Tom a little, and I want you to know that, so far, you've played your hand with intuitive skill."

"How can you possibly know that?"

"You're here, aren't you? Tom's only eighteen and already you've faced the problem. It's been diagnosed and you've found excellent help. Do you have any idea how many hooked kids there are out there whose parents can't or won't face the problem? Our son was one of them. There are thousands and thousands more. Not only are you here, but you were able to instill in Tom a positive sense of God as a helping power. He had no problem getting through his First and Second Steps. In families where God has been used for behavior manipulation, as a guilt-inducing whip, the addicts have a very difficult time altering that concept."

Beth felt overwhelming gratitude and love for this man who was saying everything she needed to hear.

He put his foot down and leaned forward. "We haven't had a chance to talk about your husband, but if you're like most of the parents we see, you've probably been so angry with him that you've hated him too, and maybe even wished he would die." Beth dropped her head.

"Hey," he said, lifting her chin, "don't start wallowing in guilt about that. When we recognize our feelings and get them out in the open, they lose their power over us."

Beth nodded, beginning to understand what he was saying. "I guess I should go," she said, but again she hesitated as if there were some unfinished business.

"Would you like to pray with me?" he asked, reading her mind. She nodded and he took her hands in his.

"Thank you, Lord, for answering prayers. Thank you for the healing you are bringing to Beth and her family. Be with them, guide them, and keep them always in your loving care. Amen." She whispered her amen and rose to leave. He walked her to the door and when she turned to thank him, he smiled. "Would you like a hug?" She nodded and they hugged warmly. Then, with his hands on her shoulders he said, "You're a beautiful person, Beth. Peace be with you."

When she entered Pat's office, Bonita was talking. Beth slipped into the empty chair between Bonita and Connie, trying to be as inconspicuous as possible.

"Now I know I'm crazy," Bonita was saying, but all the humor was gone from her voice. "What's wrong with me? First I marry a man I know is going to treat me like . . . you know what

". . . and then when I have a chance to tell him how I feel about everything, I clam up. I couldn't say a word. Nothing. Eddie, here, was great. He got everything out. But me, I just sat there like some big dummy and couldn't even read the first thing on my list." By the time she was through talking she had slid down into her chair, backbone withered, shoulders wilted.

As Beth looked at Bonita, she saw her with new eyes and felt a deep sympathy and caring for this woman — a feeling which had somehow been blocked before. She knew what Bonita was going through, what it felt like to not be able to really express your feelings. Instinctively, Beth reached over and patted Bonita's shoulder. The gesture, so simple, dissolved Bonita's last shred of internal resistance. Out poured an ocean filled with old pain and humiliation, rejection and torment. Beth wrapped her in her arms, stroking her back, seeking to calm her as she would a sobbing child. Her magic worked as it had worked so often when her children were small. Bonita thanked her and told her how much she needed that as she blew her nose loudly and wiped her eyes with the back of her hand.

"Well, I feel better, but I still haven't solved my problem. Why couldn't I talk yesterday?"

"If Jim had been your father, would you have been able to read your list?" Pat asked Bonita.

"Oh, my God, no. He would have slapped me across the face and sent me to my room." The words burst from her as from a boil just lanced. And then she sat up, a look of revelation on her face. "Do you mean to say that at age forty I'm still acting like a six-year-old, afraid to say what I think for fear of getting slapped?"

"Have you ever made peace with your father?" Paul asked.

"I tried once. What a bum trip that was. He's eighty years old now and still a stubborn old Italian goat."

"What happened?" Paul kept pressing the subject.

"I don't know. It was shortly after my divorce. I felt as if I had failed everyone, and suddenly it became ultra important to me to gain his approval. I was his only daughter, after all. You'd think he'd have cared as much as I did, but when I went to him and told him I was sorry for any pain I'd caused him and told him I loved him, he just turned on me, telling me all this trouble was my punishment for being headstrong and rebellious. He said, 'A woman has to know her place.' And when I heard that, I was thirteen again, wanting to strike out, to hurt him in the same way he had hurt me."

"So what did you do?"

"I turned and left and I've never been back. He can rot in that nursing home for all I care." She paused. "He always made me feel so worthless. The boys were everything. He listened to them and gave them the best of everything, even set them up in business. But when I went to him and asked for money to start a business, he told me to get married and have babies. I was smarter and had more business sense than any of my brothers, but I was supposed to spend my life being a good Italian mama making babies and spaghetti. God, it makes me sick thinking about it."

The group sat in silence for a time and then Pat spoke up, "But you still feel a little guilty that you weren't what he wanted?"

"Yes," Bonita said with a sigh. "I guess I do. How crazy it all is! I know it's wrong for parents to try to force their children into molds, and yet I feel as if it was my fault that I didn't fit. It's crazy, isn't it, how much people want and need the approval of their parents?" Connie began to cough and everyone looked at her for a moment thinking she wanted to talk, but when she shook her head no, the attention of the group shifted back to Bonita.

"Bonita, you say you felt as if you were at fault in your relationship with your father. What do you usually expect to have happen when you do something wrong?" Pat asked.

Bonita shrugged. That one was easy. "I expect to be punished."

"So, at some level, you've given your father the right to punish you because you felt you'd failed him?"

"I've never thought of that before, but I guess you're right." The conversation seemed to energize her.

"But you've cut your father off, so who's going to punish you?" Pat asked.

"Other men." Beth answered the question for her.

Bonita had the look of dawning revelation.

"You're right. I hated them for it, but I let them do it. I am crazy, aren't I?"

"Not crazy, just an affected person," Pat said encouragingly. "So, are you going to spend the rest of your life being a victim, letting other people punish you because your father could never accept you?"

"But how can I break the pattern?"

"Maybe she should go back to her father and try again, maybe this time he will be open to her?" Paul suggested to Pat.

"Whose need are you talking from?" she asked him with a smile.

"But maybe he's right. Maybe I should try again. I didn't really give him a chance the last time."

"I guess that would be all right, as long as you keep very clearly in mind that his inability to accept you for what you are is *his* problem, not yours, *his* failing, not yours. He may never change, but that doesn't mean you have to go through life feeling guilty because you weren't the kind of daughter he wanted."

"Maybe if she goes with the thought very clearly in her mind that she is doing this for him and not for herself, maybe then she won't be hurt again," Beth commented.

"Remember, Beth," Pat cautioned. "We are only responsible for ourselves. She needs to do what would be best for her."

"I don't think she should go at all," Connie said, joining the discussion for the first time. "She has her own life to lead. Why should she care about some incompetent father sitting in a nursing home?" The vehemence of her comment brought the eyes of the group upon her. She seemed uncomfortable with the attention. "Well, isn't that right? We only owe our parents so much, and if they've been as bad as he was, we don't owe them anything."

"Is that the way you feel about your father?" Eddie asked.

"My father has been totally irrelevant to my life since I left home when I was sixteen. I haven't seen him. I never think about him. And I certainly would never try to get in touch with him again."

Beth looked at Connie's hard, self-confident face and wondered what was underneath. She had not questioned this exterior before, but no one else in the group had been as they appeared so why should Connie be the exception. Surely she must have been deeply affected by alcoholism. Hadn't her husband been an alcoholic? And now her daughter was also.

"What was he like?" Beth asked, wanting to help Connie.

"I don't remember," she said in a tone that indicated the conversation was over.

"Well," said Pat glancing at her watch, "we're not doing very well on our goals this morning, but I think what we've done has been very important work. I'm pleased you're all starting to react to each other, to help each other grow. Maybe we have time for one more report. Eddie? Since Bonita mentioned your success, do you want to fill us in on what happened?"

Eddie seemed pleased to have a chance to talk. "After our meeting yesterday I went down to that little lounge on the first floor and sat there all by myself. I'd never felt so confused, but it was a different kind of confusion than I'd lived with before. My life was still in a thousand pieces, but I had the feeling that at last all the pieces were there, that all I needed to do was to take time to put them together. Maybe they aren't really all there and maybe I won't ever get them all together, maybe that's an impossible goal, but I think I can put together enough to be able to lead a reasonable life.

"I did what you said and began with my anger toward Dad about this Fifth Step and then went back, writing everything down. I couldn't believe the things I thought about, things I hadn't remembered in years, like the time when I was in sixth grade and he promised me he would help me with my math when I got home from collecting for my paper route. But by the time I got home, he was drunk. I didn't know it then, but I do now. And all of the answers he helped me with were wrong. I flunked the damn assignment . . . my only F of the year.

"And I thought of other things all the way back to when I was little. I don't know if they were all related to his drinking or not, but I guess that doesn't really matter."

"What were some of those things?" Paul asked.

"One time my friends and I were playing tag in the basement, and someone knocked over one of his sawhorses. It didn't hurt anything, nothing was broken, but he came storming down the stairs and spanked me in front of them and then sent them all home. I never dared to have kids play at my house after that when he was home.

"And then when I was in peewees and little league, either he wouldn't come or when he came he'd get so angry at the umps, or at me, that I wished he'd stay home. Stuff like that."

"And then you read the whole list to him?" Kris asked.

"I didn't think I would ever dare to do that, but it all just came out. And he seemed so understanding and so sorry. It had never occurred to me that he realized what he was doing or that he felt badly about it, but I guess it's right that an alcoholic knows guilt we have never heard of. He hated himself for what he was doing to me, but he didn't know how to stop.

"Then last night I got started on the book, *It Will Never Happen to Me*. It's all about problems that children of alcoholics have, especially the ones, like me, who think they'll never end up like their parent, they'll never become drug abusers. I still have a lot to read, but what I read was enough to convince me that I should take the assessment to see if I'm chemically dependent. The thought of it makes me sick. But I guess it's better to know now than after I've screwed up a wife and kids."

He paused as if wondering whether he should go on. Then he said, "And last night I wrote a letter to my mother." Again he hesitated. "Bonita, I don't want you to think this has anything to do with you. You've been wonderful to me, and I'll always love you. But I love her too." He folded his hands and inverted them, bending his fingers back, cracking all his knuckles at once, then he reached into his folder and took out a sheet of paper. His eyes moved down the sheet and back to the top. He cleared his throat, looked again at Bonita, and then began.

"Dear Mom, If anyone had told me a week ago I'd be writing to you, that I would even be thinking about you, I would've told them they were crazy. But here I am, sitting in the room where you used to come to tuck me in and read to me, sitting here wanting more than anything to be in touch with you again, to touch you again." He sniffled, then tried to cover the sound by again clearing his throat and looked up at Pat who gave him an encouraging nod. He went on. "I want you to know how sorry I am for what I said to you. I hated and blamed myself for so long and then I just quit thinking about it, but I know how much it must have hurt you.

"Maybe you know that Dad remarried. She's a great lady and I love her a lot, but that doesn't mean I ever quit loving you. He's in treatment now for his alcoholism. He admitted himself after almost losing his job. Bonita and I are here, too, sorting out what living with an alcoholic has done to us. In the process, I can better understand what it did to you.

"I've been so angry with Dad these past years . . . really hated him. But I guess I've hated you, too, hated you for leaving and not taking me with you, hated you for not keeping in touch. You could've at least done that. It's really strange how loss and guilt and hate and love can all get mixed together and come out as anger. I'm trying to sort out my feelings toward both you and Dad.

"I don't know what your life is like now or if you even want to be reminded of the past, but I just want you to know I love you and if you want to see me, it would make me very happy. Your son, Ed."

As he folded the paper thoughtfully and put it back in his folder, the box of tissue was passed from person to person.

Pat waited, not breaking the mood, and then noted it was time for lunch. "Bonita, we've rescheduled a family conference for you this afternoon at four. This time you're going to get it all out. Right? See you all back here at one o'clock." The members of the group stood up and stretched. Connie moved toward the door, but all the others flocked around Eddie, hugging him, patting him on the back, telling him how proud they were of him. And then they broke into small groups and headed down to the dining room.

As the group moved out the door, Beth paused to give Paul a chance to catch up with her. "It's been quite a morning, hasn't it?" she said, smiling at him.

"Yes, I guess it has, but where did you disappear to? I was worried about you," he said, putting his arm around her shoulder.

"I'll tell you about it later," she responded as they walked down the stairs.

The group members picked up their food and gathered around their usual table in the corner. After the comments about the relative merits of the food, Beth spoke up. "So, tell me about the movie."

"You skipped the whole movie?" Kris exclaimed, surprised.

"Did I ever say I was perfect?" She responded, her voice joking but her eyes deeply serious.

"No, but you always were." Mother and daughter locked their gaze momentarily over a table cluttered with trays of partially eaten food. The moment passed quickly, unnoticed by anyone else. But for Beth, it marked the beginning of something. Understanding, perhaps. Maybe even an adult relationship.

"Didn't you see any of it?" Rick asked.

"I saw the beginning, the part in the parking lot where all these people were tailgating."

"That was nothing. You should've seen the end when everyone was in this huge stadium. There must have been millions of people and they were all chemically dependent people or from dependent families."

"Not millions," Paul corrected, "but the place was packed, everyone joking and singing. That song they were singing at the end keeps running through my mind . . . 'living free, one day at a time.' "

"The song I liked," Bonita chimed in, "was the one Dick Van Dyke and Gary Moore did, 'How could you believe me when I said that I was sober when you knew that I'd been drinking all day?' What a stitch those two are."

"Who were they?" Eddie asked, "I've never seen them before."

"Oh, you're such a babe in arms," Bonita joked. "They were a couple of the best comedians on TV a few years ago." Then addressing Paul and Beth she went on. "It's hard to remember how young these kids are. The other day I mentioned the assassination of Robert Kennedy and he said, 'Who?' " The adults chuckled and Bonita went on. "Wasn't it great to see Hubert again?" she said, addressing Paul, "standing up there talking to all those people, giving them encouragement. I thought at first, 'Was he an alcoholic?' But then I figured he was there because it was in Minnesota. That must not have been long before his death. What a shame that man was never president."

"Hubert who?" Rick asked, genuinely interested, and then realized what he had said. The whole group laughed.

"The part in the movie that really hit me was seeing that family in family court with their son. What memories that brought back." Paul turned to Beth. "Remember the first time we had to go to court? We parked in the ramp below the Hall of Justice and then walked up the rear exit stairwell to the third floor so no one would see us. We got up there and discovered that the whole floor contained family courtrooms except for one door. So, we stood in front of that door checking up and down the hall to be sure no one we knew was around before slipping into our family courtroom."

"And then to have to sit there," Beth picked up the scene, "with a probation officer and a social worker and a judge all staring at us, assuming we had been totally incompetent parents."

"I'm sure they weren't really thinking that," Bonita argued. "I mean, they must see so many different kinds of families that they wouldn't just assume that."

"Oh, probably not, but at that stage, I was so paranoid I thought the whole world was talking about me, judging me."

"And how do you feel now?" Paul asked, but before she had a chance to answer, Eddie, who hadn't heard the question, set down his glass and said, "You know, the thing about the movie that really blew me away was how everybody seemed to be so proud of themselves. I mean, people would say, 'I'm so and so, and I'm an alcoholic' or 'I'm so and so and my father is an alcoholic.' I couldn't get over it. I've been so ashamed of my dad all my life that I've never told anyone he had a drinking problem. I still can't imagine what it would be like to invite some friends over and say, 'I'd like to have you meet my father, a recovering alcoholic.' Weird."

"But when you think about it," responded Bonita, "those people have every right to be proud of themselves. Think of what they've been through. And they're making it."

"*We* people," Beth corrected her. "Think of what we've been through."

"You're right," Bonita laughed. "If all this had happened a few years earlier," her gesture swept the room, "we might have been there in that stadium singing with the rest of them."

"Maybe they will have another festival sometime," Kris mused, "and we can all go and have a reunion."

Mention of a reunion reminded the group that the week was almost over, and they would soon be returning home. A gloom settled over the group and was not broken until Pat came by and said, "Group in ten minutes."

When they had assembled, Pat handed the Al-Anon book to Eddie and asked him to read. The group listened thoughtfully as he began.

> *If a sharp thorn or a splinter pierces my hand, what do I do? I remove it as quickly as I can. Surely I wouldn't leave it there, hurting me, until it festered and sent its infection*

throughout my body . . . True, resentment and hatred are more difficult to pull out of our thoughts than the physical thorn from a finger, but so much depends upon it that I will do my best to eliminate them, before their poison can spread.

After the reading, Pat asked, "What was going on downstairs? You were laughing and talking, but by the time I came over you all looked like you had lost your best friend."

"It just hit us all at once," Bonita responded, "that tomorrow is the last day, and we'll probably never see each other again."

All but Connie joined in with comments about how fast the week had gone and how close they felt and how it would be like losing a best friend.

"Would you like to share addresses and telephone numbers? We usually do that for family groups. Here, I'll pass around a sheet of paper. If you want your name and number distributed, write it down, and I'll make copies of the sheet for everyone. I want you to feel free to keep in touch with me also. You can't imagine how frustrating it is for us to become so intimately involved with people for a short time and then never hear from them again. We care very much about each of you, and we'd love to hear from you.

"While I'm on the subject, I might as well add, though you will hear it all again tomorrow, that none of you will be able to make it on your own. You're going to need others who have gone through what you're going through to help you. The first few months are going to be tough, so get in touch with some kind of group support. We strongly recommend Al-Anon and Alateen." Pat paused, looking from person to person, impressing on each one the importance of what she had just said. Then she went on. "Back to our goals. Eddie, had you finished?"

"There was just one other thing. I'd like to take the assessment if it isn't too late. Could you make an appointment for me?"

"Of course it's not too late, but don't look so frightened, it's not all that bad, is it Rick?"

Rick, whose mind must have been somewhere else, said, "Bad? What?"

"The assessment, dum-dum," Kris responded. "They want to know if it was so bad."

"Oh, no. It was a breeze."

Eddie seemed to relax a bit and Pat said, "Well, who's next? Beth?"

"Actually, I've hardly begun my goals."

"What were they?"

"I was supposed to do the list of blocks I feel in my relationship with Tom. I did get a little of that done. But last night when Paul wanted to do the dyadic encounter, I told him I was too tired. The truth was, I didn't want to talk to him. And I was supposed to write letters to Kris and Erik telling them whatever seemed important. I started writing both those letters, but, again, I couldn't do it. I didn't want to do it. I didn't want to communicate with my own children. I felt like I was being smothered. All I could think about was getting away from them all."

She paused and looked at Kris and then Rick both of whom had looks of bewilderment on their faces. "I didn't really feel that way, of course, I mean, I would never have left."

"Wait a minute," Pat interjected. "Don't apologize. You've been doing that for far too long. Of course you wanted to run away, to escape. That's the most common of all feelings."

Beth sat, not knowing what to say. "So you went to bed. What happened this morning?" Pat asked in order to continue the discussion.

"I woke up early after a terrible nightmare. I was being crushed and I couldn't even call for help. Nobody cared." She stopped, overcome by her own words.

"It's unfair, isn't it, after spending your whole life caring for others, that when you need help, no one is there for you?" Pat's words kept her going.

"I was all alone," she choked. The peace and relief she had felt such a short time ago was slipping away. Out of the corner of her eye she saw Paul move toward her, but Pat must have signaled him back.

"Do you think someone would have come if you had called for help?"

"I don't know." Her voice was a whisper followed by a long pause.

"You know, Beth, you rob your family of something very important when you don't let them know when you need them. There is a very thin line between being a self-sacrificing nurturer, which most mothers are, and being a martyr, which many mothers become. Why did you leave the movie?"

"I don't know. I guess I just couldn't stand to see all those happy people. I was feeling so miserable."

"So you went down and talked to the chaplain?"

"Yes, he said pretty much the same thing, that I had to start being honest with my family. It seems funny to think about it. I was so insistent on their being honest with me, and yet I never really let them know what I was feeling. He called that 'stuffing anger.' I guess I'd been doing that for a long time and finally I was full of anger and I couldn't love anymore. All I wanted to do was run away."

"You were angry with all of us?" Kris asked, seeming hurt.

Not wanting to hurt her, Beth began backing off. "Well, not really you . . . ."

"Beth, you're doing it again," Pat cautioned. "Kris isn't going to break if you tell her the truth. In fact, it might help her to be more honest, herself." Beth nodded, trying to break deeply ingrained patterns.

"I had reached a point where I was empty, empty of love, that is, and full of resentment and hate. It was mostly toward Tom, of course. I used to . . . sometimes I would even . . . ." She stammered, then went on. "Once in a while I would imagine him dead so I would be rid of the problem." She paused, waiting for a shocked response, but there was none. "But the anger included the rest of you, too, especially Paul. I felt as if he'd walked out on our marriage and our family and left me holding the bag. The only time he related to us, me, was when he wanted something. I got so I could hardly stand to have him touch me."

"But you never told him how you felt?"

"No, I guess I just pulled away."

"But that really wasn't her fault," Paul said to Pat, "I probably wouldn't have listened, wouldn't have understood. In fact, now that I think back, she did try to tell me time and time again about how bad things were getting with the kids, but I never believed her. In fact, I blamed her for overreacting or for not being able to control them."

"Tell her that, don't tell me."

Beth knew Paul's eyes were on her but she couldn't look up. She heard him roll his chair over to her and saw his knees in front of her. Then his hands cupped her face and he lifted her head to his. "Can you ever forgive me? I'm so sorry. Things are going to be different, I know they are." Beth nodded and he kissed her warmly on the lips, but inside, she knew, something was still wrong. She was suspicious of his sorrow, she questioned his repentance. She had been used so often that it was impossible to trust anyone anymore. Of course he'd say what needed to be said to keep her happy, to make things like they'd once been, so she would be content and take care of the home and make love whenever he wanted to. But would anything really be different?

Paul rolled his chair back, a look of happiness on his face that she hadn't seen for ages, and Beth felt guilty, knowing she had done it again, she had not been honest.

"How do you feel now?" Pat asked.

"I don't know."

"You don't know, or you don't want to tell us?"

Beth felt she was being exposed for the liar she was.

"Do you really believe things are going to be different between you and Paul?" Beth bit the side of her mouth and then quickly pressed her finger against her temple, hoping to stop the tic before anyone noticed it. "You don't trust him, yet, do you?" Beth didn't know how to answer. "Do you still feel as if the whole world used you and then turned against you?"

Turned against you. Turned against you. Blurred images and words began coming into focus, slowly, painfully until the scene was clear.

"Did you hear what he said?" Beth almost shouted.

"Who said?"

"Tom. Right here in this room. Didn't you hear him?" Beth looked from face to face, shocked that they seemed bewildered, angry that they didn't know what she was talking about. "And no one said anything. No one cared."

"What did he say, Beth?"

"You must have heard him. He called me a fool. All that time he'd been lying to me." No one responded properly. No one understood her rage. She tried to explain, "The only thing I had to hold onto during the last year was that we talked. People always said if you can keep the lines of communication open with your children, things will turn out, so I did. We always talked. It was the only thing I had left to hold onto, the only thing that showed I wasn't a terrible mother, and all the time he was lying to me, using me, playing me for a fool. Did you hear him say it? 'God you were a fool!' He said that to me. He called me a dumb guppy for sucking it all in. And then he turned to Paul, wanting his love, casting me off like some piece of garbage. After all I tried to do, all I put up with, it's his father he loves and I'm the fool. I'm the fool."

The absurdity of it all struck Beth as ultimately, hopelessly hilarious and she began to laugh, a strange, high-pitched, choking laugh and then it didn't seem so funny anymore so she just sat, staring out the window, thinking nothing, feeling nothing.

"Beth." Her name came to her from far away. "Beth," Pat's voice brought her back, "you have every right to be deeply hurt and angry over what Tom said that day. I thought it was outrageous. I almost said something, but then I caught myself and waited for you to respond."

"I felt the same way," Kris added, "He was always so mean, but that was the worst. I wanted to kill him."

"And I was so flattered that for once he was interested in me that I didn't even notice." Paul shook his head as if unable to believe his own insensitivity.

"Beth, do you realize you took that cruel comment without a whimper of protest? Tom has no idea he hurt you in any way." Pat waited and then went on. "You've got to start leveling with your family about your own feelings, your own needs. In one of our films, we learned about resentment being the emotion that burns out its container from the inside. I suspect you've been hurt repeatedly by the people in your family, and you've always tried to be the strong one, the loving one, the giving one. But, gradually, all those hurts and angers burned you out. The only other option you could see was to get away, to leave."

"But what was I supposed to do? I get so tired of these women who are always talking about their needs, always demanding their rights. They don't seem happy either. It's like trying to counter selfishness with selfishness. And I've been in other homes where the mother is always shouting at the kids and picking at her husband. The tension is so thick it's repellent."

"Have you read the little pamphlet in your folder on detachment?" Pat asked. Beth shook her head no. "I would strongly recommend it to you. When people live with a chemically dependent person, it's almost impossible not to get caught up in an either/or cycle. Either you are totally involved and controlled as you were, or you withdraw or escape, as Paul did and as you want to do now. Neither response is helpful. In fact, both are counterproductive.

"But most people don't realize there's another option. We talk about 'detaching with love' here, or about 'letting go,' or about 'emotional distancing.' These are all ways of saying the same thing. If you're going to live with a practicing alcoholic or a recovering alcoholic, you have to separate yourself in such a way that you can still love and care for the person. But you can't let the person's behavior control your moods or, especially, your self-image. You need to detach from the problem, not from the person. I hope all of you will read the book carefully. But again

I will say it, and I'll keep saying it until you are sick to death of hearing it: You can't do it alone. You've got to find support and guidance or you'll slip right back into all of the old roles.

"One of the reasons we sometimes refer to people who live with an alcoholic as codependents is that they become dependent on the behavior of the alcoholic for their own self-image. Everyone ends up used and abused from time to time in life, but the danger of codependence is when you end up in a position where you need people to use and abuse you so you can feel persecuted and somehow, self-righteous. No one can be a martyr if there aren't persecutors around. So, when your self-image becomes tied into martyrdom you set yourself up, subconsciously almost forcing those who live with you to abuse you. We've found this is one of the hardest behavior patterns to root out.

"Beth, you've come a long, long way today. But you still have a long way to go. You'll have some time after this group and before your family conference. Use that to work on your list of angers and worries and fears and resentments toward Tom. And then, tonight, try to finish your other goals. We'll have you report tomorrow. We have time for one more. Connie?"

Connie shifted in her chair, cleared her throat, looked across the room and out the window, and then said, "I think these little gimmicks you put people through are a waste of time. I can't imagine anyone taking them seriously."

"What are you afraid of?" Pat asked.

"I'm not afraid of anything. I know who I am and I'm content with my life." Connie shook a cigarette out of its pack with such force that several more shot out, landing on the floor. She bent over and picked them up.

"You've been resisting the program all week. Usually the people who resist the hardest are the people who need it the most."

"I really resent that. Just because my father and husband were alcoholics and my daughter was picked up on some stupid charge doesn't mean I'm sick like you keep implying."

"Your father was an alcoholic, too?" Paul exclaimed.

"And you think you haven't been affected by alcoholism?" Bonita added.

Realizing she had been tricked into saying more than she wanted to say, into revealing more than she had intended, Connie got up and walked out.

The group sat in silence for a time, a sense of failure hanging over them. "Do you ever have people who get nothing out of these weeks?" Beth asked.

"Of course. We're not perfect and the program isn't perfect, and even if it were, for some people the timing just isn't right. The people who come here are responsible for their own health. They have to make the decision and make the effort."

"But, doesn't that bother you? I mean, when someone just walks out?" Kris asked.

"I'd have gone crazy a long time ago if I hadn't learned to separate my self-image from my success as a counselor. Detachment, remember?" But as she said the word, she picked up a cigarette that Connie had missed and began fondling it. "Anybody here have a light?"

"I thought you quit smoking," Rick said indignantly.

"That's right, I did," she said, laughing to cover up her embarrassment as she put the cigarette on her desk. "Well, we still have time for one more goal report. Who wants to volunteer? Bonita, you had more on your goal list than just writing out your feelings toward Jim. Did you get the rest finished?"

"I read the pamphlet about detachment. It's really good. In fact, it makes a lot more sense to me today than it did yesterday. I really recommend it," she said, turning to Beth. Beth nodded and Bonita went on. "And then I was supposed to make a list of ten specific ways I can be good to myself. That was hard when all I could think about was how I had failed at that conference, but I did get a few." She pulled a sheet of yellow legal size paper out of her folder and started reading.

"I'm going to quit putting myself down and telling myself I'm crazy. I'm going to start going to Al-Anon and I'm also going to start taking time to go to an exercise class." She stopped reading and explained. "I feel so much better about myself when my body is in good shape, but for the last year or so, I just haven't cared." She looked down at her body, laughed, and said, "Obviously."

Returning to her list she read, "I'm going to start reading everything I can get my hands on about alcoholism." Again she looked up from her list and explained herself to the group. "Remember that comment in the film? He said when a retarded child was born into a family, everybody read everything they could about the subject. But when someone has a drinking problem, people tend to suffer in ignorance. I may still have to suffer, but it won't be in ignorance." Then she went back to her list. "Every time Jim says or does something that hurts me, I'm going to say to myself, 'That's his problem, it has nothing to do with me.' "

Again, Bonita couldn't resist explaining herself. Turning to Beth she said, "One of the things it said in the detachment pamphlet is that the two most difficult actions to detach yourself from are sneers and mockery. I thought about that when you were talking about what Tom had said. Jim is really good at that, too. Nothing that big, but little things, barbs, putdowns. I used to get so upset I could hardly stand it. Well, no more. I will simply disregard all such comments."

"Excuse me a minute, Bonita," Pat interrupted. "What you just said is going to be extremely important for all of you when you get home. You have probably all gotten rather good at those sneering, mocking, or sarcastic comments. It's a defense the whole family picks up rather quickly. You will all have to work on both ignoring such comments when they are directed at you, and not using them on others. Go ahead," she nodded toward Bonita.

"This is my last one and I got this idea from that pamphlet also. I'm not going to assume that just because I've been through this process that I have all the answers or any of the answers. I'm not going to try to advise or control others. I'm just going to worry about myself, at least for a while." She looked up and grinned. "That's it."

"That's a good list," Pat responded. "Stick it on your refrigerator so you won't forget any of it." Pat glanced at her watch and sighed. "There's just never enough time, is there? We still haven't heard from you, Paul, or Kris, or Rick, and *you* still have work to do, don't you?" she asked, looking at Beth who nodded yes. "I think we should try to get started a little early tomorrow morning. Can you be here and ready to go by eight-thirty? There will be a short talk by a woman from Al-Anon and then we'll have the rest of the morning for goals. In the afternoon we'll have our graduation ceremony."

Kris and Rick looked at each other and started to laugh, recalling their comments the day they arrived. "What's so funny?" Eddie asked.

"On the morning we came, our cab driver mentioned he had gone through treatment here and that he had met his wife at an alumni party. We couldn't believe it and started making jokes about the graduation ceremony they must have," Rick answered.

"Do you still think it's funny?" Pat asked.

Rick thought a moment and then said, "I remember the little graduation ceremony we had when we finished junior high. You know, I feel like I've learned more in a week here than I learned in three years of junior high. That wasn't exactly the junior high's fault, you understand," he said, grinning at Pat, "but it's true. I'm going to be proud to graduate tomorrow." The rest of the group members nodded agreement as they picked up their folders and began getting ready to leave.

"The family conference for the Inghrams will be in about twenty minutes. Eddie, you're scheduled for your chemical use assessment at four o'clock, and Bonita, we'll call Jim down and give you another chance with him. Donna will meet with you along with Jim's counselor."

Beth hurried out the door and found herself a quiet corner in the meeting room. She needed to work on her list and there wasn't much time. But this time the words poured out and her pen hardly left the paper until she heard Paul calling to her, telling her the meeting was about to begin.

When she got to the room, everyone was seated, leaving her the chair next to Tom. She hesitated and then sat down.

"You all remember the ground rules," Dan, Tom's counselor, began the meeting. "No violence, nobody leaves the room, try to avoid verbal abuse, and always address your comments to the person you are referring to. Okay? Did any of you have any trouble thinking of what the blocks are in your relationships?" He looked from person to person noting their smiles, as they assumed his question had been a joke. "Good," he said, "You know, once in a while we get people in here who are so out of touch with their feelings that they insist the chemically dependent person has never done anything they resent, they have never been hurt, they never worry. I know it sounds incredible, but it happens. Once in a great while, it might even be true, if they haven't been very involved with the person. But ninety-nine times out of a hundred, if a person insists he or she has been unaffected, we are correct in assuming that the person is out of touch with his or her feelings.

"The rationale behind this conference is that you can't build a firm house on a shaky foundation. Or to use another metaphor, a little rotting garbage smells as bad as a whole can full. In order to clean out the air, we have to take out all the garbage, all the resentments and hurts and angers. After that, there's a possibility for a clean start. So, who wants to go first?" No one volunteered. "Tom, you're an old hand at telling people what you think of them by now, why don't you go ahead."

Tom took out his list, started the first sentence, then stopped, looked up and explained, "I didn't make out separate lists for each person like I was supposed to. It was easier to just write down things as they came to me, so it's kind of a jumble." Then he went back to his list.

"Dad, I really resent you for cutting me out of your life, for never being there when I needed you. I know I didn't try to talk to you very often and when I did, I wasn't very rational, but I always felt like you didn't care, like I was wasting your precious time.

"And Mom, I hated the way you would always correct my grammar, especially when you would do it in front of my friends, and the way you would always ask me where I was going when I would go out at night and then stay up till I got home. I hated even coming home knowing you would be standing there looking sad and angry, making me feel guilty. And I really resent how you were always going to church. Sometimes when I would come home on Sunday mornings and want to talk, you wouldn't be there.

"Rick, I couldn't think of much to say about you. You were a pretty good kid brother. I guess I only resented the fact that I never knew if I could trust you or not. Sometimes you and Kris seemed so close, and I was afraid you would tell her what you knew and she would tell Mom.

"And Mom, it always seemed as if you favored Kris. Just once I wanted you to be proud of me like you were of her. And Dad, too, always talking about his little princess. It was sickening.

"Kris, almost everything you did made me gag. I resented your goody-goody attitude and how you would always rat on us and that you were Mom and Dad's favorite because you always got *A*s and did everything right."

Beth had felt herself getting more and more angry as Tom attacked Kris. Then, unable to control herself, she blurted, "Wait a minute. How can you sit there saying you resent us for the things we were doing that were good, like Kris getting good grades, or me asking you where you were going and waiting up for you until you got home? Isn't that what mothers are supposed to do?" The last question was addressed to Dan, Tom's counselor, not to Tom.

"Of course it is," Dan said in a calming voice. "But of course Tom resented it. He was afraid you'd figure out what was going on and try to stop it. Remember, at that stage of his life, all he was thinking about was how to get and use drugs in such a way as to keep people off his back. Also, remember, feelings are not right or wrong, and often they're totally irrational, but if they are there, then it's important to get them out. Okay?" he asked, looking at Beth. She nodded, feeling embarrassed. "Anything else, Tom?"

"No, that's it."

"Any other responses to Tom's list?" Dan waited a moment and then went on. "Who would like to go next?" Dan asked. "I will," Kris said emphatically. Beth looked at her and saw that she, too, had been angered by Tom's comments.

"I never realized until this week how much I've resented you all these years." She read from her paper and then looked up at Pat. "I can't believe he thought I was the favorite. He's the one who got all the attention." Pat nodded with understanding and then signaled her to continue reading. "I resent you for all the times you put me down and told me I was ugly and stupid. It's no wonder I have such a poor self-image. In your eyes, nothing I ever did was right. I resent you for all the times you made fun of me for getting good grades and how you'd always tell me how unpopular I was and that everyone thought I was a real dork.

"I resent you for always picking fights, and then when Mom would come, we would both get blamed and you would laugh at me when I cried. And I still get angry when I think of all the times you pinched me or twisted my arm or snapped me with rubber bands. We could never be in the same room without you doing something to hurt me.

"And I hated you for what you did to Mom, for all the times you screamed at her and swore at her and even hit her. When I would hear her crying in her room because of you, I wanted to do something to help her, but nothing I could ever do was enough to make her feel better.

"And you ruined things for me at school, too. It was like I had to be twice as good at the beginning of the year in order for teachers to accept me because they hated you so much, and they just assumed I would be like you. I couldn't stand to have everyone think so badly of our family, so I ended up having to be the good one. I really hated being the good one, not being able to be normal and have fun like everybody else, but because you were so bad, I had to be good. But even then, you got all the attention. I tried and tried, but everyone just expected me to be good and all they did was think about you." Beth, who had never seen her daughter so open, so forceful, watched in amazement as Kris put her paper down and looked directly at her brother. "And just now when you said I made you sick because I was such a goody-goody, I wanted to smash your face in."

All but the counselors sat in stunned silence. Finally, Tom's counselor said, "Is there anything you want to say to your sister, Tom? How do you feel after hearing all those resentments?"

Tom looked at him, shaking his head. "I don't know what to say. I mean, I guess I never thought of her as having feelings before. She was just there, a bratty sister. I really feel sorry . . . ."

"Tell her that."

Tom looked at Kris, back to his counselor who nodded encouragingly, and then back to Kris. "I never really meant to hurt you. No, that isn't true. I did mean to hurt you, but I never thought I had any power over you. You never did anything I said, and you were so different from me. I know I kept at you all the time, but I never realized until now that you were affected. I'm really sorry, Kris."

"Kris, how about you? How are you feeling now?"

Kris wiped her eyes and nose with the tissue someone had handed her. "Great. I've been holding that in for so long, and I never thought I would have the courage to say it. But I hope I didn't hurt your feelings," she said, addressing Tom. "I would never want to set you back. Maybe I was exaggerating."

"Whoops." Pat cut in. "Here we go again. You don't need to back off from your feelings. Tom treated you badly for years. We know it wasn't really his fault, but that doesn't alter the fact that he did it and he has to bear the responsibility for his actions."

Then, addressing the whole family, she went on. "As long as the subject has come up, let me mention the real tendency there is for recovering chemically dependent people to use a sort of subconscious blackmail on their families. Family members go around like they're walking on eggs, thinking they can't do this or they better not say that for fear they will trigger the person's chemical use again. Just remember, your only responsibility is to be honest with yourself and with your family. You don't have the power to cause him to begin using again any more than you have the power to prevent it. Okay? Okay.

"One more thing, Kris. We've been talking this week about how no one has the power to make you feel anything. Others may do hurtful things, but we choose to let those things hurt us, and we choose, maybe not consciously, but we choose nonetheless, to let that hurt turn into anger and hate. Sometime before tomorrow, I'd like to have you go through your list again and sort out those things which are really your problems. You can't ever change Tom's behavior, but you can change your response to it."

Kris looked a little confused so Pat explained more. "For instance, I heard you blame Tom for the fact that you have a poor self-image. Many people in your life were giving you positive reinforcement, but you chose to let Tom's opinion of you determine your opinion about yourself. That's something you can change. See what I'm getting at?" Kris nodded and began skimming her list. "Okay. Who's next?"

Beth glanced from Paul to Rick wondering if either of them wanted to go. Finally, Paul reached down, picked up his folder, and took out his list.

"The first thing I wrote was that I deeply resented Tom for putting our family through this experience, but even as I wrote it, I realized it was no longer true. I'm not thankful he has a drug problem, but I am thankful for the opportunity it has given us to regroup as a family." Paul spoke, looking from one counselor to the other.

"Can I interrupt a moment?" Pat stopped him before he could go on. "I want you to look at Tom and address your comments to him. Say, 'I resent you for . . .' or, 'I'm angry about . . . ,' okay?" Paul nodded and then swiveled his chair so he could look at his son.

"Tom, I resent you for all the times you hurt your mother, and for the way you drained her of all her emotional energy, leaving little for the other children or myself. I resent you for all the times I came home from work, wanting nothing but to sit and relax, and the house was so filled with tension I just wanted to leave. I resent you for all the fights you would start whenever we tried to do something as a family. I still get angry thinking of the embarrassment of having to go to parent/teacher and parent/principal conferences, and family court, especially family court. I couldn't stand that. I don't think I've ever felt like such a failure as I did the first time we had to appear before that judge."

He stopped and addressed Tom's counselor. "I guess, like any father, I wanted my son to grow up to be at least a little like me, with some of my values, some of my priorities. It's been an overwhelming disappointment to me to find out how he's been living, what he's been doing." The counselor nodded understanding and then, with a gesture of his head, directed Paul's attention back to Tom.

Paul began reading again, "I resent you for the ways you hurt Kris and for trying to make Rick just like you. It makes me feel angry and guilty that I have to go back to Rochester knowing my son was a part of the drug distribution chain, a part of the problem. I still can hardly face that myself, and I'm not sure how I'll be able to face others, especially my patients who come in hysterical because their twelve- and thirteen-year-olds are getting drugs from somewhere and they don't know what to do. I resent you for turning me into a workaholic." He began to fold his paper and then looked up at Pat. "Maybe that's not fair. Maybe I would have been one anyway. I don't know."

Paul carefully set one sheet of paper aside and looked at the next. "You mentioned we were to think about our fears or anxieties," he said, addressing Pat. Then, turning back to Tom he began reading. "I've never felt so fearful about the future. On the one hand, now that I know what is going on, I know I can be of more help to you. But, on the other hand, life has never seemed so complex."

"Anything you want to say to your father, Tom?" Dan asked.

"I don't know," he said with a little laugh. "I was expecting so much more. I always thought you were down on me all the time, that you would come in here with pages. I mean, Mom put up with me and was always there to talk to, but you just cut me off. I thought you really hated me. I guess I feel a little relieved.

"But one thing, Dad. Sure you can be of help to me, but my life is my problem. I don't want you thinking you can take over and start telling me what to do. You're going to have enough of a problem taking care of yourself. Remember, 'Let go.' "

Paul folded his paper angrily and then turned to Tom's counselor. "Is that what you teach kids here? How to be insolent to their parents?"

"Was it what Tom said or the way he said it that seemed insolent to you?" Dan asked.

"It couldn't have been the way he said it," Rick answered, defending Tom. "I mean, I've never heard Tom say anything with more respect."

"He was just saying what we've been learning, Dad," Kris added.

"You don't need to tell me what we've been learning," Paul snapped and Kris responded as if she had been slapped.

Beth, furious with Paul, was about to jump in to defend her children when Pat stopped the action.

"Okay. Here you have a good example of the kind of interactions that are going to come up when you get home. Let's take a look at what happened and see if there are better ways of handling it. First of all, Beth, you were about to say something, to get involved. Is this your problem?"

Of course it is, Beth thought. *Anything that happens to my children is my problem.* But then she caught herself. "No, I guess it really isn't."

"And, Kris, you jumped in to help out your brothers. Was it your problem?" Kris shook her head, no. "Has it become your problem?"

"What do you mean?" Kris asked.

"Are you now emotionally hooked into the situation?" Kris nodded. "Why?"

Tears began to well up in her eyes. "I just made a simple observation. He didn't need to yell at me."

"I didn't yell," Paul said defensively.

Pat ignored him and concentrated on Kris. "And you let him hurt your feelings, so now you're angry and defensive." Kris nodded. "Would you say your getting involved in this problem just caused more problems?" Again, Kris nodded agreement.

"What about you, Rick, was this your problem?"

"No, I guess not."

"Do you think maybe your dad began feeling as if he was being ganged up on?" Rick gestured, "I don't know . . . perhaps."

"Now, Paul, think back. Something Tom said upset you. Toward whom did you direct your anger?" Paul muttered a response. "What might have happened if you had said directly to Tom, 'I feel hurt or put-down or upset when you . . . ,' and then told him what was bothering you?"

"I don't know what would have happened."

"Why don't you try it?"

"I think you've made your point, and besides, I don't remember what I was angry about. I think we should go on. We're running out of time."

Pat glanced at her watch. "You're right. It's too bad we can't pursue this a little further . . . we need time for everyone to read their lists. But Paul, I want you to think about what just happened. Okay? Okay. Let's move on with our lists."

Beth began to feel nauseated, thinking of the pages of resentments she had in her folder. *What irony,* she thought, as she recalled Tom's comment about the difference between his parents. *The parent he thought hated him was simply not thinking about him, and the parent he thought loved him was wishing he were dead. Maybe I should leave that part out.* She felt panicky, trying to decide. One of the counselors was asking who wanted to go next. Beth looked at Rick. He shrugged and picked up his folder.

"I mostly resent you for always being the center of attention. Whenever you were around it was like no matter what I did, you were always the important one. And even now, you take over and everything revolves around you, like the other night when we went out to dinner. And when you come home, I can see it now, you'll get all the attention for being good just like you used to get all the attention for being bad. And it made me feel so inferior because you were better at everything than I was. There was nothing I could do better than you. I resent you for always ridiculing me and calling me names if I wouldn't do whatever you wanted me to do or whatever you were doing. You called me a fag so often I almost started believing I was one.

"I resent you for the way you treated Mom and for making me think I had to choose sides. I never wanted to treat my parents like I did, but I thought I had to in order to be accepted by you because that's what you did. I resent you for the way you would make fun of any friend I had that wasn't tough like you. And you teased me so much about things I was involved in that I quit everything. I could have been really good in music, but you made me think only wimps went out for band and chorus so I quit.

"I resent you for all the times you got me in trouble," and he read a long list of specific instances beginning with the party where he had gotten into a fight. Then he paused, glanced at Tom, and quickly looked back at his list.

"I resent you for making me think I had to choose between you and Kris. I really liked Kris when we were little, but you made me think I had to be as cruel to her as you were. I hated myself whenever I did mean things to her, but it was like you had a spell over me, like you controlled me." He stopped and looked at the counselor.

"I know we learned that everyone in a family where someone is chemically dependent falls into roles, but I can't get the thought out of my mind that if I had been a stronger person, I wouldn't have gotten so sucked in. I mean, I was really sucked in."

"Rick," Tom's counselor said sympathetically, "don't tear yourself apart with that thought. You're going to have enough to worry about without wondering whether you're strong or weak. We're all weak. We're all victims. Especially Tom. He was so weak he couldn't live without chemicals. Think about that. He was so weak he had to prove his self-worth by always trying to manipulate others. Don't think in terms of strength or weakness. Think in terms of direction. You were going in one direction for a time, and now with the help of your Higher Power and others who've been through experiences similar to yours, you're going to go in another direction. You're no longer going to be enslaved by Tom's behavior in the same way he was enslaved by drugs. You're going to walk free." He reached over and put his arm around Rick's shoulders and gave them a squeeze. "You're a great kid. And you've got your whole life ahead of you. Hang in there."

"Tom, did you want to respond to Rick's list?" Pat asked.

"It's crazy. I guess I had never thought of either Kris or Rick as real people. They were just there, either helping me or in my way. It's hard to believe he was really thinking all that, feeling all that. He always seemed like he wanted to be a part of my group. I don't know, I just feel kind of confused."

"You know we'll be going over these resentments in our group, don't you?" Dan responded. "That will give you a chance to sort out which of the problems mentioned are things you should try to make amends for and which things you aren't responsible for. Well, one left," he said as he glanced at his watch.

Beth took out her list, feeling pressured by time, sensing that everyone was bored with the whole process and wasn't interested in her. All of a sudden it all seemed terribly unimportant, she seemed terribly unimportant.

Pat, who must have sensed her mood, said, "Beth, we have plenty of time. You have a lot to say to Tom and this is the time."

Beth opened up her revised list and began rolling down the corner.

"Beth, it's very important that you do this," Pat's voice was stern.

Beth took a deep breath and looked at her firstborn son. "Tom, I have to say something to you first, because of all the things you have done over the years, for some reason, it hurt the most. I don't know if I can ever forgive you for what you said last Monday when you called me a fool and told me you had been lying to me during all those talks we used to have. I don't know if I can ever trust you again. I don't know if I can ever trust my own judgment again. When you said that, I was so hurt and angry I wanted to kill you." Beth saw the look on Tom's face turn to surprised shock, but once started, she couldn't stop.

"I often used to lie in bed at night and wish you would die. Nothing I did worked and everything was so hopeless that it seemed like the only way out. I hated you for making me feel like such a failure. I had given my life to raising my family, and everything had gone wrong." She was no longer reading. "Can you understand what that's like? I loved you Tom, and you just used me and lied to me and turned my home into a battleground. You'll never know how deeply I resent you for that." She paused, trying to control her breathing, and then returned to her list.

"I resent you for what you did to both Kris and Erik. I could see it happening, but no matter what I did to prevent it, it happened anyway. And I let you become a barrier between Paul and me. We began disagreeing about how you should be handled years ago, and it just got worse and worse. Maybe he was right. I don't know. It doesn't really matter now.

"It used to make me so angry, the way you would never take responsibility for your actions. Nothing was ever your fault. You could always find someone or something else to blame. And you made every change in our lives so difficult. You seemed unable to handle change, and when it was forced on you or us, you always took it out on us.

"I resent you for all the times teachers looked at me accusingly, blaming me for your behavior. And I resent you for making me have to pick you up at the police station and for having to go to family court. I still feel sick thinking of how our family life became bridge club gossip, and our home became a case study for social workers to pick apart and analyze. It was so ironic." Again Beth looked up from her paper and spoke, this time to Tom's counselor. "I thought I knew what I was doing. I had all the theories and I'd always been good with children. But nothing worked. And then to have to sit, as a failure, in front of some young social worker who knew all the theories, who was as sure as I had once been that good parenting produces good kids. It's crazy."

Dan sat back in his chair and chuckled. "You're right," he said. "There's no theory that works with these kids." Grateful for his understanding, Beth went back to her list and began reading.

"I still get angry thinking of all the times you embarrassed me in front of my friends by being abusive and totally disrespectful, until I finally quit having friends come over. And then I quit going out. I got so paranoid, wondering what people were thinking of us, what they were saying, that it was easier to just stay at home." She stopped, her mind drifting back to those years of self-imposed isolation.

Movement by someone in the group brought her back. She continued reading. "Your language was always so terrible. I got so I could hardly stand to hear you talk. I always felt you used that gutter grammar and those gutter words because you knew how much it bothered me. I kept thinking, if I just quit reacting, you'd quit talking that way, but even when I tried I could never get over being offended and repulsed by your language and you never did change.

"And I resent you for all the times you interfered with my disciplining of the other children, especially Erik . . . when you'd tell him he didn't need to listen to me, that there was nothing I could do, that I had no power. And it was true.

"Your terrible behavior even made me think I'd lost my faith. I prayed and prayed for a miracle and all that happened was more fights and more arrests. Finally I quit going to church. I'd leave the house on Sunday morning, but I would go and sit in a coffee shop. I couldn't stand being in church. All it did was remind me of my failure, my failure as a wife, my failure as a mother, the failure of my prayers, the failure of my faith. For a time I believed in demon possession. It was the only thing that could explain your behavior. And then I looked at myself and realized evil is everywhere. You twisted, perverted, corrupted my vision until finally all I could see was darkness." Beth set her paper down and looked up. All of the members of her family were staring at her as if she were a stranger.

"Beth, how are you feeling, now?" Pat's voice cut through the silence.

"I don't know," Beth said, trying to decide how she felt. "Scared, I guess. Like I've finally taken off a mask, but I don't know if people will like what's underneath."

"Do you like what's underneath?"

"No, not particularly." She began folding her paper first in halves then quarters then eighths and sixteenths. "But for some reason I feel more hopeful than I have for years."

"I can't believe you really quit going to church," said Rick voicing the outrage and disillusionment of all children when brought abruptly face-to-face with the humanity of their parents.

"You remember the film about family illness?" Pat asked. "One of the things he mentioned was that many people either become fanatics or lose their religious faith. It's a symptom of the disease."

"One of the problems," Dan continued, "is that chemical dependency is a disease that has to get worse before it can get better. So when you start praying for a miracle, the answer to that prayer seems like a nonanswer because things get more and more difficult. Well, I've become a believer in miracles since working here. We see them happen all the time. And, in fact, we're seeing one happen right here." The Inghram family looked at him with puzzled, questioning eyes. "It's not a 'zap miracle' where all your problems are solved in an instant. It's a miracle of process. I believe deeply in the Power of God. Trust me. You've all come a long way. I feel extremely optimistic about your chances for healthy, whole lives." His eyes moved authoritatively from person to person around the circle, convincing them that, all evidence to the contrary, he was right. There was a God who was in control. They were experiencing a miracle.

"Tom, do you want to respond to your mother or to anyone else in your family?" Tom, with downcast eyes, resumed a habit he had broken years before — biting the skin along the side of his thumbnail, first one strip of skin and then another, tearing it off then spitting it onto the floor. Finally he looked up. "I don't know what to say," he said to the counselor. The room was quiet. Then he looked at his mother.

"Mom, I had no idea." His voice quivered and then cracked. He cleared his throat, trying to regain control. "You've got to believe me. I really never meant to hurt you. When I realized I was hurting you, I hated myself for it. But I never had any idea of what you were going through. Everything you said, I deserved and probably lots more. When I called you a fool the other day, I didn't really mean it. No, that's not true. I did mean it. I always thought you were a fool because you kept caring about me when I knew I didn't deserve it. And it seemed so easy to pull the wool over your eyes. But just because I thought of you as a fool, doesn't mean that you were one." Tears began pouring from his eyes. "I love you, Mom. I always have. You've meant more to me than anyone. I could never have made it through all this if it hadn't been for you."

Beth sat, dry-eyed, looking at her son, knowing some sort of response was expected of her, but unable to feel anything.

"Would you like to close this meeting in the same way we close our group sessions?" she heard Dan ask Tom, and she saw him nod yes. Tom and Dan stood and moved to the center of the room, gesturing for the others to join them. Beth stood, feeling awkward, not knowing what to expect. Tom came and stood next to her and put his arm around her shoulder and his other arm around Kris. Soon everyone was in a huddle, arm in arm, and Dan led Tom and Pat in the Serenity Prayer.

"God grant me the serenity
to accept the things I cannot change,
Courage to change the things I can,
And the wisdom to know the difference."

And then he began the Lord's Prayer. For Beth, who had not prayed with her family for years, the effect was instantaneous and overpowering. She held her boys, one on each side, touched Kris' arm, and felt Paul's hand on her shoulder. They were together again. It *was* a miracle. She heard the amen and then turned, wrapping Tom in both arms, weeping into his neck, assuring him that she loved him too, thanking him for understanding, telling him everything was going to be okay. Then, remembering the others, she turned and hugged Rick and Kris, and finally Paul.

The mood was broken when, as if from another world, she heard Dan saying, "Paul and Beth, I'd like to talk to you for a few minutes before you leave. Would you come down to my office on first floor?"

Several minutes later they were seated with him in his office. "I thought you'd want to have some idea of how we assess Tom's progress and what our recommendations are for him. The program here generally takes about four weeks, but often teenagers need more time to begin working on their social skills. You've probably heard sometime during the week that a person stops maturing when he or she begins using drugs as an escape. That means Tom is at about the maturity level of a twelve-year-old as far as being able to make decisions or relate to people or control his emotions.

"We want to keep him here at least another week, and then we would strongly, strongly recommend that you arrange for him to stay in a halfway house for a few months until he's a little more sure of himself and more adjusted to a life of sobriety. I think they have several such places in Rochester, but it might be better for him if he stayed in the Minneapolis/St. Paul area if we can get him in some place. He has no contact with people in the drug scene here, so it will be easier for him to stay clean."

Beth was taken aback. Just minutes before it had seemed as if they were ready to conquer the world. She looked at Paul who seemed just as puzzled. They had both forgotten their conversation with Tom at the restaurant.

"I really hate to mention this after what you've been through this afternoon, but you'll be leaving tomorrow, and we do need your written permission for whatever we do. Will you give it some serious thought tonight? I can tell you Tom's chances for recovery will be infinitely increased if he doesn't have to go back to the old setting right away. He isn't ready and he won't be for some time. You have no idea the kind of pressure he would be under to return to the drug scene. We feel he just isn't strong enough yet, and his new behavior patterns are not firm enough."

"I hadn't thought of it that way," Paul said.

"It's very important not to underestimate the struggle Tom is going to have with himself to stay sober. He may never lose his desire for drugs. We never use the term *recovered* or *cured* when referring to addiction because it never ends. Each day is a new struggle, and we take it one day at a time."

Paul shook his head in amazement. "How does anyone stay sober?"

"It's not easy. The alternatives to a life of sobriety always have to be made more painful than the discomfort of a sober life. And no one can make it alone. Tom is going to need the support of A.A. and N.A. groups all his life, but it's especially important during this very crucial stage. N.A. is Narcotics

Anonymous," he explained as if reading the question in the minds of Paul and Beth. Then he went on, "Tom will always be chemically dependent. What he has to do is transfer his dependency from alcohol and other drugs to his Higher Power through the help of A.A. and N.A. groups." He paused, twisting the hair in his beard into little ringlets.

"You also have to think about yourselves and Kris and Rick. You will all go through some painful, sensitive times during the weeks and months ahead. It will probably be much easier for you to regain your emotional health if Tom isn't around for a time. Then, when you're all stronger, all more secure, you can regroup as a family."

Paul and Beth both nodded. What he said made sense. Paul, speaking for both of them, said, "We'll talk it over and get back to you tomorrow." As they stood up, Paul reached out and shook the counselor's hand. "Thank you so much for all you've done for Tom."

"For all of us," Beth added.

Several hours later, after waving good-bye to Eddie and Bonita as they got on the elevator, the Inghram family regathered in Kris and Rick's room where the two families had spent the evening rehashing the events of the day.

"Didn't Eddie seem unusually quiet?" Beth asked as she stacked plastic glasses and threw empty pop cans into the wastebasket.

"I tried to talk to him a little about the assessment for chemical dependency, but he just changed the subject," Kris responded.

"I wonder what they told him?" Rick, who had flopped back on his bed, his arms hanging over the footboard, joined the conversation.

"It must not have been good news or he'd have said something." Kris sat on the edge of her bed and pulled off her shoes as Paul and Beth relaxed in the two easy chairs.

"But could you believe Bonita?" Paul followed suit, pulling off his shoes and putting his feet on the bed next to Rick's head.

Rick gasped, acting as if he were going to pass out, and Paul responded by tickling him under the arms with his toes. "She was floating so high you'd have thought she'd popped a pill before coming."

"It was so great to see her happy again," Beth responded. "That must have been quite a conference."

Kris curled up on the end of her bed, pulling the spread over her feet. "You know, I was thinking while she was talking that she was back to normal, like she was the first day, bubbly and funny, but the more I think about it, the more I realize it was different. I can't explain it. Like a happy funny, not just a funny funny."

"That's very perceptive," Paul responded thoughtfully. "You're right, but I could never have put my finger on the difference. At the beginning of the week, her humor was a defense."

"I don't get it. Funny is funny." Rick propped his head up on his elbow and looked first at his sister and then at his father. But it was Beth who responded.

"In many ways, you've changed in the same way Bonita has."

"I have?" Rick looked puzzled.

"You've always been funny, too. But your humor was angry, a way of putting people down, hurting them. I haven't noticed any of that in the last day or two." Beth smiled at her son as Kris and Paul affirmed her observation with nods.

"Golly, gee, folks," Rick said as he tucked his head in his arms, "and I can't even think of anything funny to say." Everyone laughed and then sat in silence, as if wondering how they could hold onto this moment.

"We should probably tell you kids about our talk with Tom's counselor," Paul changed the subject and the mood passed. "They want to keep Tom here for at least another week and then put him in a halfway house for a few months here in Minnesota."

"You mean, he won't be coming home with us?" Rick seemed dismayed.

"We were disappointed too, son," Paul said, "but what the counselor said made sense. We're going to have enough to do just keeping ourselves on the right track without being responsible for him, also."

Beth noticed a look of fear on Rick's face. "What are you worried about?" she asked.

"You know how that guy told me I would have to make new friends, friends that don't use drugs?" Beth nodded, remembering the report.

"I just never thought I'd have to do it by myself. I mean, I always thought Tom would be there, so at least I wouldn't be alone, so we could help each other."

"I guess we hadn't thought of it from that angle," Beth sighed, looking at Paul, wondering if they were making the right decision.

"But, what if Tom starts using again, there's no guarantee he won't, you know, what then?" Kris countered. "Then it will be twice as hard for you. You'd never survive that."

Beth felt a deep gloom creeping over her. Paul, as if reading her mind, reached over and stroked her arm. "That's not going to happen. I won't let it happen."

"But, Dad . . . ," Kris started and then stopped.

"I just couldn't stand it," Beth responded. "Not after all this, not after seeing what a warm, caring, sensitive person he can be, I couldn't stand to see the old Tom come back."

"But, at least if we have to go through it again, we'll know better what to do," Kris tried to cheer her mother up.

"Back to you, buddy," Paul said, nudging Rick with his toes. "How can we help you get through this?" Rick shrugged an I-don't-know and Paul went on. "You know, I've been thinking. Maybe it's time I took on a partner. There's a young man just out of his residency who approached me a couple of weeks ago. I told him I wasn't interested, but I don't think he's made arrangements anywhere else. I really want to start being a more active husband and father, not just because I feel guilty for having shirked my responsibility in the past, though, of course,

I do, but because I've gotten to really like you all." He immediately realized that what he said could be taken wrong so he tried to backtrack. "I mean, it wasn't that I didn't like you before...."

"It's okay, Dad," Rick responded patting his father's feet. "We didn't like you much before, either." As Kris and Rick and their father laughed, Beth reflected on how impossible such an admission would have been even a few days ago. The week had changed them. It had been hard to measure any progress when everyone was so enmeshed in feelings, but something had happened. Things were better. Beth smiled to herself and then caught the end of Paul's comments.

". . . days off, I could work with you on your riding. Maybe we could start going to some of the shows and races. Kris, have you ever thought of learning to ride?"

Before she had a chance to answer, Rick said, in surprise, "She's good, really good, didn't you know that?"

Paul glanced at Beth and shook his head in embarrassment, "Boy, I have been out of touch." Then he looked at Kris, "That's great. We can make it a family event."

Finally Beth looked at her watch and said, "I hate to break this up, gang, but we have a long day tomorrow. Did you kids finish your goals?" They nodded yes, and then she turned to Paul, "But we haven't done that encounter yet."

"It's too late now," he responded as Kris and Rick joked about incompetent people who don't get their assignments done. "We'll have to save it for the flight home."

Telling their children to get right to sleep, Paul and Beth left them and went into their own room. Some time later, as she soaked in a hot bath trying to relax, Beth had time to reflect on the events of the day. She tried to recapture the wonderful sense of release she'd felt in the chaplain's office, but the moment was gone and in its place was a deep soreness, the infection gone but the wound gaping.

However, thinking of the group session and her hysterical outburst was more embarrassing than painful. She wondered how she'd be able to face the others tomorrow. And all those angers and resentments toward Tom. How could she have ever dumped all that on her own son? She didn't think it was because she had intentionally been trying to conceal, to mask her real self, and now couldn't handle exposure. Rather, it was as if that woman, so angry and hurt and repressed, was a stranger, a person who had somehow gotten into her skin, taken over for a time, turned her into a stranger even to herself. She wanted to be treated as her old self, her real self.

But, what was that? Beth tried to reconstruct the shattered image: competent, calm, loving, a good sense of humor. Beth stared at her naked flesh, touched her small breasts, ran her hands across her stomach and thighs, searching for reassurance in the familiar, the tangible, the real. Who was she now?

The water turned cold. She reached for the hot water faucet, then changed her mind and climbed out of the tub. As she opened the door to their room, she wondered if Paul had waited up for her. Again she was plagued by ambivalence: wanting and not wanting, needing him and needing time.

He was in bed, propped up against his pillows, the soft headlamp casting shadows across his face. Beth sat down nervously on the edge of her bed.

"Can we talk?" she asked. The tic in her eye began quivering and automatically she pressed her finger against it.

"Sure." He pulled back the covers inviting her in, but when she didn't move, he returned them brusquely, tucking them up under his arms.

"Honey, I'm sorry. I'm just not ready."

"And what is it going to take to get you ready?" He was angry. She was spoiling his day.

"It's like a thousand feelings are still at war inside me." She wondered if he understood. "Just tonight when we were sitting and talking to the kids, most of me was feeling wonderful, realizing we were together again, having fun. But a part of me was feeling resentful toward you. You walked back into their lives, and they accepted you and loved you as if you had never withdrawn. It just doesn't seem fair. Like you haven't paid your dues, but you got in anyway."

"So, as far as the kids are concerned, in your eyes, I'm damned if I do and damned if I don't." His tone was questioning and tired, not bitter as she had expected.

"I know, I must be crazy," she responded, imitating Bonita. They laughed. The tension eased. Beth reached over and touched her husband's hand. "I need more time, Paul. Can you understand? I'm all torn apart right now. I have to heal." Her eyes pleaded with his for understanding and he responded as she had hardly dared hope he would.

"Sure, honey, take all the time you need."

She crawled into her bed, shivering against the cold sheets. He turned out the light, settled down into his bed, and called across the chasm in his Groucho Marx imitation, "You've got until tomorrow night."

Beth rolled over on her side, curling her legs against her chest. She felt her muscles relax, one by one, sinking her deeper and deeper into the mattress. Closing her eyes, she started to pray, "Thank you Lord for . . . ." Her mind sank further and further down, below thoughts, below feelings, until all that was left was a voice saying, "peace."

DAY FIVE

But for the clanging sounds of pots and pans in the kitchen, the dining room was quiet and empty when the Inghrams entered. "Looks like we're the first ones here," Paul commented.

"And for the first time all week we're actually on time. That may be a good omen," Beth responded.

"We wouldn't have been if that taxi driver hadn't been trying to outdo Evel Knievel," Kris noted.

"The guy must have popped a little speed this morning," Rick added.

The family settled around the end of one of the tables and Kris went on, "Wouldn't it be ironic if we had been wiped out in a car accident on our way to a drug treatment center because the driver was high on some drug?"

"Can you see the headline?" Rick held up his hands as if he were holding a paper and was about to read the imaginary headline when the door swung open, and Bonita bustled in.

"Boy, did I sleep like a baby last night," she exclaimed, plopping down next to Paul. "I could hardly wake up this morning." She shook her head, trying to shake out the sleep, and then called to Eddie who was just coming through the door. "Would you get me a cup of coffee, hon, before you sit down?" He headed toward the large coffee pot, and she turned back to the Inghrams. "Gotta get a little caffeine cruising through my system or I'll fall asleep the minute I sit in one of those chairs," she chuckled. "Good thing we don't have a movie today."

A few minutes later, Pat walked into the dining room, glanced around the table and queried, "Connie's not here?"

The group members shook their heads. "Not yet anyway," Beth responded.

Pat sighed, walked toward the table, and then looked alarmed. "Eddie's not back either?"

"Over here," he called. "Can I get you some coffee, too?"

Pat exhaled, a smile of relief crossing her face. "Sure. Well, did you all have a good evening?"

"The best," Rick responded, as the others grinned up at her.

"The first thing this morning," Pat explained, "will be a short talk by a member of Al-Anon who was willing to share some of her experiences with you. As soon as she's through, we'll meet in my office for our morning group. Up and at'em," she said with a broad gesture of her arms. "We've got lots of work yet to do. I hope you weren't all sitting around feeling so self-satisfied that you didn't finish your homework."

"What homework?" Paul asked with a twinkle in his eye.

"Dad, you loser," Rick joked back and Paul grabbed him in an armlock. They tussled affectionately all the way up the stairs, the others keeping a safe distance behind just in case one of them lost balance and came crashing down.

Shortly after the group had settled in the front rows of the meeting room, a woman entered who was probably in her early 40s. She walked to the front of the room and sat down on the edge of the table, crossing her legs, and smiling at each person. "Hi, my name is Corinne and I've been a member of Al-Anon for about five years. My task this morning is to tell you something about Al-Anon, and I thought the best way to do that would be to tell you a little of my story." She paused long enough to receive affirmation from the group and went on.

"I'm married to a very bright, gifted, sensitive man who's a respected member of the professional community in our city and who is also a practicing alcoholic. I know that must seem like a contradiction to you, but the facts are that most alcoholics are practicing, not recovering, and many of them are reasonably competent, professional adults. For a long time I tried to convince myself that this man I love didn't have a drinking problem because if he did, how could he appear to others to be so free of problems? He never abused me or the children in any way. He never embarrassed us with public drunkenness. And he always managed to come through on major responsibilities.

"But there was something wrong. I could feel it more than I could see it. He drank daily, into the night, alone. 'Need it to relax,' he would explain. He had a stressful job, and I tried to be understanding. But gradually he withdrew from the family, and I began to get more and more angry. Sometimes I wanted to smash his wine bottles. And sometimes I wanted to smash him. And then I would swing to the other extreme, explaining him to the children, running defense for him, taking over more and more of the household responsibilities. In the early years of our marriage we had been each other's best friend, but the friendship withered, and I found myself reaching out to others more often for companionship and support.

"One of those people was a man who, it turned out, was a recovering alcoholic. I had met him through a volunteer committee we were both involved with. We sat around after a meeting one night and I found myself pouring out my soul to him. When I was through, he asked, 'Has it ever occurred to you that your husband might be an alcoholic?' I insisted that couldn't be true. After all, we had none of the problems usually associated with an alcoholic family. But he kept asking me questions, probing questions. I went home that night and collapsed in weeping despair. Some time later, I did what he had strongly encouraged me to do. I joined Al-Anon.

"I went to that first meeting with the hope or, I guess, the desperate need, for the group to fix my husband, to solve the problem. But what I found out was that Al-Anon is an individual recovery program for the family member. They couldn't fix him. But they offered the kind of help I needed to lead a reasonable life while living in an unreasonable situation.

"Of course, I deeply hope and pray my husband will stop drinking. I believe his life would be so much more satisfying for him if he did. It appears to me that his career is beginning to suffer and certainly his relationships with me and the children are not what they could be. But whether he sobers up or not, I need to keep from letting his illness infect me. And I couldn't do that without the support, advice, insights, and encouragement I get from Al-Anon.

"I know I'm supposed to keep this short, but I want to say a few words about the Twelve Step recovery plan that we use in

Al-Anon." She went on to briefly describe the path to emotional health which members of Al-Anon walk, and then she continued. "Of course, each group is different. We encourage you to shop around until you find a group of people with whom you feel comfortable.

"And, one other thing. It's easy to leave a place like this totally caught up in the unique set of problems caused by alcohol and other drug abuse. But, really, you are a part of the mainstream. Everyone has problems. Everyone has been traumatized in one way or another. Many, perhaps most, people live at least a part of their lives in high stress situations. The main difference between you and many of them is that for alcoholics and their families, there's a wide network for effective help and a track record which can do nothing but give hope."

She spoke with such calm assurance that it was difficult to believe all her problems had not been solved. After asking if there were any questions, she wished the group well, and reminded them there was a meeting right away in Pat's office.

Pat was already seated as the group members chose their places in the circle. She opened the Al-Anon book to a pre-marked page and asked if anyone would like to read. Bonita volunteered and read, tripping on words from time to time as the meaning of what she was reading hit home.

If I believe that it is hopeless to expect any improvement in my life, I am doubting the power of God. If I believe I have reason for despair, I am confessing personal failure, for I do have the power to change myself, and nothing can prevent it but my own unwillingness.

After the reading, Pat looked around the group. "Well, let's go. Who wants to report first?"

Bonita nearly jumped off her chair. "I will, and it'll just take me a minute because everyone here has heard the whole story a dozen times. Jim and I met. I did it. And I feel great. You're looking at a new woman. No one is ever going to walk all over me again." She grinned and nodded her head as if to say, that's it. Mission accomplished. Then her expression changed, sobered.

"But, I have to confess something. When I woke up this morning, I could feel something was bugging me. I wondered if I'd had a dream, you know the kind where you wake up upset with someone for something they did in a dream and you can't even remember the dream. But then it came to me. I was brooding in the back of my mind over the crack Jim made about all my headaches, trying to make it my fault that he'd had an affair. I thought at the time I handled it so well."

She looked at the group for support, and they all nodded. The night before she had told them how she had calmly turned to him and said, "I resent your attempt to make me feel guilty for your wrongdoing." He had seemed amazed that his tactic hadn't worked, and she had turned back to her list and continued reading.

"But now, today, here I am, letting that dumb comment bother me. I remember our talk about how mockery and put-downs are the hardest things to deal with. It really is true. I want to punch his face in."

"To somehow get even," Pat reflected her feelings.

"Yes, isn't that childish? And I know it wouldn't work. I could never hurt him as much as he's hurt me, and even if I could or did, he would just hurt me back and it would never end."

"So, what are you going to do with your anger?" Pat asked.

"I think she should tell him that he really pissed her off," Eddie said sullenly.

"But it's not Jim's fault that Bonita is angry," Paul argued.

"He deliberately made her angry," Kris responded indignantly.

"Hold on a minute," Pat stopped the discussion. "Let's take a look at the situation. Jim did what people often try to do . . . shift responsibility for their actions onto someone else. Bonita refused to take that responsibility or guilt and that was great. But in the process of trying to shift the fault, Jim also hurt Bonita and she's responding to that hurt with anger. You're right, Paul, that isn't Jim's problem. It's Bonita's. No one can make you angry. People can say hurtful things, but you allow those things to hurt your feelings and then you allow that hurt to turn into anger. And anger is always harder on the possessor than on the object."

"But that doesn't help me," Bonita responded.

"You still want to pop him in the nose?" Pat asked.

"It does seem a little silly doesn't it?" Bonita began to laugh. "Maybe I'll just pull out his fingernails one by one." Everyone laughed with her. Then she went on, "Hey, gang, do you realize what has happened? Not only did I handle his put-down effectively yesterday, but now I don't feel quite so angry. Boy, am I learning fast."

"Bonita," Pat seemed pleased about what had just happened. "Put into words for the group exactly what it took for you to defuse that anger."

Bonita thought for a minute. "I guess I had to first realize why I was angry . . . exactly why. It was because my pride had been hurt. And then, I had to talk it out. Be honest about it."

Pat nodded and then addressed the whole group. "You've all felt a lot of anger in the past and that problem is not going to go away. Things are going to continue to happen that are hurtful and the almost automatic response to hurt is anger. We hope you'll leave this place with two tools. The first is the ability to recognize something as another person's problem before you take it on as your own. And the second tool is the ability to defuse anger once it has taken hold. For Bonita, simply talking it out helped. Others write down their feelings. Some people go out and jog ten miles. Just remember you can't just wish anger away, you have to give it an escape hatch." Pat looked around the room to see if the group members understood. Seeing affirmative nods, she went on.

"Anything anyone wants to say to Bonita?" Pat asked.

"I just hope she can hold onto that self-image when she starts living with my dad again." Eddie's words swung the mood of the group from optimistic to apprehensive.

"I'm sure it won't be easy," Beth said, underscoring the mood.

"Nothing is going to be easy for any of you," Pat interjected, matter-of-factly. "We think of the treatment process as working through about ten percent of what needs to be worked through from your pasts, then there are all the problems of daily living that are going to come up." Pat sighed and looked around the group. "I'm sorry. I'm making everything seem very depressing. It's just that I know what an ongoing struggle I have to keep moving in the right direction. Just this morning I got so angry with my male friend that I stormed into my office at home and smoked two of his cigarettes before even realizing what I was doing."

The energies of the group members shifted to Pat. They seemed to want to help her with her problems in gratitude for all she had done for them. Quickly she redirected the focus of the group by saying, "Kris? Rick? Did you get your letters written?"

Kris already had hers out. As she unfolded her papers, Pat said, "First tell the group what your goals were."

"I was supposed to write letters to Mom and Dad and then read as much as I could of *Why Am I Afraid to Tell You Who I Am?* The book was really interesting. I didn't get it all read, but I read enough to realize how I have always covered up my real feelings because I was afraid people wouldn't love me or accept me if they knew what was inside. I was getting to be like a computer."

"Well, you had a good role model," Beth interrupted. "I had to read that book also and it really hit home. What strikes me so funny, now that I think about it, is that we all want to be loved, but we think the road to love is paved with impressive actions and good deeds. We confuse being admired with being loved. So we cover up everything about ourselves that we think shows weakness or vulnerability and play up our strengths. When I think about the people I love, it's not the impressive, superior, perfect people who get into my heart, it's the warm, vulnerable, human ones."

"That's really true, isn't it?" Bonita responded. "I've never thought of this before, but, do you suppose that's why alcoholics are so easy to love? Because their weakness is so obvious and their needs so great?" Then she chuckled. "I know they're easy to hate also, but, think about it, all of us so deeply love a chemically dependent person that it almost ruined our lives."

"That's a good point," Pat commented. "I swore to myself a thousand times I wouldn't get involved with anyone who had anything to do with chemical dependency, but I, too, am in love with a recovering alcoholic." Then quickly shifting her chair, she directed the attention of the group to Kris.

"What about your letters, Kris? Do you want to read them to us?"

"Sure," Kris answered. Her voice was steady, but her shaking hands rattled the papers.

"Dear Mom," she glanced at her mother and then quickly looked back to her paper. "I was going to wait and write this in the morning, but I couldn't sleep, so here I am, wrapped up in a blanket, sitting in bed thinking about you. Today was the strangest day of my life. Sometimes I thought it was the worst and sometimes the best . . . like when we were talking about the horses . . . but mostly it was just strange. It was as if the person I thought I knew the best in all the world turned out to be somebody totally different. I couldn't believe you ever really wanted Tom dead. I thought I was the only one who had those thoughts. At first I was disappointed in you, like somehow you had failed me. I'd always wanted to be perfect like you, but here, it turns out you aren't perfect at all. But now, as I'm sitting here thinking about it, I realize I feel closer to you and love you more than I ever have. I just want you to know that. I still need you to be my mother, but I would also like to have you for a friend. Thank you for always being there, for loving us and taking care of us, and never really giving up. Love always, your daughter, Kris."

What happened next had happened hundreds of times before in that room. Mother and daughter hugged and wept, giggled at their tears and then sat down, giggling again as they reached for the tissue box.

"Look at those two," Bonita laughed. "They don't know whether to laugh or cry."

"Maybe they want to do both," Rick responded looking as if he, too, might cry.

Kris took out her letter to her father. She seemed more comfortable with this one. "Dear Dad, I want you to know how great it has been to feel like I'm beginning to get to know you. It has been so helpful to me to realize that it wasn't because you disliked me that you seemed so distant. I always thought it was my fault and I tried so hard to win your attention back. Now that I realize you were responding, as we all were, to what Tom was, I really feel better about myself. Thank you for being my father, for being someone I can be proud of. That's another thing I never realized before . . . how great it is to have a father I can be proud of." Kris and Eddie exchanged a knowing look. Kris continued reading. "I hope when we go home we can build on what we've started here. I love you, Dad. Your daughter, Kris."

Before Paul had a chance to reach over and hug Kris, Pat asked him, "How does that make you feel?"

"Great," he responded. "Like people in my family are finally starting to understand me a little."

"And you're willing to let Tom's illness take all the blame for your withdrawal from the family?"

"Isn't that what we've been learning here?" he countered defensively. "People respond in extreme ways to the behavior of the chemically dependent person. Perhaps I did withdraw from the family, but that wasn't my fault."

"Why don't we take the discussion out of the arena of fault and put it into the arena of choice. A difficult, stressful situation evolved in your family. There was no way things could go on as they had been, so you were faced with a number of options. You chose to emotionally withdraw. Now you're responsible for the consequences of that choice."

Pat's voice had slipped into a lecture tone. She smiled at Paul as if trying to make amends for being so hard on him. "Does that make sense?"

Before he had a chance to respond, the door opened, and Connie walked in. "I'm sorry to interrupt. Please go ahead with what you were doing." But the mood was broken. Paul reached over and squeezed Kris' hand and whispered something to her as Connie pulled her chair into the circle and sat down.

Everyone sat and waited, expecting, almost demanding some sort of explanation from the group dropout. Pat watched her carefully, as if looking for any sign that she was now ready to take the process seriously. But Connie seemed cool, remote, in control, as she shook a cigarette out of her pack, lit it, inhaled deeply, and then smiled at the group.

"I owe you all an apology for walking out on the group yesterday. I don't usually take out my frustrations on others, but it had been a bad day. I had gotten a call in the morning from my older daughter who had a thousand pressing problems. I'm sorry, my mind was just on other things. Please go ahead."

Connie blew another stream of smoke into the air, her defense system intact. It would take hours, perhaps days, to get close to her source of pain again. It was a shame. There simply wasn't time.

"Your timing was perfect, we're between people. Would you like to go next with your goals?" Pat asked, giving no indication of her frustration.

"Sure." The group members all seemed surprised. In concert they leaned forward, expectant, waiting. But Connie didn't take out any papers, in fact, she didn't even have her folder with her. She stubbed out her cigarette and spoke a calm, prepared speech.

"I was to read all of the pamphlets in our folders and then whatever I could get finished of *Why Am I Afraid to Tell You Who I Am?* I did all the reading but, I must say, I found it quite disappointing. There was really nothing I hadn't already learned in my counseling sessions and in popular, self-help books I've read. In fact, I've actually found other books more helpful. Then, I was to write letters to my daughter and to my ex-husband. I decided to wait with that so I would have something to do on the plane trip home. By the way, I'll have to leave at noon in order to catch my plane. I tried to get another flight, but there was nothing open."

The group sat in disappointed silence as Connie dug in her purse for another cigarette. Tense silence, and then an angry voice. "Then, why the hell did you bother to come back?" Eddie shouted. "You don't need us and we sure as hell don't need you."

"Apparently the week hasn't helped you much, either." Connie caught and held Eddie's eyes. He withered but didn't apologize.

"You seem pretty uptight this morning, Eddie. Is something bothering you?" Eddie shrugged a response to Paul's question.

"Is there any way we can help?" Beth asked, "We've grown to care about you a great deal." Pat glanced quickly around the group, Connie stared out the window, and everyone else focused on Eddie in sympathetic concern. They had taken a stand. If Connie wanted to wall off her emotions, they would let her. She had offended an important member of the group, and now the others no longer were concerned about her.

Eddie cracked his knuckles, one at a time, shifted in his chair, and finally looked at the group with a dejected, whipped look. "God, I don't know. I don't think anyone can help me. I've been so bummed since I took that assessment yesterday." He paused for so long they feared he wouldn't go on.

"Do you want to tell the group about it?" Pat asked.

His eyes, deep in his head, stared at his shoes for a time and then he shrugged. "I bombed it. The guy thinks I'm an alcoholic or becoming one." Bonita gasped and everyone's eyes shifted to her and then quickly back to Eddie. He didn't look up.

"The man's crazy. That boy is no more an alcoholic than I am."

"What do you think, Eddie?" Pat asked.

Again, the pause was so long it was as if he hadn't heard the question.

"I don't know. I've been thinking and thinking and I keep coming back to the question, how can they know? I don't drink any more than my friends. There's no way they can say I'm going to be a drunk."

"So you're going to blow it off and continue on with your usual drinking patterns?" Pat pressed.

He dropped his head, rubbing the back of his neck, and then looked up, his voice pleading. "More than anything in the world, I don't want to end up like my father. But do you have any idea how hard it would be to just quit drinking? I'd lose all my friends. I wouldn't have any place to go at night. And I'm supposed to go through all that just because some guy thinks I might have a problem? They can't tell for sure. He told me that himself."

"I think this whole assessment business is crazy," Bonita exclaimed as if stating it would make it so. Everyone looked at Pat, expecting her to agree or disagree.

The question of dependency assessment was a loaded one and the source of constant debate around the center and most everywhere where serious work with chemical dependency was going on. Is it possible to diagnose alcoholism before the disease is full-blown and all kinds of people have been hurt? And, if it is, is it possible to convince potential alcoholics of the diagnosis so they can prevent the ravages of the disease? Even the questions were dependent upon the unproven theory that some people are predisposed to alcoholism. If you believed most other theories, then, of course, the questions become irrelevant.

Pat avoided a theoretical discussion of the causes of chemical dependency by simply asking, "So, Eddie, what are you going to do?"

Again, he sat in silence, his shoulders sloped. Then, as if he hadn't heard the question, he said, "You know, the thing that scares me the most is that last night when I was sitting in my room trying to think this whole thing through, all I wanted to do was to go out and have a drink. I could almost taste it. And then, I thought, he's right. I am a drunk. God, I can't stand to even think the thought. I am what I hated most in my father." Bonita was about to console him, about to say, "No you're not, don't worry about that, you're not like your father," but Pat signaled her to silence and spoke in a firm voice to Eddie.

"Being an alcoholic is not the worst thing in the world, you know, especially if you catch it early before it destroys your life. We all know that assessment isn't foolproof, and if you're like almost everyone else who takes it and has positive results, you will deny its validity and go out and drink and use drugs. But please remember, when your life gets miserable enough that you want to change, we're here and we can help you. We all care very much about you, Eddie, and we don't want to see you throw your life away. If you don't want to come here, there are many other treatment centers or groups where you can go to get help." Eddie sat in morose silence, consumed with self-pity.

Then a voice, unexpected and maternal, broke the silence. "Eddie, you asked me a few minutes ago why I came back. Maybe the reason will be helpful to you." At first Pat didn't even recognize the voice. Then, turning in her chair, she noticed Connie's hands twisting nervously on her lap. "The call I had Wednesday night was from the halfway house where Trisha was staying. She had run away. I'd never really wanted her to go there in the first place, but it was upsetting not knowing where she was or what she was doing. Last night I started calling her friends in Rochester to see if they'd heard from her. No one knew anything about her, but I gave them my number in case they should see her or hear from her. I didn't really expect to hear anything, you know how kids stick together, but for some reason I couldn't leave my room this morning. Then the call came. One of her friends who'd been like a daughter to me had seen her on the street late last night. She was obviously high, but they'd talked for a time." At this point it seemed as if Connie's voice was about to break. She paused, trying to gain control.

"She found out that Trish is living with a pimp. My little Trishie is a whore." The pain was raw, but still she held onto her emotion.

"At first I was angry, blaming the halfway house and this treatment center. After all, I'd spent a fortune getting her the best treatment in the country and it hadn't worked. Then I thought about you people," she nodded toward the Inghrams, "and you," she looked at Bonita and Eddie, "here as families struggling together to get things worked out. And I didn't even take her problem seriously enough to adjust my schedule to come here when she was here. We've never really talked. And now it's too late." She stopped talking, and then, remembering why she had started in the first place, she went on.

"Eddie, I know I haven't really been a part of the group this week and there's no reason why you should listen to me, but I've been listening and watching you all change and grow, especially you, Eddie. There's something about you that caught my heart. I guess all I can say to you is, don't underestimate the power of drugs. They're poison. They kill. Everyone I've ever loved has been destroyed by alcohol or some other drug. You don't need to drink to have a good life. You don't need to drink to have fun or have friends. Please, Eddie, before it's too late . . . ." Her voice trailed off and again the group sat in silence.

Pat reached over and squeezed Connie's cold hand. "Thank you for coming back and sharing that with us. I know how difficult this has been for you." Then she caught Connie's eye. "What do you want from this group? From me?"

Connie looked away and shrugged. "I don't know. I just didn't know what to do. I have my ticket to go home, but when I get there, what can I do? I have no power over her, no authority. She hasn't listened to me for years."

"Isn't she under age?" Paul asked. "You could alert the juvenile authorities. They might step in."

"Or," Beth added, "you can hope and pray that her life gets miserable enough that she will come home."

"With young people, especially," Pat said, trying to be encouraging, "it often takes a second time around with treatment before they really take their problem seriously. But in the meantime, you have yourself to think about. Your life doesn't need to be destroyed because the people around you are destroying theirs. Will you start attending Al-Anon?" Connie nodded and smiled a weak but grateful smile. At least she had something to do, something to hold on to.

Pat glanced at her watch. "Why don't you all take a quick break, get some coffee or whatever, and we'll meet back here in about five minutes." The group members stood and stretched and then wandered, one by one, out the door, each, it seemed, deep in thought. But Eddie lingered until Connie had lit a cigarette and started moving toward the door.

"Thanks for what you said," he reached a hand toward her and then pulled it back, unsure. "I'm sorry I yelled at you. This hasn't been my best day." He grinned at her, that shy, little boy grin.

"Nor mine," she responded. There was only a moment's hesitation and then they hugged, spontaneously, warmly.

"I'm really sorry about your daughter," Eddie said as they separated.

"So am I." She turned slightly to include Pat in the conversation. "But I'm glad I came back this morning. I do feel better, or at least not so alone."

"You don't ever have to be alone in this, you know." Pat put her arm around Connie's shoulder. "Everywhere in this country there are parents going through what you're going through. Reach out to them. They'll provide strength for your weakness and you can provide strength for their weakness."

The rest of the group began returning, everyone taking the place they had had earlier. When they were all settled, Pat said, "Connie, or Eddie, is there anything else you would like to talk about?" Both responded in the negative. "Then, let's see, we still haven't heard Rick's goals or part of Beth's. Did you have a chance to finish?" She looked first at Beth and then at Rick. Both nodded. Then they looked at each other deferring back and forth until it became funny. Rick finally picked up his folder and took out two sheets of paper.

"I was supposed to write letters to Mom and Dad and, if I had time, to Kris. I started trying to write to Dad, but I couldn't think of anything important to say. We've been talking so much in the past couple of days that it seems as if it's all been said." Then he stopped and looked at his father. "I just want you to know that I think you're a great guy, and I really hope you were serious when you said you would help us with riding. That's going to be so much fun." Paul nodded, assuring Rick he was serious. Then Rick opened up the folded letters and looked for a moment at the one on top.

"Dear Kris, I decided to write to you because I knew I could never say the things I wanted to say to you. I'm really sorry for the way I treated you, especially during the past few years. I thought of you as a mother and then rebelled against you, taking out on you all the frustration I was feeling toward myself. When we were little I always felt so close to you and I hope we can have that closeness again. In fact, if I'm going to quit partying, you'll probably be my only friend when we get back."

"If?" Paul interrupted with raised eyebrow.

Rick laughed and held up his hand as if to reassure his father. "I meant 'when,' of course." Then he went back to the letter. "Thank you for all you've done for me and meant to me. Love always, Rick." He looked up at Kris and smiled, receiving the hoped for warm response. Then he shuffled the pages and turned his chair to face his mother.

"Dear Mom," his voice seemed deep and somehow, more mature. "I never realized until yesterday what we've put you through. In fact, I never really thought about you as a person before. You were just there. I can't tell you how bad I feel that your life has been such a bummer for the past few years. I know it wasn't all my fault, but I did do my share. I'm sorry for all the times I hurt you and caused you to worry. I hope things can be like they were before, when we were young, when you were happy and took care of us. I'll always love you and I promise to try to behave from now on. Your son, Erik."

Pat began to say something and then stopped and waited

while Rick slid his chair over to his mother and gave her a big hug.

"Rick, one of the things you said made me a little nervous."

"The part about things being like they were before, I bet," Bonita jumped into the conversation.

Pat nodded at her and looked back at Rick who appeared confused and put-down. "It's a very natural and understandable response for people who have gone through a bad time to want things to be like they were before. And there seems to be a subconscious pressure exerted to try to force each other into those molds. But you've all changed too much for things to ever be like they were, and if you stop to think about it, it's a good thing. Seeing your mother as vulnerable and human was a frightening thing for you as it is for all young people when they finally see their parents for what they really are. It's natural for you to want to reject that mother and try to reclaim the mother you thought you had when you were little, that all-loving, all-knowing, always there, perfect person. And it might be a temptation for your mother to want to fall back into that role, also, but to do so would be at the expense of the emotional well-being and maturity of both of you. Does that make sense?"

"I guess so," Rick answered, now looking embarrassed that he had written the statement in the first place.

"Hey, kiddo," Bonita said, "don't look so glum. Aside from that, it was a beautiful letter, one I'm sure your mother will treasure for the rest of her life."

He looked at his mother who nodded agreement and he was satisfied.

The attention of the group then focused on Beth. Her hands were calm as she opened her folder and took out two sheets of paper.

"Paul and I still haven't done the encounter, but only because we got so busy talking about horses last night that there just wasn't time. I'm honestly looking forward to doing it. I looked over the questions and I realized that even though I've been living with him for twenty years, I have no idea how he'll answer some of them. It really is amazing, isn't it, how little we really know about the people in our families . . . or about ourselves, for that matter?

"I did get letters written to Kris and Erik, though, I must admit, it was more difficult than I would ever have guessed. I wanted to say so much, but I just couldn't put together adequate words. But this is what I ended up with." As she opened her paper she turned to her daughter.

"Dear Kris, I remember when you were younger how I would say to you, 'What would I do without you?' I said it so often it must have become meaningless, or even worse, it became a part of the pressure you felt to be the responsible one, the perfect one. But I want you to know I couldn't have made it through the past few years without the love and support I felt from you. I know a parent is not supposed to lean on a child in that way, but I needed someone to lean on and you were there, strong and dependable. Thank you for that, Kris. From the bottom of my heart, thank you.

"But I also need to ask your forgiveness. I realize now how adversely affected you were by my behavior. I'll do whatever I can to make that up to you. But for now, I just want you to know you're free to get on with being a teenager, with finding your own way in life. We'll always be behind you, loving you and supporting you, rejoicing with your joys and weeping with your sorrows. You're a beautiful girl, almost a woman, and I'm so proud to have you as my daughter. Love always, Mom."

Beth put down her paper and looked at her daughter. "Thank you, honey, for being you." Tender cheeks touched. Warm tears mingled.

After wiping her eyes, Beth turned to the other letter. She turned her chair so she could face her son.

"Dear Erik, this has been quite a week, hasn't it? I've watched you leave behind the cocky, smarty-pants kid that you were and become a sensitive, perceptive young man. I can't tell you the joy and relief I feel when I see you now. For a long time I thought I was going to lose both my sons. Tom had always been difficult, it somehow seemed almost inevitable with him. But with you it was different. Being wild and tough seemed so out of joint with your nature, with the you I had given birth to and raised for thirteen years. But there you were, following right after your brother. It nearly broke my heart. I wanted to pull you back, to hang onto you, to scream at the world to leave you alone. But I couldn't. I had lost the power. Maybe I never had it. Maybe the power parents feel when their children are small and things are going well is illusory. I don't know. Pat keeps telling us that the way won't be easy, that there will be many snares and traps, but I know if we all stick together we'll make it.

"I'm sorry for all the times I was too distracted to take your problems seriously, or the times I took out my frustrations about Tom on you, or the many times I acted in what must have seemed like very irrational ways. I was trying so hard to be everything to everyone, but it just doesn't work to live that way. Everyone suffers. I just want you to know how much I'm looking forward to the weeks and months ahead as we all begin a new journey in a new direction.

"I also want to say I love you very much. I treasure you as a son, and look forward to discovering the man you are becoming. Love, Mom." All of the love and tenderness a mother feels toward a son, especially when that son is the baby in her family, came out in those words and Rick's response was what one would expect. Deeply moved, he threw his arms around his mother and gave her a bear hug that began grandiose, almost formal, and ended tearful and gentle.

As they hugged, Pat quietly got up and reached over to her desk for a stack of papers. At the same time, Connie glanced at her watch and stood up. "I really am sorry to have to go. Not just because I'm beginning to feel as if I know you, as if you're my friends, but because I don't want to go home and face what must be faced." She began moving toward the door. Quickly the others in the group stood and shook her hand or hugged her awkwardly, wishing her well. Eddie was the last to say good-bye and as he hugged her stiff, tight body, she unwound a bit, swallowed the fear in her throat and said, "Take care of yourself, kid." And then she was gone.

"What do you think is going to happen to her?" Eddie asked, assuming Pat would have an answer.

Pat shook her head. "I don't know. I knew Trish a little when she was here. She's a beautiful girl, but her wall is as high and thick as her mother's. Who knows? We'll just have to hope for the best." The expressions on the faces of the remaining group members indicated their perception of the situation — a situation in which "the best" seemed so far from the present reality, so impossible to attain. "Well, since you're all in a depressed mood, I guess it's as good a time as any to do these survival sheets." Pat patted the papers on her lap.

"Survival?" Paul questioned, not sure he had heard her.

"We want you to leave here confident of the best, but prepared for the worst. As I'm sure you realize, the battle Jim and Tom are going to have to wage in order to stay sober is awesome, indeed. They may not make it. In fact, it's more the rule than the exception for people who leave treatment to crash hard once before they really, deeply accept the fact that they can never use mood-altering chemicals again. You have to be prepared for that, or they may bring you all crashing down with them. And you have to be prepared for the possibility that they may never live a life of sobriety.

"What we want you to do is fill out this plan of action so that if the person you love starts using again, you'll know exactly what you're going to do. That plan might include contacting Jim's or Tom's sponsors in A.A., notifying legal authorities, marital separation, and so on. Let me remind you one last time that if that person has any reason at all to suspect you're not deadly serious about your plan, that you can be manipulated in the old ways, or that you'll play the enabler role again, if he's not growing in his own program, he'll use you and you'll be right back where you started. You have to have the thought indelibly clear in your mind that you will not accept anything less than a sober life from that person, and that to do so is to bring ultimate destruction upon both him and yourselves. So, with that in mind, think through what you'll do if it becomes clear to you that Tom or Jim is drinking or using other mood-altering chemicals again.

"Then turn the page over and work out your own aftercare plan. The first question involves thinking of a change you can make in your daily routine which will help you reduce the stress level you're living with. Some people set aside time for meditation and prayer, or for physical activity, or they organize their time so they can get more sleep. Just think of one change you can make that will help you.

"Then make a commitment to yourself to get continuing help and support from others.

"Finally, think of one specific action you can take to improve your self-esteem. It might be something as simple as getting your hair done regularly, or losing a few pounds, or signing up for a course, or learning a new skill. All of your egos have taken a real beating in the past few years, so think of ways you can be good to yourselves. When you have your plans finished, bring them to me and I'll go through them with you, and then we can both sign the bottom of the page. And please don't forget that once you've gone through our treatment program, you are a part of a network of support and help. Don't ever hesitate to call."

Pat sat and watched as the six group members stared into space, isolated from each other by their thoughts, and then, one by one, began writing.

It was Beth who broke the silence, her voice quivering. "I can hardly stand to think about it, about Tom using again. I keep thinking about our home filled with tension, about angry scenes at the dinner table, about arguments between Paul and me over what to do." One by one, the members of the group quit writing and began listening.

"But what haunts me the most is to think about those horrible nights walking the floor, listening for cars, hoping, imagining, dreading, fearing." Her voice broke. Then she went on, looking at Pat, pleading for an answer. "How can people live knowing that the person they love so much could, overnight, turn back into that ugly, abusive, irresponsible, unpredictable person they lived with before? Knowing what a warm and sensitive and loving person Tom can be when he's not using drugs makes me think I'd rather die than lose that Tom again."

The others in the group nodded understanding and agreement.

"Beth," Pat spoke quietly. "I can understand how you feel. It's a terrible letdown when an addicted person relapses. But you survived his drug use the first time. Hold onto that. And you'll be able to survive it again, not only survive, but continue your own life, growing in wisdom and serenity." Then she addressed the whole group. "I hope you've all picked up the slogan which you've heard from time to time during the week. The only way you're going to be able to live is to live 'one day at a time.' Don't hold onto the pains of the past or borrow the problems of the future. Just today. That's all. Remember, one day at a time."

"But, that's so hard," Bonita responded. "Think of the decisions I would have to make. Separation. Divorce. Living alone again. Starting over. I almost get sick realizing that in a week or a month or a year we could be right back to square one." Bonita sighed.

"Jim may be back to square one, but you don't ever have to be unless you choose to be. You don't have to be a victim again." Pat spoke, her voice firm and authoritative. Bonita grinned and nodded as Pat touched her arm and added, "And don't you ever forget that."

Then Paul asked a question he had been curious about since coming to the center but had never felt free to ask, or had been afraid to ask. "What, exactly, is the prognosis for Tom? What sort of cure rate do you actually have here?"

"Let me answer the second question first. We never talk about a 'cure rate' because chemical dependency is never cured. The disease goes into remission and keeping it there is serious, lifelong work. If you want to know what percentage of our residents lead a life of sobriety after leaving here, we don't know for sure. We do as much follow-up as we can, but we lose track of some people. We know the first year is the hardest. Many people convince themselves they aren't really chemically dependent, that they understand the problem of excessive use now, and so they begin using again, thinking they can control their use. Of course, it doesn't work, and it's at this point that family and friends must be extremely firm, not believing any excuse, not tolerating anything but total sobriety."

"That's where our survival plan comes in," Eddie commented, holding up his sheet of paper.

"Right," Pat went on. "One relapse is often enough and after that a life of sobriety is freely chosen. One of the terms you will run into at Al-Anon meetings is *dry-drunk*. Sometimes a person reverts to all the old behavior but isn't drinking or using drugs. That can't be tolerated either."

"How will we know?" Beth asked.

"Knowing is the least of your problems. Believe me, you'll know," Pat answered. "The problem is knowing what to do. And again I encourage you to call anytime. Also, you can get in touch with graduates of our program. There are some wonderful families in Rochester," she said addressing the Inghrams, "who've gone through all that you're going through and can give you some real support and advice."

Then she looked at Paul. "About the prognosis for Tom. If he sticks with the program, his chances for a life of sobriety are better than fifty/fifty. Perhaps much better."

Paul seemed impressed and relieved. The odds were in their favor. In his practice he had rarely lost a mother or a baby when the odds were with him. They weren't going to lose Tom either. He knew it.

Then, as if reading his mind, Pat added, "But, remember, Tom's sobriety is his problem. You can't do it for him. All you can do for him is not tolerate drug use. Your problem is yourself, your own growth in love and wisdom." Then she looked at her watch.

"You all better get going on your survival plans. Be sure your plan includes getting outside help and support from us or from Al-Anon people, and also confronting Tom or Jim about their behavior. You also have to have a statement, 'If he doesn't change, I will leave him, divorce him, throw him out,' whatever action will save you from being sucked into his illness again."

The group wrote for a time and then Rick spoke up. "You know, I just realized that I'll probably be the first one to find out if Tom starts using again. I can't get the vision out of my mind of walking down the hall at school and seeing Tom surrounded by all his old friends with that jeering, taunting look on his face. What should I do? Talk to him? Tell Mom or Dad?"

"Has he ever listened to anything you've said before?" Pat asked.

Rick grinned. "You're right," and he wrote, "Tell Mom and Dad," as the first step in his survival plan.

"You may not ever have to worry about that, son," Paul interjected. "Tom might not get home in time to go back to school."

"That's right," Rick responded, remembering the talk about the halfway house.

"It would probably be better for him if he didn't ever go back," Kris added. "I don't know how he could possibly survive being a part of that scene but not really a part of it."

Rick nodded agreement and Paul shrugged, glancing quickly at Beth. "We'll just have to see how things work out."

Pat smiled as she looked over the group. It had been a good session. They had all done well. They were on their way to a new life.

When they had finished their survival plans and talked them over with Pat, she handed out a form on which they were to evaluate their experience during the week and give to the center any suggestions for improving the program. Then it was lunch time and the group left to have their last meal together.

Jim greeted them at the door to the dining room. "Great, you made it out in time today. How was your morning session?"

Without waiting for a response, he went on, "Tom and I are at the corner table. The food looks pretty sick, but it'll fill you."

As the family members went through the lunch line, Jim squeezed between tables, greeting old friends, and patting the shoulders of new residents. "How's it going?" "Hang in there." "You're looking good today," the confident, almost arrogant banter of a person nearly through the treatment process who has not yet faced the difficult, humbling problems of a sober life.

Jim took the place at the head of the table. Tom was already sitting in the center on one side. As they chatted about the food, Bonita and Eddie arrived, taking the places on either side of Jim. Beth came and sat next to Tom, followed by Paul who sat opposite Jim. Rick and Kris lifted their trays high and eased into the two remaining spots, Kris next to Eddie, and Rick on the end next to his father.

All but Jim seemed passive, almost melancholy, weighted by private thoughts and fears. Finally Eddie broke the silence. "When will you be going home, Dad?"

Jim swallowed his food and answered. "I was hoping to go home with you today, but it looks as if they're going to keep me for a few more days. Final polishing," he said with a laugh.

"Making you a perfect gem," Bonita joked back. "Oh boy, I can't wait. I've never lived with a perfect person before."

Jim held his hands up in a grand gesture of humility. "Well, maybe not perfect, but close. Close."

Eddie seemed not to hear. Looking at his father with that sad, intense expression, he said, "Dad, I've got to talk to you about something."

"Well, go ahead," Jim responded, still jovial.

"Not here, not now."

"Why not? You're among friends. Spit it out." Jim patted him on the shoulder and Eddie recoiled.

"No, it's nothing." By that time everyone at the table was watching and listening.

Finally Bonita realized what Eddie was trying to do. "You're not still worried about that assessment, are you?"

"What's going on here?" Jim looked around the group. "I feel like odd man out."

"You and me," Tom interjected.

"Forget it," Eddie said. "I shouldn't have brought it up."

"Of course you should've brought it up and of course your father should know." The voice came from the end of the table where Paul was sitting, leaning forward, elbows on the table.

Eddie glanced around the table and then fixed his eyes on his plate. "It probably doesn't mean anything. I mean, maybe it doesn't." He stopped, finding it much harder to talk to his father than it had been talking to the group. "Pat thought I ought to have an assessment to determine whether or not I was chemically dependent. They can't really tell for sure, you know," he caught his father's eye for a second as if to reassure him and then looked away. Jim sat back in his chair, folding his arms across his chest.

"This is silly," Bonita chimed in. "Let's not spoil our last meal together." She picked up her fork, broke off a piece of her fish patty, and put it in her mouth, hoping everyone would follow. No one noticed.

"So what happened?" Jim asked, the question more a statement meant to delineate the response than an indication of curiosity or caring.

Eddie might have changed the subject had Kris not touched his arm and said, "Go ahead."

"Dad," he cleared his throat. "I'm an alcoholic." The unequivocal statement surprised even Eddie.

"That's impossible. I won't hear of it," his father responded. "How could you be? I've never seen you drunk."

"You wouldn't have known the difference." Father and son stared at each other in defensive silence and then Jim picked up his tray and left the table, sitting down with a group of his friends, joining them in their banter.

Bonita stood up to follow him, looked back at Eddie, appeared torn, and then sat down again. "You shouldn't have brought it up now," she said.

Eddie started to apologize but Paul cut him off. "Wait a minute. You're blaming Eddie for Jim's bad behavior. Of course he should've told him and Jim should've responded better, but don't take it out on Eddie because he didn't."

"Nothing's changed," Bonita sighed. "Here I am, still caught in the middle, forced to take sides."

"Why do you even have to be involved?" Kris asked. "It's not your problem."

"Detachment, remember?" Rick added.

Beth laughed. "Out of the mouths of babes . . . ."

"Almost adults," Rick corrected her.

"Well," continued Beth, "we've had our first little test in living with an alcoholic under the new rules."

"And I flunked," Bonita responded disconsolately.

"No you didn't," Beth tried to encourage her. "You wanted to involve yourself, to be the go-between, but you didn't."

"But I might have, eventually, if you people hadn't caught me. And I did take out my frustrations on Eddie."

"Well, we're all learning."

Tom, who had remained silent through the entire interchange, finally spoke up. "What have you been using?" he asked Eddie.

"Oh, beer, pot, all the usuals," Eddie shrugged, "and I never used that much, at least compared to my friends, it didn't seem like so much . . . you know how it is, you can always find someone around who uses more than you do and seems to be getting along fine." Tom nodded and Eddie went on. "I guess that's not the question. It's more when you use and why and what effect it has on you."

Again Tom nodded agreement and then turned to Bonita putting his arm around her. "And you can't quite face having two alkies in the family?"

Bonita's eyes glazed momentarily but quickly she joked. "I hadn't quite bargained for double trouble." Then, turning to Eddie, she said, "Don't worry, kid. I'm nuts about you. Whatever I can do to help, just let me know. I'll always be there for you."

For a time all that was heard from the family table was the clicking of silverware against china. Then Tom spoke up, "I'll have to go in a minute, and I probably won't see you again for a while."

Beth was immediately alert, tense. "We'll have a chance to say good-bye."

"Probably not. I'll be in group then, and you know how this place is run . . . like a prison camp." He tried to make a joke of it, but no one laughed. "I guess I'll be here another week, and then I'll move to a halfway house for a while. You think that's best, don't you?" He looked first to his mother, then to his father — a child needing assurance.

"Yes. Yes, of course. We've made the decision," Paul responded.

Quickly Beth asked, "Will you need more clothes? What about bedding or towels?"

"I don't know. I'll let you know later." He turned around, noting that all of the residents of the center were leaving. "I'll have to go in a minute," he said again, this time making a token effort to scrape and stack his dishes on the tray. Finally he stood and everyone stood with him.

He reached across the table and shook Eddie's hand. "Good luck, man," he said, and then added, "Don't worry about your father. I'll confront him in group this afternoon. He'll get himself straightened out. We alkies take care of our own. Maybe I'll see you around . . . at an A.A. meeting or something."

Eddie nodded, "Good luck to you, too."

Then Tom turned to Bonita, gave her a hug, and said, "Hang in there. Don't let the men in your life get the best of you."

"Don't worry," she said, taking his face in her hands and kissing him squarely on the mouth. "Never again."

Then Tom turned to his family. Thrusting his hands deeply into his pockets, he looked not so much like a child as like a defendant, standing before judge and jury, convicted of his guilt. "I couldn't sleep much last night. I kept thinking about all you had said yesterday. I'm really sorry — "

Before he had a chance to go on, Paul interrupted. "Tom, we're all sorry for what we've done, but we're going to put the past behind us, and we expect you to do the same. The problems of the day will be more than enough."

"You're starting to sound like Pat," Rick pointed out.

"Is that a compliment or an insult?" Paul queried.

"Would I insult my dear old dad?" Rick and Paul laughed together as Tom looked on.

Beth sensed his feelings, as she had always sensed them, and quickly brought the focus back to Tom. "Will you call us tonight? We'll be home by early evening."

Tom turned to his mother, reached over and gently wiped her cheek with his fingertips. His hand moved down to her shoulder, and he swayed toward her, but pulled back as if trying to resist some primal magnet. "Sure, Mom, I'll call after our meeting." Then he went around the table, hugging each member of his family, thanking them for coming, and wishing them a safe trip home. All the residents had left the dining room by the time Tom said his last good-bye, brought his tray back to the kitchen, and hurried out without looking back.

Bonita moved down to sit next to Beth, patted her arm and tried to console her. "He'll be okay. Don't worry. He'll be home in no time. You'll hardly realize he was gone."

Then wanting to distract them, to ease their melancholy, she said, "Could you believe it when Connie came back this morning?"

"And she finally opened up a little," Kris added.

"It's really funny," Eddie commented, leaning forward so everyone could hear him. "All week I really disliked her. I kept thinking I should try to be understanding and sympathetic, but all I could think about was how she didn't care enough about her daughter to come here while Trisha was in treatment. It made me so angry I couldn't see any of her good qualities — "

"She didn't have many," Kris interrupted.

"Or show many," Paul corrected.

Eddie went on. "But this morning, by the time she left I had this strange sense of closeness toward her, like we had been friends in another life."

"Maybe she reminded you of your mother," Rick said, proud of his newly developed powers of analysis, and then was disappointed when everyone acted as if the statement was so obvious it hardly needed to be spoken.

"There must be something we can do to help her," Beth mused.

"Rochester can't be that big," Bonita replied. "You could maybe get together."

"I wonder if Trish would be open to Rick or me. Sometimes it's easier to talk to someone your own age," Kris added thoughtfully and the conversation went on, each contributing an idea or possible action — anything at all that might be helpful to Connie or Trisha.

As they were talking, Pat approached. "You all ready for graduation?"

"Sit down a minute," Paul said. "We'd like to talk to you."

Pat wondered what was up, they all seemed so serious.

"We got started talking about Connie and Trisha," Paul went on.

"We all feel so bad about what's happened to them," Bonita added.

"What we were wondering is if you think it would be appropriate for us to get in touch with Connie when we get back to Rochester and try to help them," Paul continued.

"There must be something we can do," Beth added.

Pat looked at their intent, concerned faces and sighed. "I'm sure Connie would appreciate getting a call from you," she said, addressing the Inghrams, "or a letter from you," she looked at Bonita and Eddie. "Be there for her if she needs to talk, but please, don't set yourselves up as her saviors. You're still a bunch of greenhorns yourselves, and when she's ready for help she's going to need some tough, experienced help. We have a group of alumni of this center in Rochester which I assume you'll become a part of. Rely upon them and their judgment."

The group appeared crestfallen. "Hey, I know how you feel right now, like you could conquer the world. I don't want to put gravel in your shoes, but I'm afraid you'll find that within a week or two, you'll need all the help you can get just keeping your own journey going. Connie and Trish both know what they need to do to regain their health. When they're ready, they also know where to get help. It's their problem. Their responsibility." Then Pat smiled at them encouragingly and added, "You're really a great group to be sitting here, on your last day together, trying to think of ways to help someone else. I love and admire you all for that. But, it's after one o'clock and we still have our graduation ceremony. Let's go."

The mood of everyone lightened as Bonita began singing the familiar graduation march and the group members strode, in step, up the stairs and took their seats in Pat's office for the last time. Pat counted out six medallions, picked up the Al-Anon book, and sat down between Bonita and Beth. Opening the book, she read the passage she had carefully selected.

Let me learn to settle for less than I wish *were possible, and be willing to accept it and appreciate it. I will not expect too much of anyone, not even of myself. Contentment comes from accepting gratefully the good that comes to us, and not from raging at life because it is not better. This wholesome attitude is by no means* resignation, *but a realistic acceptance.*

Pat closed the book and looked up, catching the eyes of each member of the group. "Your graduation from the family program is a very special time. You've all worked hard this week, passing through dark and painful valleys. I feel so good about each one of you. The progress you've made here is an important and dramatic first stage in your journey toward healthy, loving relationships with yourselves and with each other. I'm proud of you all, and I've found that working with your two families has been as helpful to me in my own personal journey as, I hope, it has been for you." She paused and then smiled broadly, "I don't say that to every group, I want you to know that. You've been very special to me." Then, as she looked from one face to the other, her eyes filled with tears. "Please keep in touch. I really want to know how you're all doing. And we're always here to help you in any way we can."

Pat set the Al-Anon book on the floor next to her chair and picked up one of the medallions. "Each of you will receive one of these medallions today. On one side is the emblem of this center and on the other side is the Serenity Prayer which I hope will become a very special prayer for each of you. I want you to choose some other member of the group to give you your medallion. That person will say a few words to you, give you the medallion, and then you'll have a chance to respond. Okay?"

Pat glanced around the group to see if there were any questions, and then asked, "Who would like to go first?" There was a long pause. She waited. Finally Bonita spoke up.

"As usual, I'll be the fool to jump in first."

"That wasn't a put-down of yourself, was it?" Pat asked, teasing her.

"Old habits die hard," Bonita responded with a laugh. Then she swiveled her chair so she could face Eddie who was on her right. "Eddie, I'd like to have you give me my trophy." He nodded agreement and Pat handed him a medallion.

He fingered it for a time, rubbing his thumb over the rough surface. "Bonita, there's no way I can tell you how much you've meant to me over the past years. I really don't know what would have become of me if I hadn't gotten to know you. I'm really sorry for all the trouble we've caused for you. More than anything in the world, I don't want to see you hurt by either Dad or me, but I know you've been and probably will continue to be." He looked down at the medallion, turning it over and over between his thumb and forefinger, and then looked up again, this time with tears in his eyes. "I guess all I can say is thank you and I love you very much." He handed her the token of her graduation and then hugged her.

She sniffed loudly, laughed loudly, and then said, "Oh boy, do I feel I've earned this. Eddie, honey," she said as she reached over and grabbed his hand, "don't ever apologize for the trouble I've had since meeting you and Jim. The trouble couldn't begin to outweigh the joy and meaning you've given me. And even the trouble has helped me learn about myself and grow. We've both got a thousand miles to go, kid, but we'll make it. I know we will." Then she looked at Pat and at each of the Inghrams. "And you guys have all been just great. Pat, thank you a million times over for all you've done for me." Pat nodded, reached over, and squeezed her hand and then Bonita went on. "And you people. What a great family you are. Don't you ever forget it. Believe me, I know. I've seen all kinds and you're really something else. And if you don't write, I'm going to fly to Rochester and live with you for a month." She laughed loudly, her deep voice reverberating off the walls. "With a threat like that, I can't miss."

"That's a promise, not a threat," Beth responded and the rest of the Inghrams joined in with invitations and encouragement. Finally the chatter died down and it was time for the next presentation.

"I guess I can go next," Eddie said, and then, turning in his chair, he looked at Kris who was on the other side of him. "Would you mind giving me mine?"

Kris blushed as she nodded agreement. Pat slid her chair across the circle to Kris and handed her Eddie's medallion. A hush settled over the group.

Finally Kris spoke. "I don't think I've ever had my opinion of someone go through such extreme swings in so short a period of time. Knowing you has taught me something I'll never forget, and that is there's always more to people than what we see and therefore we shouldn't be so quick to make positive or negative judgments." She paused and stammered a bit, and then went on. "What you did that night made me so angry and upset, but it also made me realize I'd been only living half a life because I was so afraid of doing something wrong. Because of you I've learned enough about myself and about life to start growing up." She looked down, began giggling, and then looked at her parents. "Don't worry, Mom and Dad, I'm not going to turn into a big partier, but I'm not afraid or so naive anymore." She checked with Pat who nodded encouragingly. "Thank you for that, Eddie. I really hope your life goes well. You have so much potential and will be a wonderful man." She handed him the medallion, touched his hand, hesitated as if wondering if she should hug him, and then sat back, blushing again.

    Eddie held the treasure tightly in his fist and looked at Kris. "Thank you for saying that. I haven't been able to get over feeling guilty for being such a jerk that night. I'd never met anyone like you before, and I just didn't know how to act." Then he shrugged and sighed, "I guess I really didn't know myself well enough to know how to relate to anyone very well." Then addressing her again, he went on. "Anyway, I just wanted you to know I think you're an incredible girl. I don't know what direction my life's going to take. I just haven't had time to sort things out very well, but I'd like to write to you if you don't mind." Kris reached over and squeezed his hand, assuring him that she would write also. Then he looked at the others in the group. "I want to thank all of you for being so great, for taking a special interest in me, and helping me. So much has changed this week that I can hardly believe I'm the same person who came here." The others nodded, smiling agreement with him. "I guess that's it. Just thanks and I'll never forget any of you." His eyes scanned the group, focusing finally on Bonita, who immediately slid her chair next to his and hugged him.

    A pattern had now been established. Before Pat had a chance to ask for the next volunteer, Kris said, "Well, I guess it's my turn," and she turned to the person on her right, grinned, and said, "Hey, little brother, will you give me my medallion?"

    "Sure, if you don't ever call me 'little brother' again," he responded jokingly. Pat handed him a medallion, and he turned his chair toward Kris and sat, trying to think of what to say.

    "This has been a crazy week. I'd never have believed it if anyone had told me that in a few days time I'd end up feeling good about myself or close to my dad or shocked by my mom or worried about you." He stopped to emphasize the last clause, smiling at his sister in a teasing way. "You were always like a mother to me, and I expected you to be responsible and take care of things. I guess I was a part of the pressure you felt to be perfect. I just never could've conceived of you in any other way. To realize you'd been drinking that night and to see you throwing up made me furious. For some reason I needed to think of you as some sort of solid, unbending leaning post. But I don't know, it's different now. I'm glad you're human and I hope we can be friends. In fact, if I'm going to avoid the drug scene, I'll probably be hanging around with you and your friends all the time." He chuckled a little and so did she, and then the tone turned serious. "Anyway, thanks for being such a great sister. Right now I feel like the luckiest guy in the world to have such a wonderful family." He handed her the medallion, hugged her and whispered "Love ya" into her ear.

Kris took the medallion, wiped her eyes with the back of her hand, and turned to the group. "I just want to thank you all for everything that has happened this week. Pat, you seemed to know me long before I knew myself, and you were such a help. And, Mom and Dad, I love you both so much." Tears began pouring down her cheeks. "And Rick . . . ." She reached over and held his hand, but no more words could come out. Bonita handed her the tissue box and as she wiped her eyes and blew her nose, she signaled to Pat that she was through. Without a pause, Rick, assuming it was his turn, turned to his right and asked his father to give him his medallion. Paul nodded agreement and Pat handed him the small packet.

"Erik, Rick . . . ."

"It's okay, Dad, I like Erik." Father and son exchanged a look that said more than any speech or hug could say. Paul seemed, for a moment, unable to speak, and then he went on.

"Erik, you will likely graduate from high school and you'll probably graduate from college and you may even go through graduate school, but I don't think I could ever be as proud of you as I am right now. It's been like watching a metamorphosis, seeing you shed your old self and emerge, altered and changed, in some obvious and many not so obvious ways. You've begun your journey on the road to compassionate manhood and I'm so looking forward to sharing with you the rest of the journey. I've missed so much of your lives," his eyes went from Rick to Kris and back again. "But all that's going to change. I may need you to remind me of that from time to time if I start slipping back into my old workaholic self." Both children nodded and grinned. Then putting his hand on Rick's shoulder, he said, "I'm so proud to be your father and thankful to have been given you as a son." He handed him the medallion and then wrapped him in his arms. "I love you, son." They hugged — strong, adult, male hands patting pliant, immature shoulders.

Rick sat, knowing he was expected to respond, but too moved to think of anything to say. Finally, shrugging his shoulders and looking across the group to Pat, he said, "I can't think of anything more to say except thanks to all of you." His eyes scanned the group. "This has been the greatest week of my life. I just wish there was some way to hold onto the feelings I have right now." He looked down and then back at Pat to let her know he was through.

Then Paul turned to Beth, wordlessly asking her to be his presenter and wordlessly she agreed. Pat handed her the medallion.

"It's so hard to put what I'm feeling into words." Beth reached over and took her husband's hand, turning it over, rubbing her thumb across the skin kept soft, almost childlike, by surgeon's rubber gloves and indoor work. "I feel as if we're one of those lucky couples who've been given a chance at a second marriage without having to dissolve the first, and given a second chance at parenting with the same children we experimented on the first time around. I was hopeful and optimistic when we started our first marriage, but it was an innocent, naive optimism. In spite of all we've been through, or maybe because of it, I'm even more hopeful and optimistic now. I want more than anything to have a close, growing relationship with you, Paul. And I guess we both have a much better understanding of how much time and effort and honesty it takes to make that happen. It's strange, isn't it? All those years we lived together, and I never really knew you, and I guess you never really knew me. Maybe it's not possible to really know another person, but I think we've come closer to that goal now than I ever thought we could." She stopped, put the medallion into his open hand and closed his fingers over it. Then, looking into his eyes she said simply, "I love you, honey," put her hand on the back of his neck, and kissed him warmly, affectionately, as if there was no one else in the room.

Kris and Rick exchanged looks and smiles, while Eddie and Bonita both watched the scene with tender longing.

Then Paul turned his chair so he could face the whole group, held the medallion in the air, and said, "I feel like Bonita, this little piece of metal is a giant trophy for a race well run. This is more important to me than all the diplomas hanging on my wall at the office because it represents a real turning point. I technically became a husband when I got married and a father when my children were born, but I don't think I ever really knew what either word meant until this week. I can't tell you how thankful I am that we were, as Beth said, given this second chance. I'm so looking forward to being a good husband to you, Beth," he touched her shoulder, "and a real father to you two." He grinned at his children. "And when Tom comes home," his voice started to crack as he thought of his oldest son who would be left behind. "When Tom comes home, I'll be there for him to make sure he doesn't get off the track again."

He looked at Pat who raised an eyebrow. "Tom will have to make his own choice," she said softly.

"I know. Of course I know that." Paul seemed upset, but it was unclear whether he was upset with himself for falling into the same trap again, or with Pat for pointing it out to him. "But . . . ," he stopped and then went on in his original tone. "I guess that's all I have to say except thanks to all of you." He looked specifically at Bonita and then Eddie and finally Pat. "I know I have a long way to go, but you've been very helpful."

The attention of the group focused on Beth. She looked past Pat to Bonita. "Would you mind giving me my medallion?"

"I'd love to. There's something I've been wanting to say to you and this will give me the chance." She accepted the medallion from Pat and then rolled her chair toward the middle of the circle until she was directly in front of Beth.

"For the first couple of days I thought of you and Connie in the same way. You were both sort of cool and aloof and negative like you thought you were too good for the group. I understood that attitude in Connie, but I couldn't figure you out. Here you had this great husband and two great kids and another one who was really working at getting his act together and still you seemed critical and into yourself. I guess I was jealous of what you had and it made me angry that you didn't seem to appreciate it." Bonita stopped and looked at Beth closely, hoping she wasn't hurting her feelings. "But then, along came yesterday, and what you said and what happened to you nearly blew me away. I can't really explain it. It's almost as if there are certain feelings women share even if they haven't had the same experiences. When you talked about your hurt and your anger, it was my hurt and my anger, and when you cried, it was my tears. And when the tears stopped and calm settled in, I could feel the calm inside of me.

"This sounds really silly, I guess, but I just wanted you to know how grateful I am to you for being so open and honest and for giving me that experience." Then she rolled her chair back so she could encompass the whole family. "I've said it before, but I'll say it again. You guys don't know how lucky you are to have a family like the one you have. Just hang in there, and when the doorbell rings and there's a middle-aged, Italian mama standing on your doorstep, you better open up and let me in." She laughed uproariously and then pulled her chair forward again and handed Beth her medallion. "Here you go, dear. Wear it next to your heart so you'll never forget this week or forget us."

Beth took the medal as Bonita wheeled her chair back to its place. "While you were talking, I was thinking of my first impressions of you. I was jealous. You seemed so easygoing and funny, and you were never at a loss for something to say. You got along with my husband better than I did, and I really resented that. But it was your openness that triggered something in me. I know what you meant when you said my anger and hurt and tears were yours. I felt the same way about you. Sometime, somewhere we'll have to sit and talk this all out. We all feel so close to both of you that I can't imagine we won't maintain a long and deep friendship." Beth sat back and looked over the whole group, trying to think of something that hadn't already been said. "I wish there were something special I could say as a fitting end to this week, but all I can think of is what you've all said. Thank you. Thank you all so much. You'll never know the freedom you've helped me gain. Yes, I will wear this next to my heart, and all of you will be in my heart. God bless you all." Soft, happy tears poured from her eyes as the group members and Pat stood and all began hugging each other, wishing each other well, promising to write and, finally, saying together the Serenity Prayer.

And then it was over. Pat followed the group down the stairs to the lobby catching bits of the conversation. "Can we give you a ride to the hotel?" "No, we're going straight to the airport. The cab should be here in a minute."

The scene in the lobby was one of slow-motion chaos as the Inghrams retrieved their luggage from a back office and everyone pressed around the coatroom. Then the Inghrams were saying their last good-byes to Bonita and Eddie. Final promises to call or write were made followed by "Good luck," and "We'll be thinking about you," and "I know things are going to go well," and "Remember, one day at a time."

As Bonita and Eddie walked to the parking lot, a yellow cab pulled up and the driver jumped out and hurried up the sidewalk to the door. The Inghrams began picking up their luggage, but stopped when the driver waved to Pat and asked, "How's life?"

"Just great. And yours?"

"Couldn't be better," he said with an impish grin, but then looked sober and came close to her, talking confidentially. "Well, actually, it could be better. My wife hasn't been feeling well for the past few weeks." Then he grinned again. "Expecting, you know."

"You're going to be a father?" Pat exclaimed giving him a congratulatory hug. The receptionist joined the group asking questions about when the baby was due and how long his wife planned to keep working. Then Pat caught Paul's eye and said, "Your cab driver is a special friend of ours."

"Yes, I know, we've met," Paul said warmly as he reached out to shake hands and threw the other arm around the man's shoulder. "So, you're going to be a father. I know a good doctor, but you'll have to move to Rochester." Everyone laughed as the cab driver shook hands with the other family members, asking them about their week, nodding approval as he heard their glowing reports. Then he took the bags Beth had intended to carry and the group crowded out the door.

Assembled in the taxi, the Inghrams looked out the window and saw Pat standing on the sidewalk, rubbing her arms to keep warm. She waved and they all waved back, first out one side of the car, then the other as the cab made a giant U-turn, and finally, out the back as they drove down the street.

Within seconds, Pat and the center were out of sight. The family members sighed, turned, and looked ahead as the taxi jerked and jolted through mid-afternoon traffic, heading for the freeway, and then the airport.

"Looks like we might be getting some bad weather," the driver commented matter-of-factly. Beth peered anxiously out the side window, but could see little besides buildings and an occasional cement sound barrier separating neighborhoods from the interstate. The driver flipped on his radio and began moving the dial from station to station trying to get a weather report. Finally, as he turned onto the last stretch of freeway leading to the airport, he shut it off.

"Guess we'll just have to hope your flight gets off," he said to Paul.

"Don't worry about us," Paul responded as the taxi skidded to a stop in front of their airline's door. "We'll make it. I'll see to that."

Under the shelter of the canopy, the Inghrams unloaded their luggage and said "Good-bye" to the taxi driver, while out on the runways small planes shuddered and pilots double checked their instrument panels as heavy, wet snow, driven by strong winds, swept in from the northwest.

The driver leaned against his taxi and watched the Inghrams vanish behind sliding glass doors. "Good luck to you all," he called as the wind muffled his voice. "Take care of yourselves, now, you hear?"

AUTHOR'S NOTE

I suspect it would be impossible to read this book without wanting to know what happened to the people involved. Did Tom stay sober? Did the Inghrams maintain and build on the open communication fostered by their week of family program? And what happened to Eddie? Bonita? Jim? Connie? Trish?

I wish I could tell you, but the characters are fictitious, modeled after composites of real people. What I can tell you is something of my own experience that led me to write this book in the first place and something of the process involved in writing it, all of which might help you project the fate of the characters you have come to know through your reading.

Our son, the first of five children, went through treatment for chemical dependency at Twin Town Treatment Center in St. Paul, Minnesota, when he was a senior in high school. At the time, we were living in a small Minnesota community where my husband was the pastor of a Lutheran congregation. Our family was experiencing the enormous strain and disintegration such a situation inevitably produces. I searched for something I could read to help me understand, not so much our son — there was such material available — but myself and the other members of the family. There was nothing. After experiencing the family program at Twin Town, I vowed if our lives ever cleared enough for me to think straight, I would write something to help others. I had been keeping a daily journal of my feelings and experiences and began adding those of others in similar situations with whom we came in contact.

I knew I wanted to capture the family experience at both an intellectual level and an emotional level and do it in such a way that it would be accessible to people as young as thirteen or fourteen. I began doing research, reading everything I could find on the subject and interviewing people involved in treatment programs.

At the same time I began experimenting with form. None of the usual forms worked. Articles or essays were capable of communicating some of the information, but the emotional impact of living through such a situation was difficult to capture. The short story, while capable of capturing feelings, limited information and multiple points of view.

The traditional novel, while an attractive option in some ways, would not have the authority or the flexibility to present reliable, factual information. I considered autobiography or documentary, but ruled them out, not willing to expose my family or break the confidence of the many people with whom I had talked over the years.

The answer to the question of form — a cross between documentary, fiction, and autobiography — was so obvious it was difficult. By creating fictitious characters and having them experience a week of family treatment as it actually happens, I could present the information and give some sense of the emotional anguish such families experience.

This form solved an additional problem, also. The Minnesota model of treatment is based on the disease theory of alcoholism. While internationally recognized and respected, it is not the only model, nor is the disease theory the only theory. I wanted the book to present the Minnesota model because it is the one I am most familiar with and personally ascribe to. But I also wanted the book to be helpful to people who have had contact with treatment programs based on other theoretical assumptions, or who simply disagree with the disease theory.

As I set out to write this book, I had as my working material my own personal journal, a folder filled with information about alcoholism and its effects on the family, and character profiles and experiences of dozens of people whose lives had touched mine during the past years. I also had the hour-by-hour agenda of the treatment center family program and a general character sketch of each of the seven people I had decided to create for the book.

While writing, I realized the form, which had solved all of my original problems, created a whole new set. It wasn't long before the characters took on life, as fictitious characters can and should. I needed them to travel a very prescribed and intricate path, but they kept wanting to move on in their own directions. That tension permeates the book, sometimes adding to its impact and sometimes detracting from it.

In an effort to have the information be as up-to-date as possible and the methods described reflective of the most current methods practiced, I spent a week at the family treatment program at Hazelden, a residential community for alcohol and other drug treatment, family treatment, counselor and chaplain training, research, and publishing, located in a beautiful lakeside wooded area about fifty miles northeast of Minneapolis, Minnesota. The time was well spent. Theories and methods had changed as they will continue to change. The book, then, reflects the structure of a family program as practiced at Twin Town in 1983 and the theories and some of the methods as practiced at Hazelden in 1985. While theories and methods are fluid, moving in new directions as research and experience dictate, the kinds of experiences families have when one member is chemically dependent tend to be frighteningly, or perhaps reassuringly, universal.

So, what can I tell you of the Inghrams and the other characters? What are their chances for a whole life? If their lives were to follow the patterns I have seen in the real people I know, their chances are very good — if they use the tools they have been given. As Dan said to the Inghrams, "I've become a believer in miracles since working here. We see them happen all the time . . . . It's a miracle of process. I believe deeply in the Power of God . . . . I feel extremely optimistic about your chances for healthy, whole lives."

Following is a list of publications mentioned in the story:

Adult Children of Alcoholics, Janet Geringer Woititz (Health Communications, Hollywood, FL, 1983). Available through Hazelden Educational Materials, order no. 5001.

Detaching With Love, Carolyn W. (Hazelden Foundation, Center City, MN, 1984). Available through Hazelden Educational Materials, order no. 1253.

Grief: A Basic Reaction to Alcoholism, Joseph L. Kellermann (Hazelden Foundation, Center City, MN, 1977). Available through Hazelden Educational Materials, order no. 1297.

It Will Never Happen to Me, Claudia Black (Medical Administration Company, Denver, CO, 1981). Available through Hazelden Educational Materials, order no. 8123.

One Day at a Time in Al-Anon, Al-Anon Family Groups (Al-Anon Family Group Headquarters, Inc., New York, NY, 1973). Available through Hazelden Educational Materials, order no. 3120. Meditations used in story: January 5, August 4, 21, 22, and 29.

The Promise of a New Day, Karen Casey and Martha Vanceburg (Hazelden Foundation, Center City, MN, 1983). Available through Hazelden Educational Materials, order no. 1045. Meditation used in story: January 15.

Why Am I Afraid to Tell You Who I Am?, John Powell (Argus Communications, Niles, IL, 1969). Available through Hazelden Educational Materials, order no. 6670.

Hazelden

Other titles that will interest you...

Today's Gift

Today's Gift is our first daily meditation book written with the family in mind. A collection of readings written specifically to help us, as individuals, deal with our family concerns, *Today's Gift* is an excellent companion for those of us involved in A.A., Al-Anon, Alateen, Adult Children of Alcoholics, and other self-help groups. *Today's Gift* will inspire discussion among family members — child and adult alike — and help us all to pause, regain a sense of balance, and recognize the riches we have within and around us. (400 pp.)
Order No. 1031A

Kids, Drugs, and the Law
by David G. Evans, Esq.

Can a minor consent to chemical dependency treatment? Can teachers be sued for trying to help a student with drug problems? This highly informative book will help treatment providers, school officials, parents, and lawyers understand the legal rights and responsibilities of kids who use alcohol and other drugs. (88 pp.)
Order No. 1341A

Setting Limits:
Parents, Kids and Drugs
by William LaFountain

Setting Limits was written specifically to help the parents of adolescent drug users. Such parents often struggle and suffer while trying to understand behaviors foreign to their own experiences. If parents are to succeed, they must set clear, firm limits on what is expected of their children and of themselves. These thirteen statements and examples enable parents to more clearly identify and deal with their own situation. (36 pp.)
Order No. 1418B

For price and order information, please call one of our Customer Service Representatives.

Hazelden Educational Materials

Pleasant Valley Road
Box 176
Center City, MN 55012-0176

(800) 328-9000
(Toll Free. U.S. Only.)
(800) 328-0500
(Toll Free. Film and Video Orders. U.S. Only.)
464-8844
(Toll Free. Metro Twin Cities.)
(612) 257-4010
(MN, AK, & Outside U.S.)